SOUS VIDE

Cookbook for Beginners

600 Recipes
Effortless Everyday Meals to Make at Home

Charles Jordan

CONTENTS

INTRODUCTION 9

RED MEATS 11

1. Cilantro-Garlic Beef Roast....................................11
2. Beef Rib Eye Steak 11
3. Tasty Mediterranean Meatballs 11
4. Traditional French-Style Steak............................12
5. Yummy Smoked Beef Brisket..............................12
6. Perfect Roast Steak 12
7. Chipotle Beef Steak Coffee Rub 13
8. French-Style Stuffed Beef Burgers 13
9. Herby Skirt Steak 13
10. Tamari Steak with Scramble Eggs 14
11. Tasty Short Ribs with BBQ Sauce 14
12. Caribean Chili Steak Tacos 14
13. Chili Beef Tenderloin 15
14. Saucy Beef Sirloin..15
15. Fire-Roasted Tomato Tenderloin........................15
16. Soy Garlic Tri-Tip Steak 16
17. Greek Meatballs with Yogurt Sauce...................16
18. Dijon & Curry Ketchup Beef Sausages 16
19. Jalapeno–Tomato Rib Roast................................16
20. Baked Korean-Style Marinated Beef Ribs...........17
21. Chili Beef Meatballs 17
22. Sirloin Steak with Mashed Turnips.....................17
23. Stuffed Bell Peppers 18
24. Chili Seared Tenderloin 18
25. BBQ Beef Brisket 18
26. Garlicky Prime Ribs 18
27. Flank Steak with Tomato Roast 19
28. Shredded BBQ Roast 19
29. Beef Steak with Shallots and Parsley.................19
30. Prime Rib with Celery Herb Crust 20
31. Sirloin Steaks with Mushroom Cream Sauce.........20
32. Beef Pear Steak 20
33. Tomato Stuffed Mushrooms 21
34. Simple Corned Beef 21
35. Beef with Onions...21
36. Beef Sirloin in Tomato Sauce.............................22
37. Beef Chuck Shoulder with Mushrooms 22
38. Honey-Dijon Brisket 22
39. Classic Beef Stew 23
40. Red Wine Beef Ribs 23
41. Beef Pepper Meat 23
42. Beef Stroganoff 24
43. Garlic Burgers 24
44. Beef Fillet with Baby Carrots 24
45. Ground Beef Stew 25
46. Beef Bites with Teriyaki Sauce & Seeds.............25
47. Delicious Cheesy Steak Roll................................25

48. Lemony & Peppery Flank Steak 26
49. Beef & Veggie Stew 26
50. Zesty Beef Steak 26
51. Rosemary Ribeye Stew 26
52. Worcestershire Meatloaf 27
53. Drunken Beef Steak 27
54. Divine Sirloin with Sweet Potato Purée.............27
55. Beef Pie with Mushrooms 28
56. Classic Cheese Burgers 28
57. Creamy Veal Marsala 28
58. Rib Eye Noodles with Cauliflower 29
59. Kimchi Rib Eye Tacos with Avocado...................29
60. Liver with Garlic 29
61. Easy-to-Make Tenderloin with Cayenne Sauce 30
62. White Wine Veal & Mushroom Chops.................30
63. Peppercorn Veal Chops with Pine Mushrooms.......30
64. Dijon Veal Liver 31
65. Saucy Veal with Port Wine..................................31
66. Lamb Meatballs with a Yogurt Sauce 31
67. Portobello Veal 32
68. Veal Chops 32
69. Veal Gravy..32
70. Minted Lamb Chops with Nuts 32
71. African-Style Lamb Chops with Apricots..............33
72. Spicy Shoulder Lamb Rice...................................33
73. Sweet Lamb with Mustard Sauce........................33
74. Mustard & Honey Marinated Rack of Lamb 34
75. Lemon Mint Lamb 34
76. Lamb Shank with Veggies & Sweet Sauce 34
77. Herb Crusted Lamb Rack 35
78. Pancetta & Lamb Stew..35
79. Popular South African Lamb & Cherry Kebabs 36
80. Lemon Lamb Chops with Chimichurri Sauce.........36
81. Spicy Lamb Kebabs 36
82. Bell Pepper & Lamb Curry 37
83. Peppery Lemon Lamb Chops with Papaya Chutney 37
84. Garlic Rack of Lamb 37
85. Goat Cheese Lamb Ribs.......................................38
86. Herby Lamb with Veggies....................................38
87. Thyme & Sage Grilled Lamb Chops.....................38
88. Lamb Shoulder...39
89. Jalapeño Lamb Roast 39
90. Chili Lamb Steaks with Sesame Seed Topping.......39
91. Lamb Chops with Basil Chimichurri 40
92. Harissa Lamb Kabobs 40
93. Lamb & Bean Stew...40

PORK 41

94. Sweet Mustard Pork with Crispy Onions 41
95. Delicious Basil & Lemon Pork Chops 41
96. Boneless Pork Ribs with Coconut-Peanut Sauce   41
97. Baby Ribs with Chinese Sauce 42
98. Jerk Pork Ribs 42
99. Maple Tenderloin with Sautéed Apple 42
100. Balsamic Pork Chops 43
101. Lime and Garlic Pork Tenderloin 43
102. Flavorful Pork with Mustard & Molasses Glaze 43
103. Spicy Tenderloin with Sweet Papaya Sauce 44
104. Roasted Pork Neck 44
105. Herby Tenderloin with Spicy Pineapple Sauce   44
106. Smoked Paprika Pork Belly 45
107. Pork Tacos Carnitas 45
108. Pork Ribs 45
109. Thyme Pork Chops 45
110. Pork Cutlets 46
111. BBQ Pork Ribs 46
112. Sage & Cider Chops 46
113. Sweet Pork Chops with Pear & Carrots 46
114. Tomato Pork Chops with Potato Puree 47
115. Rosemary Pork Tenderloin 47
116. Paprika Tenderloin with Herbs 47
117. Paprika Pancetta with Pearl Onions 48
118. Toasts with Eggs & Crispy Pancetta 48
119. Tasty Potato & Bacon with Scallions 48
120. Bell Pepper & Carrot Pork Chops 48
121. Sweet Chops & Zucchini with Almonds 49

122. Pleasing Pork in Salsa Verde 49
123. Asian-Style Pork with Rice & Ginger 49
124. Spicy Coconut Pork Ribs 50
125. Crispy Pork Chops 50
126. Savory Pork Chops with Mushrooms 50
127. Sweet Spare Ribs with Mango Soy Sauce 51
128. Loin Pork with Almonds 51
129. Sweet Sausage & Grapes 51
130. Creamy Cognac Pork Loin 52
131. Tasty Tenderloin with Avocado Dip 52
132. Sweet Lemongrass Pork Chops 52
133. Pork Chops with Bell Pepper & Corn Stir-Fry   52
134. Pork & Mushroom Ramen Noodles 53
135. Tomato Pork Shanks with Carrots 53
136. Pork Chop with Spiced Coffee Sauce 53
137. Spicy Tenderloin 54
138. Pancetta & Corn Cream Soup 54
139. Cumin & Garlic Pork Kabobs 54
140. Sweet Apple Sausages 54
141. Awesome Pork Chops with Balsamic Glaze 55
142. Red Cabbage & Potatoes with Sausage 55
143. Garlic Pork Fillets 55
144. Mexican Pork Carnitas with Salsa Roja 56
145. Juicy BBQ Baby Ribs 56
146. Pork Chops with Mushroom Sauce 56
147. Savory Thyme & Garlic Pork Tenderloin 57
148. Sweet Orange Pork Tacos 57
149. Pork with Vegetables 57

POULTRY 58

150. Chili Chicken & Chorizo Tacos with Cheese 58
151. Easy Spicy-Honey Chicken 58
152. Crunchy Homemade Fried Chicken 58
153. Classic Chicken Cordon Bleu 59
154. Spicy Chicken Breasts 59
155. Delicious Chicken Wings with Buffalo Sauce   59
156. Savory Lettuce Wraps with Ginger-Chili Chicken 60
157. Aromatic Lemon Chicken Breasts 60
158. Mustard & Garlic Chicken 60
159. Yummy Chicken Legs with Lime-Sweet Sauce 61
160. Pepper Chicken Salad 61
161. Orange Chicken Thighs 61
162. Chicken Stew with Mushrooms 62
163. Chicken Thighs with Carrot Puree 62
164. Whole Chicken 62
165. Simple Spicy Chicken Thighs 63
166. Whole Chicken 63
167. Chicken Breasts with Cajun Sauce 63
168. Basic Chicken Breasts 63
169. Sriracha Chicken Breasts 64
170. Parsley Chicken with Curry Sauce 64
171. Parmesan Crusted Chicken Breast 64
172. Ground Chicken with Tomatoes 64
173. Thyme Chicken with Lemon 65

174. Buffalo Chicken Wings 65
175. Shredded Chicken Patties 65
176. Lemon Chicken with Mint 66
177. Chicken with Cherry Marmalade 66
178. Sweet Spicy Chicken Drumsticks 66
179. Zesty Chicken 66
180. Stuffed Chicken Breasts 67
181. Mediterranean Chicken Thighs 67
182. Paprika Chicken Lunch 67
183. Chicken Breasts with Harissa Sauce 68
184. Garlic Chicken with Mushrooms 68
185. Chicken Thighs with Herbs 68
186. Almond Butternut Squash & Chicken Salad 68
187. Chicken Pudding with Artichoke Hearts 69
188. Cilantro Chicken with Peanut Butter Sauce 69
189. Chicken & Walnut Salad 70
190. Sweet & Sour Chicken Wings 70
191. Crispy Chicken with Mushrooms 70
192. Citrus Chicken Breasts 71
193. Vegetable Chicken with Soy Sauce. 71
194. Layered Cheese Chicken 71
195. Mustardy Chicken Legs 72
196. Chinese-Style Chicken Salad with Hazelnuts 72
197. Artichoke Stuffed Chicken 72

198. Rosemary Chicken Stew 73
199. Chicken & Leek Stew 73
200. Cheesy Chicken Salad with Chickpeas 73
201. Oregano Chicken Meatballs 74
202. Herbed Chicken with Mushroom Cream Sauce 74
203. Rice & Berry Loaded Cornish Hen 74
204. Crispy Fried Chicken 75
205. Green Chicken Salad with Almonds 75
206. Crispy Chicken Bacon Wrap 75
207. Chessy Rolled Chicken 76
208. Green Chicken Curry with & Noodles 76
209. Herby Chicken with Butternut Squash Dish....... 76
210. Pesto Chicken Mini Bites with Avocado 77
211. Cheesy Chicken Balls 77
212. Cherry Tomatoes, Avocado & Chicken Salad 77
213. Milky Coconut Chicken................................... 78
214. Chicken with Sun-Dried Tomatoes 78
215. Chinese-Style Chicken 78
216. Roman-Style Bacon & Chicken Dish................. 78

217. Minted Chicken & Pea Salad........................... 79
218. Chili Chicken 79
219. Honey Flavored Chicken Wings 79
220. Cheesy Turkey Burgers 80
221. Bacon & Nut Stuffed Turkey Wrapped in Ham 80
222. Caesar Salad Tortilla Rolls with Turkey 80
223. Sage Turkey Roulade 81
224. Thyme & Rosemary Turkey Legs 81
225. Thyme Turkey Breast 82
226. Pesto Turkey Meatballs Burgers 82
227. Turkey Breast with Pecans 82
228. Turkey Breast with Cloves 82
229. Spice Turkey Dish 83
230. Turkey in Orange Sauce 83
231. Dill & Rosemary Turkey Breast 83
232. Roasted Sweet Duck 84
233. Thyme Duck Breast 84
234. Orange Goose Confit 84

FISH & SEAFOOD 85

235. Halibut with Sweet Sherry & Miso Glaze 85
236. Crispy Salmon with Sweet Ginger Glaze 85
237. Tasty Trout with Tamari Sauce 85
238. Citrus Fish with Coconut Sauce 86
239. Lime-Parsley Poached Haddock....................... 86
240. Crispy Tilapia with Mustard-Maple Sauce........ 86
241. Swordfish & Potato Salad with Kalamata Olives 87
242. Buttery Red Snapper with Citrus Saffron Sauce 87
243. Sous Vide Halibut 88
244. Sesame Tuna with Ginger Sauce 88
245. Mustardy Swordfish.. 88
246. Spicy Fish Tortillas 89
247. Cilantro Trout 89
248. Tilapia Stew 89
249. Basil Tuna Steaks.. 90
250. Smoky Salmon 90
251. Speedy North-Style Salmon 90
252. Curry Mackerel 90
253. Wild Salmon Steaks....................................... 91
254. Halibut with Shallots & Tarragon 91
255. Minty Sardines 91
256. Grouper with Beurre Nantais........................... 92
257. Herb-Marinated Tuna Steaks 92
258. Sea Bream in White Wine............................... 92
259. Herb Butter Lemon Cod 93
260. Tuna Flakes 93
261. Salmon & Kale Salad with Avocado 93
262. Gingery Salmon 94
263. Chili Smelts 94
264. Marinated Catfish Fillets 94
265. Lemon Butter Sole 94
266. Honey Salmon with Soba Noodles.................... 95
267. Savory Creamy Cod with Parsley..................... 95
268. Thai Salmon with Cauliflower & Egg Noodles 96
269. Basil Cod Stew 96

270. Easy Tilapia 96
271. Sesame-Crusted Cod Fillet 96
272. Salmon with Asparagus 97
273. Creamy Salmon with Spinach & Mustard Sauce 97
274. Egg Bites with Salmon & Asparagus 97
275. Salted Salmon in Hollandaise Sauce 98
276. Herby Lemon Salmon..................................... 98
277. Light Sea Bass with Dill................................. 98
278. French Pot de Rillettes with Salmon 98
279. Sage Salmon with Coconut Potato Mash 99
280. Amazing Lemon Salmon with Basil................... 99
281. Squid Rings.. 99
282. Crabmeat Patties... 100
283. Mussels in Fresh Lime Juice 100
284. Parsley Prawns with Lemon 100
285. Shrimp with Spicy Sauce................................ 100
286. Sweet Buttered Scallops with Pancetta 101
287. Cheesy Lemon Shrimp Pasta........................... 101
288. Creole Prawn Kabobs 101
289. Chili-Lemon Calamari Linguine 102
290. Crabmeat with Lime Butter Sauce.................... 102
291. Paprika Scallops with Fresh Salad.................... 102
292. Divine Garlic-Lemon Crab Rolls 103
293. Spiced Charred Octopus with Lemon Sauce 103
294. Octopus Grill 103
295. Buttered Scallops 104
296. Rosemary Squid.. 104
297. Fried Lemon Shrimps 104
298. Buttery Cockles with Peppercorns 104
299. Chili Shrimp & Avocado Salad........................ 105
300. Saucy Scallops with Mango 105
301. Savory Buttery Lobster Tails 105
302. Leek & Shrimp with Mustard Vinaigrette 106
303. Coconut Shrimp Soup..................................... 106
304. Dill Baby Octopus Bowl................................. 106

305. Gourmet Lobster with Mayonnaise 107
306. Party Shrimp Cocktail 107
307. Garlicky Mustard Shrimp 107
308. Sweet Chili Shrimp Stir-Fry 108
309. Fruity Thai Shrimp 108
310. Dublin-Style Lemon Shrimp Dish 108
311. Juicy Scallops with Chili Garlic Sauce........... 109
312. Curry Shrimp with Noodles 109
313. Yummy Cheesy Lobster Risotto 109

EGGS ... 110

314. Ground Beef Omelet 110
315. Light Vegetarian Frittata 110
316. Avocado & Egg Sandwich 110
317. Devilled Eggs 111
318. Hard-Boiled Eggs 111
319. Pickled Eggs 111
320. Dill & Turmeric Egg Scramble................... 111
321. Soft and Chili Eggs 112
322. Eggs Benedict 112
323. Poached Eggs 112
324. Eggs in Bacon 112
325. Cherry Tomato Eggs 113
326. Pastrami Scramble 113
327. Tomato Shakshuka 113
328. Arugula & Prosciutto Omelet 113
329. Spinach Omelet.................................. 114
330. Ginger Spring Onion Omelet 114
331. Leek & Garlic Eggs 114
332. Spinach & Mushroom Egg Quiche................. 114

APPETIZERS AND SNACKS ... 115

333. Italian Chicken Fingers............................ 115
334. Cherry Chicken Bites.............................. 115
335. Herby Italian Sausage Pannini..................... 115
336. Cinnamon Persimmon Toast 116
337. Chicken Wings with Ginger 116
338. Beef Patties 116
339. Carrots & Nuts Stuffed Peppers 116
340. Easy Spiced Hummus 117
341. Green Pea Dip 117
342. Mustard Drumsticks 117
343. French Fries 118
344. Stuffed Collard Greens 118
345. Lemon & Garlick Artichokes 118
346. Ginger Balls 118
347. Sweet Tofu Kebabs with Veggies 119
348. Onion & Bacon Muffins 119
349. Tarragon Asparagus Mix 119
350. Cod Bite Balls 120
351. Panko Yolk Croquettes 120
352. Chili Hummus..................................... 120
353. Turkey Salad with Cucumber 120
354. Eggplant Rounds with Pistachios 121
355. Creamy Artichoke Dip............................ 121
356. "Eat-me" Fruity Chorizo 121
357. Radish Cheese Dip................................ 122
358. Celery Dip 122
359. Chicken & Mushrooms in Marsala Sauce 122
360. White Wine Mussels............................... 122
361. Scallops with Bacon 123
362. Chicken Liver Spread 123
363. Sweet & Spicy Duck 123
364. Glazed Baby Carrots.............................. 123
365. Tamari Corn on The Cob 124
366. Shrimp Appetizer................................. 124
367. Gingery Squash Veggies.......................... 124
368. Lobster Tails 124
369. BBQ Tofu 125
370. Tasty French Toast 125
371. Milky Mashed Potatoes with Rosemary........... 125
372. Sous Vide Pickled Rhubarb 125
373. Hot Chicken Wings............................... 126
374. Sweet Thighs with Sun-Dried Tomatoes 126
375. Dijon Chicken Filets 126
376. Adobo Chicken 126
377. Bacon-Wrapped Turkey Leg....................... 127
378. Mexican Butter Corn 127
379. Vanilla Apricots with Whiskey 127
380. Kaffir Lime Drumsticks........................... 127
381. Orange Duck with Paprika & Thyme 128
382. Spicy Cauliflower Steaks.......................... 128
383. Cayenne Potato Strips with Mayo Dressing 128
384. Cheesy Pears with Walnuts 128
385. Nutty Baked Sweet Potatoes...................... 129
386. Tasty Parsnips with Honey Glaze 129
387. Buttery & Sweet Duck............................ 129
388. Paprika & Rosemary Potatoes 130
389. Buttery Yams 130
390. Broccoli & Blue Cheese Mash 130
391. Turkey Meatballs 130
392. Curried Zucchinis 131
393. Spicy Pickled Beets 131
394. Spicy Butter Corn 131
395. Jarred Pumpkin Bread 131

SAUCES, STOCKS AND BROTHS ... 132

396. Spicy BBQ Sauce 132
397. Peri Peri Sauce 132
398. Onion Pomodoro Sauce 132
399. Ginger Syrup..................................... 132
400. Chicken Stock.................................... 133
401. Jalapeno Seasoning............................... 133

402.	Honey & Onion Balsamic Dressing	133
403.	Seafood Stock	134
404.	Fish Broth	134
405.	Garlic Basil Rub	134
406.	Tomato Sauce	134
407.	Mustard Asparagus Dressing	135
408.	Vegetable Stock	135
409.	Beef Broth	135

VEGETARIAN & VEGAN 136

410.	Cream of Tomatoes with Cheese Sandwich	136
411.	Garlic Tabasco Edamame Cheese	136
412.	Citrus Corn with Tomato Sauce	136
413.	Sage Roasted Potato Mash	137
414.	Maple Beet Salad with Cashews & Queso Fresco	137
415.	Celery & Leek Potato Soup	137
416.	Cheesy Bell Peppers with Cauliflower	138
417.	Herby Mashed Snow Peas	138
418.	Buttered Asparagus with Thyme & Cheese	138
419.	Fall Squash Cream Soup	138
420.	Lemon Collard Greens Salad with Cranberries	139
421.	Ginger Tamari Brussels Sprouts with Sesame	139
422.	Buttered Peas with Mint	139
423.	Beet Spinach Salad	140
424.	Garlic Greens with Mint	140
425.	Brussel Sprouts in White Wine	140
426.	Cauliflower Broccoli Soup	140
427.	Bell Pepper Puree	141
428.	Radish with Herb Cheese	141
429.	Smoked Paprika Veggie Wontons	141
430.	Tomato Soup	142
431.	Brussels Sprouts in Sweet Syrup	142
432.	Beetroot & Goat Cheese Salad	142
433.	Eggplant Lasagna	143
434.	Mushroom Soup	143
435.	Poached Tomatoes	143
436.	Ratatouille	144
437.	Green Soup	144
438.	Mixed Vegetable Soup	144
439.	Radish & Basil Salad	145
440.	Bell Pepper Mix	145
441.	Cilantro Turmeric Quinoa	145
442.	Vegetarian Parmesan Risotto	145
443.	Potato & Date Salad	146
444.	Quinoa & Celeriac Miso Dish	146
445.	Curry Ginger & Nectarine Chutney	146
446.	Minty Chickpea and Mushroom Bowl	147
447.	Braised Beetroot	147
448.	Paprika Grits	147
449.	Oregano White Beans	147
450.	Cabbage & Pepper in Tomato Sauce	148
451.	Balsamic Braised Cabbage	148
452.	Grape Vegetable Mix	148
453.	Vegetable Caponata	148
454.	Braised Swiss Chard with Lime	149
455.	Root Veggie Mash	149
456.	Mustardy Lentil & Tomato Dish	149
457.	Buttery Summer Squash	149
458.	Bell Pepper Rice Pilaf with Raisins	150
459.	Yogurt Caraway Soup	150
460.	Rosemary Russet Potatoes Confit	150
461.	Honey Apple & Arugula Salad	150
462.	Rice & Leek Pilaf with Walnuts	151
463.	Delicious Chutney of Dates & Mangoes	151
464.	Mandarin & Green Bean Salad with Walnuts	151
465.	Tangerine & Green Bean Platter with Hazelnuts	152
466.	Curry Pears & Coconut Cream	152
467.	Soft Broccoli Purée	152
468.	Green Pea Cream with Nutmeg	152
469.	Chili Cabbage Goulash	153
470.	Broiled Onions with Sunflower Pesto	153
471.	Red Chili Broccoli Soup	153
472.	Easy Broccoli Puree	154
473.	Allspice Miso Corn with Sesame & Honey	154
474.	Creamy Gnocchi with Peas	154
475.	Light Broccoli Sauté	154
476.	Nutmeg Sweet Pea Cream	155
477.	Sesame Zucchini Miso	155
478.	Chili Garbanzo Bean Stew	155
479.	Buttery Agave Carrots	156
480.	Buttery Artichokes with Lemon & Garlic	156
481.	Tomato & Agave Tofu	156
482.	Sweet Red Beet Dish	156
483.	Medley of Root Vegetables	157
484.	Provolone Cheese Grits	157
485.	Effortless Pickled Fennel with Lemon	157
486.	Simple Broccoli Rabe	158
487.	Garlicky Truffled Potatoes	158
488.	Homemade Giardiniera Picante	158
489.	Crispy Garlic Potato Purée	158
490.	Easy Two-Bean Salad	159
491.	Tasty Spicy Tomatoes	159
492.	Easy Vegetable Alfredo Dressing	159
493.	Garlicky Snow Bean Sauce	159
494.	Lovely Kidney Bean & Carrot Stew	160
495.	Flavorful Vegan Stew with Cannellini Beans	160
496.	Spicy Black Beans	160
497.	Glazed Pickled Carrots	160
498.	Delightful Tofu with Sriracha Sauce	161
499.	Cheesy Arugula & Beet Salad	161
500.	Herby Balsamic Mushrooms with Garlic	161
501.	Pickled Cucumbers Pots	162
502.	Coconut Potato Mash	162
503.	Tempting Buttery Cabbage	162
504.	Sweet Daikon Radishes with Rosemary	162
505.	Shallot Cabbage with Raisins	163
506.	Mixed Beans in Tomato Sauce	163
507.	Thai Pumpkin Dish	163
508.	Lemon-Sage Apricots	163

DESSERTS & DRINKS 164

509. Fresh Fruit Créme Brulée 164
510. Vanilla Berry Pudding 164
511. Mocha Mini Brownies in a Jar 164
512. Orange Pots du Créme with Chocolate 165
513. Vanilla Ice Cream 165
514. Chocolate Pudding..................................... 165
515. Honey & Citrus Apricots 165
516. Light Cottage Cheese Breakfast Pudding 166
517. Sous Vide Chocolate Cupcakes 166
518. Easy Banana Cream..................................... 166
519. Apple Pie 166
520. Dulce de Leche Cheesecake 167
521. Sugar-Free Chocolate Chip Cookies 167
522. Raisin-Stuffed Sweet Apples 167
523. Bread Pudding 168
524. Rice Pudding with Rum & Cranberries............ 168
525. Lemon Curd 168
526. Crème Brulee 168
527. Lemony Muffins 169
528. Raspberry Mousse 169
529. Apple Cobbler... 169
530. Mini Strawberry Cheesecake Jars.................... 169
531. Wine and Cinnamon Poached Pears 170
532. Coconut and Almond Oatmeal 170
533. Banana Buckwheat Porridge 170
534. Coffee Buttery Bread 170
535. Almond Nectarine Pie 171
536. Basic Oatmeal from Scratch 171
537. Mini Cheesecakes 171
538. Bubble Raspberry Lemonade 171
539. Carrot Muffins 172
540. Peach and Almond Yogurt 172
541. Raspberry Lemon Créme Brulée 172
542. Fresh Cocktail with Ginger Beer 172
543. Oatmeal with Prunes and Apricots 173
544. Balsamic Honey Shrub 173
545. Indian Lassi with Papaya 173
546. Maple & Cinnamon Steel Oats 174
547. Asian-Style Rice Pudding with Almonds 174
548. Gingered Peaches with Cardamom.................... 174
549. Maple Potato Flan..................................... 174
550. Homemade Vanilla Pudding 175
551. Honey Tangerines 175
552. Coconut Banana Oatrolls with Walnuts............ 175
553. White Chocolate & Banana Popsicles 175
554. Cinnamon Quince Bourbon 176

555. Rum Cherries... 176
556. Pumpkin Mini Pies with Pecans 176
557. Savory Banana & Nuts Cups 176
558. Homemade Compote of Strawberries................ 177
559. Orange Cheesy Mousse 177
560. Vanilla Apricot Crumble 177
561. Vanilla Cava Fudge.................................... 177
562. Vanilla Cheesecake.................................... 178
563. Coconut Blackberry Tart.............................. 178
564. Grand Marnier & Rhubarb Mousse 178
565. Spiced Pears with Raisins............................. 178
566. Greek Yogurt Cheesecake with Raspberries..... 179
567. French Vanilla Custard Dessert 179
568. Mint Rum Pineapple 179
569. Cream Chocolate Pudding 180
570. Cinnamon Pineapple with Cheese Yogurt 180
571. Lemon & Berry Mousse 180
572. Creamy Blueberry Mousse 180
573. Fruity Chocolate Flan 181
574. Maple Lemon Brioche Pudding....................... 181
575. Cinnamon Almond Rice 181
576. Aromatic Nectarines with Mascarpone Topping 182
577. Sweet Potatoes with Maple & Cinnamon Sauce 182
578. Cinnamon Poached Pears with Ice Cream........ 182
579. Simple Lemon Jam 183
580. Rich Orange Curd 183
581. Vanilla Ice Cream with Mango Jam 183
582. Cinnamon & Citrus Yogurt 183
583. Banana Cream... 184
584. Lime Thyme Liquor.................................... 184
585. Rum Raisin Rice Pudding.............................. 184
586. Incredible Coffee Dessert 184
587. Warm Vanilla Quince.................................. 185
588. Honey Baked Cheese 185
589. Berries Vodka Tonic................................... 185
590. Maple & Lemongrass Drink 186
591. Vanilla Coffee Liquor................................. 186
592. Homemade Vanilla Bourbon........................... 186
593. Rhubarb & Blueberry Shrub Cocktail 186
594. Christmas Hot Wine.................................... 187
595. Summer Mint & Rhubarb Mojito 187
596. Gingery Gin Tonic with Lemons 187
597. Minty Vodka Melon.................................... 187
598. Sous Vide Limoncello.................................. 188
599. Spicy Agave Liquor.................................... 188
600. Citrus Piña Colada..................................... 188

INTRODUCTION

SOUS VIDE COOKING

Sous Vide is a cooking method that utilizes slow, precise cooking temperature and results in restaurant-grade meals that are not only consistent, but are also incredibly delicious. This cooking technique has been around for a long time, but it only reached its hype recently, thanks to the simple-to-use and pocket-friendly Sous Vide equipment.

Sous Vide, which means *under vacuum* in French, is the process of vacuuming the food, usually in a bag, and cooking in water at a precise temperature. This may seem fancy, but other than the fancy dishes, there is nothing complex about the cooking method. The process is super simple, and it involves only three cooking steps:

1. Attach the Sous Vide Machine to a pot of water and set the exact cooking temperature.

2. Place the food in a sealable bag, get rid of the excess air, and seal it.

3. Immerse the bag in the preheated water and cook for as long as you need to get the best results.

If you want to add a crispy exterior layer, you can finish your food by searing or grilling it.

WHY SOUS VIDE?

Sous Vide is probably the most precise cooking method, thanks to the circulation of the temperature. There is no other small kitchen appliance on the market that can offer similar results. Because it has a cooking technique that can be controlled down to a single degree, this cooking method offers tender and extremely flavorful dishes.

THE BENEFITS:

Consistency – Thanks to the extremely precise cooking temperature, you can expect consistent results.

Incredibly Tasty – Here, the food cooks in its own juices. You don't have to marinate your meat for hours prior to cooking. Why? Because you will be cooking it in marinade. Simply dump everything in a bag, seal it, immerse in the water, and let the Sous Vide machine do its thing.

Volume Increase – Don't you just hate it when your piece of meat shrinks by half during the cooking process? With Sous Vide cooking, the food doesn't lose its volume. Still in doubt? Take two equal cuts of steak. Cook one traditionally and the other one sealed in a bag with your Sous Vide. The traditionally-cooked steak will lose up to 40 percent of its volume, while the Sous Vide steak will keep its original shape and size.

Flexibility – There is absolutely no stirring or whisking involved. You simply immerse the bag with food, set the cooking temperature, tie it, and forget about it. No worries about the cooking process at all.

Money Saving – You don't have to get the most expensive cut of meat to wow your guests. The Sous Vide can cook every meat cut to perfection, providing you with a high-quality dish ready to be served.

WHAT DO YOU NEED?

To prevent evaporation and ensure that the energy transfer from the water to the food will be consistent and efficient, your food has to be properly sealed.

Here is the most beneficial packaging for Sous Vide cooking:

Ziploc Bags

Ziploc bags are resealable, versatile, and very useful for this cooking technique. And the best part? You can easily seal it with the water immersion method. Simply fill your bag with the food, liquids, and all the seasoning, and immerse it in the preheated water, but not all the way. Notice how the excess air of the immersed part has gone. Once you have vacuumed your food, you can simply seal the bag, and that's it. When using Ziploc bags, make sure they are of high quality and are BPA-free for your own safety.

Silicone Bags

If you are not a fan of plastic, you can choose resealable silicone bags instead. The cooking and sealing method here is the same.

Vacuum Sealing Bags

You don't necessarily have to have a vacuum sealer, however, keep in mind that these vacuum sealed bags are the perfect for batch cooking. And if you have a large family, well, in that case, you may find them more than necessary.

Canning Jars

Who says you have to cook in bags only? Your Sous Vide machine can also cook food in jars and cook it to perfection. From beans and grains to cakes, muffins, and custards, there are a lot of food choices that can be cooked in jars.

WHAT TO COOK?

You may wonder what foods are safe to be placed in a Ziploc bag, immersed in water, and cooked with the Sous Vide cooking technique, and the answer is – pretty much everything. Eggs, beans, grains, porridges, lentils, pork, beef, seafood, poultry, fish, veggies, and even desserts.

This book offers you 600 unique, delicious recipes so you will never run out of cooking idea. Use them as a stepping stone to becoming a Sous Vide master, and feel free to tweak them to your own taste.

RED MEATS

Cilantro-Garlic Beef Roast

Prep + Cook Time: 24 hours 30 minutes | Servings: 6

Ingredients

4 tbsp olive oil
2 pounds beef chuck
Salt and black pepper to taste
1 tsp thyme

1 tsp cilantro
1 cup soy sauce
½ cup freshly squeezed lemon juice
½ cup freshly squeezed orange juice

½ cup Worcestershire sauce
¼ cup yellow mustard
3 garlic cloves, minced

Directions

Prepare a water bath and place the Sous Vide in it. Set to 141 F. Prepare the roast and truss it using butcher's twine. Season with salt, pepper, thyme, and cilantro. Put a pan over high heat. In the meantime, baste the roast with 2 tablespoons of olive oil using a soft brush. Place the meat on the pan to sear for 1 minute on both sides. Combine Worcestershire sauce, mustard, garlic, soy sauce, lemon and orange juice in one vessel.

Slide the beef in a vacuum-bag, mix it with the previously made marinade and close the bag using water displacement method. Cook in the water bath for 24 hours.

Once ready, open the bag and pour the liquid over to a small saucepan. Cook for 10 minutes over high heat until you reach half of the volume. Add 2 tablespoons of olive oil and preheat the iron-cast pan over high heat. Gently put the meat on the pan and sear one minute each side. Take the roast out of the pan and let cool down for about 5 minutes. Slice and add the sauce on top.

Beef Rib Eye Steak

Prep + Cook Time: 1 hour 40 minutes | Servings: 2

Ingredients

1 tbsp butter
1 pound rib-eye steak

Salt and black pepper to taste
½ tsp garlic powder

½ tsp onion powder
½ tsp thyme

Directions

Prepare a water bath and place the Sous Vide in it. Set to 134 F. Rub both sides of the meat with salt, pepper, thyme, onion, and garlic powder. Slide into pieces inside the vacuum-bag, adding butter. Use water displacement method to seal the bag and put into the water bath. Cook for 90 minutes.

Once ready, get rid of the cooking liquid and take the steak out of the bag to pat dry with kitchen towel. Heat a cast-iron pan over high heat. Cook the steak for 1 minute per side. Let cool for 5 minutes before slicing.

Tasty Mediterranean Meatballs

Prep + Cook Time: 1 hour 55 minutes | Servings: 4

Ingredients

1 pound ground beef
½ cup bread crumbs
¼ cup milk

1 egg, beaten
2 tbsp chopped fresh basil
1 garlic clove, minced

1 tsp salt
½ tsp dried basil
1 tbsp sesame oil

Directions

Prepare a water bath and place the Sous Vide in it. Set to 141 F. Combine beef, bread crumbs, milk, egg, basil, garlic, salt, and basil and shape into 14-16 meatballs. Place 6 meatballs in each vacuum-sealable bag. Release air by the water displacement method, seal and submerge the bags in the water bath. Cook for 90 minutes. Heat the oil in a skillet over medium heat. Once the timer has stopped, remove the meatballs and transfer to the skillet and sear for 4-5 minutes. Discard the cooking juices. Serve.

Traditional French-Style Steak

Prep + Cook Time: 2 hours 25 minutes | Servings: 5

Ingredients

4 tbsp butter

2 pounds sirloin steak

Salt and black pepper to taste

1 shallot, chopped

2 fresh sage sprigs

1 fresh rosemary sprig

Directions

Prepare a water bath and place the Sous Vide in it. Set to 134 F. Melt 2 tablespoons of butter in a large cast-iron pan on high heat. Put the sirloin steak on the pan and sear each side for 30 to 45 seconds. Set the meat aside. Add the shallot, sage, and rosemary. Stir in butter and herbs. Cook for about 1-2 minutes until it gets bright green and soft. Slide the sirloin steak into a vacuum-bag, adding previously mixed herbs and seal the bag using the water displacement method. Cook for 2 hours.

Once ready, remove the meat and discard the cooking liquid. Put the sirloin steak on a plate lined with a paper towel or a baking sheet. Heat a cast-iron pan over high heat and add 2 tbsp of butter. When the butter sizzles, return the steak and sear for 2 minutes on both sides. Turn off the heat and leave the sirloin steak for about 5 minutes. Finally, cut into tiny pieces. Best served with vegetables and potatoes.

Yummy Smoked Beef Brisket

Prep + Cook Time: 33 hours 50 minutes | Servings: 8

Ingredients

¼ tsp liquid hickory smoke

8 tbsp honey

Salt and black pepper to taste

1 tsp chili powder

1 tsp dried parsley

1 tsp garlic powder

1 tsp onion powder

½ tsp ground cumin

4 pounds beef brisket

Directions

Prepare a water bath and place the Sous Vide in it. Set to 156 F.

Combine the honey, salt, pepper, chili powder, parsley, onion and garlic powder, and cumin. Reserve 1/4 of the mixture. Brush the brisket with the mixture. Place the brisket in a sizeable vacuum-sealable bag with the liquid smoke. Release air by the water displacement method, seal, and submerge the bag in the water bath. Cook for 30 hours. Once the timer has stopped, remove the bag and allow to chill for 1 hour.

Preheat the oven to 300 F. Pat dry with kitchen towels the brisket and brush with the reserved sauce. Discard the cooking juices. Transfer the brisket to a baking tray, put into the oven and roast for 2 hours. Once the time has stopped, remove the brisket and cover it with aluminium foil for 40 minutes. Serve with baked beans, fresh bread, and butter.

Perfect Roast Steak

Prep + Cook Time: 20 hours 20 minutes | Servings: 4

Ingredients

4 tbsp sesame oil

4 chuck tender roast steaks

1 tsp garlic powder

1 tsp onion powder

1 tsp dried parsley

Salt and black pepper to taste

Directions

Prepare a water bath and place the Sous Vide in it. Set to 130 F. Heat the sesame oil in a skillet over high heat and sear the steaks for 1 minute per side. Set aside and allow to cool. Combine the garlic powder, onion powder, parsley, salt and pepper.

Rub the steaks with the mixture and place into a vacuum-sealable bag. Release air by the water displacement method, seal, and submerge the bag in the water bath. Cook for 20 hours. Once the timer has stopped, remove the steaks and pat dry with kitchen towel. Discard the cooking juices.

Chipotle Beef Steak Coffee Rub

Prep + Cook Time: 1 hour 55 minutes | Servings: 4

Ingredients

1 tbsp olive oil
2 tbsp butter
1 tbsp sugar

Salt and black pepper to taste
1 tbsp coffee grounds
1 tbsp garlic powder

1 tbsp onion powder
1 tbsp chipotle powder
4 strip steaks

Directions

Prepare a water bath and place the Sous Vide in it. Set to 130 F. Combine brown sugar, salt, pepper, coffee grounds, onion, garlic powder, and paprika in a small bowl. Place the steaks on the previously cleaned surface and brush a thin layer of olive oil. Place the steaks into separate vacuum-bags. Then close the bags using the water displacement method. Put into the water bath and cook them for 1 hour, 30 minutes.

Once ready, remove the steaks and discard the liquid. Put the steaks on a plate lined with a paper towel or a baking sheet. Heat a cast-iron pan over high heat and add butter. When the butter sizzles, put the tenderloin on the pan again and sear for 1 minute on both sides. Let cool for 2-3 minutes and slice to serve.

French-Style Stuffed Beef Burgers

Prep + Cook Time: 50 minutes | Servings: 5

Ingredients

1 egg
1 pound ground beef
3 green onions, chopped
2 tsp Worcestershire sauce

2 tsp soy sauce
Salt and black pepper to taste
5 slices Camembert cheese
5 burger buns

Iceberg lettuce leaves
5 tomato slices

Directions

Prepare a water bath and place the Sous Vide in it. Set to 134 F. Combine the beef, onion, egg, and soy sauce using your hands and season with salt and pepper. Shape the mixture into 8 patties. Place 1 cheddar slice in the center of each patty and place another patty over the cheddar. Combine well to create a single patty.

Place the cheesy patties in four vacuum-sealable bags. Release air by the water displacement method, seal and submerge the bags in the water bath. Cook for 30 minutes. Once the timer has stopped, remove the patties and pat dry with a kitchen towel. Discard the cooking juices. Heat a skillet over high heat and sear the patties for 1 minute per side. Put the burgers over the toast buns. Top with lettuce and tomato.

Herby Skirt Steak

Prep + Cook Time: 3 hours 20 minutes | Servings: 6

Ingredients

2 tbsp butter
3 pounds skirt steak
2 tbsp extra-virgin oil
1 ½ tsp garlic powder

Salt and black pepper to taste
¼ tsp onion powder
¼ tsp cayenne pepper
¼ tsp dried parsley

¼ tsp dried sage
¼ tsp crushed dried rosemary

Directions

Prepare a water bath and place the Sous Vide in it. Set to 134 F. Brush the steak with olive oil. Combine the garlic powder, salt, pepper, onion powder, cayenne pepper, parsley, sage, and rosemary. Rub the steak with the mixture.

Place the steak in a large vacuum-sealable bag. Release air by the water displacement method, seal, and submerge the bag in the water bath. Cook for 3 hours. Once the timer has stopped, remove the steak and pat dry with kitchen towel. Heat the butter in a skillet over high heat and sear the steak for 2-3 minutes on all sides. Allow to rest for 5 minutes and cut to serve.

Tamari Steak with Scramble Eggs

Prep + Cook Time: 1 hour 55 minutes | Servings: 4

Ingredients

¼ cup milk

1 cup Tamari sauce

½ cup brown sugar

⅓ cup olive oil

4 garlic cloves, chopped

1 tsp onion powder

Salt and black pepper to taste

2 ½ pounds skirt steak

4 eggs

Directions

Prepare a water bath and place the Sous Vide in it. Set to 130 F. Combine the Tamari sauce, brown sugar, oil, onion powder, garlic, sea salt and pepper. Place the steak in a vacuum-sealable bag with the mixture. Release air by the water displacement method, seal, and submerge the bag in the water bath. Cook for 1 hour and 30 minutes.

In a bowl, combine eggs, milk, and salt. Stir well. Scramble the eggs in a skillet over medium heat . Set aside. Once the timer has stopped, remove the steak and pat it dry. Heat a skillet over high heat and sear the steak for 30 seconds per side. Cut into tiny strips. Serve with the scrambled eggs.

Tasty Short Ribs with BBQ Sauce

Prep + Cook Time: 12 hours 15 minutes | Servings: 4

Ingredients

2 tbsp butter

1 ½ pounds beef short ribs

Salt and black pepper to taste

3 tbsp toasted sesame oil

1 ½ cups barbecue sauce

10 garlic cloves, smashed

3 tbsp champagne vinegar

2 tbsp minced fresh ginger

⅛ cup chopped scallions

⅛ cup sesame seeds

Directions

Prepare a water bath and place the Sous Vide in it. Set to 186 F. Season the ribs with salt and pepper. Heat sesame oil in a skillet over high heat and sear each rib for 1 minute per side. Combine the BBQ sauce, garlic, vinegar, and ginger. Place three ribs in each vacuum-sealable bag with the BBQ sauce. Release air by the water displacement method, seal, and submerge the bag in the water bath. Cook for 12 hours.

Once the timer has stopped, remove the ribs and pat dry with kitchen towel. Heat a saucepan over medium heat and pour the cooking juices. Cook for 4-5 minutes until sticky. Heat the butter in a skillet over high heat and sear the ribs for 1 minute per side. Top with the BBQ sauce. Garnish with scallions and sesame seeds.

Caribean Chili Steak Tacos

Ready in about 2 hours 10 minutes | Servings: 4

Ingredients

1 tbsp canola oil

2 pounds flank steak

Salt and black pepper to taste

1 tsp garlic powder

2 tsp lime juice

Zest of 1 lime

Zest and juice of 1 orange

1 tsp red pepper flakes

1 garlic clove, minced

1 tbsp butter

12 corn tortillas

1 head red cabbage, sliced

Pico de gallo, for serving

Sour cream, for serving

4 serrano peppers, sliced

Directions

Prepare a water bath and place the Sous Vide in it. Set to 130 F. Season the steak with salt, pepper and garlic powder. Combine the lime juice and zest, orange juice and zest, red pepper flakes, and garlic. Place the steak and the sauce in a vacuum-sealable bag. Release air by the water displacement method. Refrigerate for 30 minutes.

Seal and submerge into the water bath. Cook for 90 minutes. Once the timer has stopped, remove the steak and pat dry with kitchen towels. Heat the oil and the butter in a skillet over high heat and sear the steak for 1 minute. Cut the steak into slices. Fill the tortilla with the steak. Garnish with cabbage, pico de gallo, sour cream and serrano. Serve and enjoy!

Chili Beef Tenderloin

Prep + Cook Time: 3 hours 20 minutes | Servings: 4

Ingredients

2 tbsp ghee
2 ¼ pounds beef tenderloin
Salt and black pepper to taste

1 tbsp chili oil
2 tsp dried thyme
1 tsp garlic powder

½ tsp onion powder
½ tsp cayenne pepper

Directions

Prepare a water bath and place the Sous Vide in it. Set to 134 F. Season the tenderloin with salt and pepper. Combine the chili oil, thyme, garlic powder, onion powder, and cayenne pepper. Brush the mixture over the tenderloin. Place the tenderloin in a vacuum-sealable bag. Release air by the water displacement method, seal, and submerge the bag in the water bath. Cook for 3 hours.

Once the timer has stopped, remove the tenderloin and pat dry with a kitchen towel. Heat the ghee in a skillet over high heat and sear the tenderloin for 45 seconds per side. Allow to rest for 5 minutes. Cut it and serve.

Saucy Beef Sirloin

Prep + Cook Time: 1 hour 50 minutes | Servings: 6

Ingredients

2 tbsp olive oil
3 pounds beef sirloin, cut into strips
Salt and black pepper to taste
2 tbsp white wine vinegar

½ tbsp freshly squeezed lemon juice
1 tsp allspice
½ tbsp garlic powder
1 onion, chopped

1 tomato, chopped
2 garlic cloves, minced
2 tbsp soy sauce
4 cups cooked quinoa

Directions

Prepare a water bath and place the Sous Vide in it. Set to 134 F. Season sirloin with salt and pepper. Combine well 1 tbsp of olive oil, white wine vinegar, lemon juice, allspice, and garlic powder. Mix together the sirloin with the marinade and place it in a vacuum-sealable bag. Release air by the water displacement method, seal, and submerge the bag in the water bath. Cook for 1 hour and 30 minutes.

Meanwhile, heat the olive oil in a saucepan over medium heat and stir in onion, tomato, garlic, and soy sauce. Cook for 5 minutes until the tomato begins to soften. Set aside. Once the timer has stopped, remove the sirloin and pat dry with kitchen towel. Reserve the cooking juices. Heat a skillet over high heat and sear for 1-2 minutes.

Combine the cooking juices with the tomato mix. Cook for 4-5 minutes until simmer. Add in sirloin and stir for 2 minutes more. Serve with quinoa.

Fire-Roasted Tomato Tenderloin

Prep + Cook Time: 2 hours 8 minutes | Servings: 4

Ingredients

2 pounds center-cut beef tenderloin,
1-inch thick
1 cup fire-roasted tomatoes, chopped

Salt and black pepper to taste
3 tbsp of extra virgin olive oil
2 bay leaves, whole

3 tbsp of butter, unsalted

Directions

Prepare a water bath, place Sous Vide in it, and set to 136 F. Thoroughly rinse the meat under the running water and pat dry with paper towels. Rub well with the olive oil and generously season with salt and pepper. Place in a large vacuum-sealable bag along with fire-roasted tomatoes and two bay leaves.

Seal the bag, submerge in the water bath and cook for 2 hours. Once done, remove the bags, place the meat on a baking sheet. Discard the cooking liquid. In a large skillet, melt the butter over medium heat. Add the tenderloin and sear for 2 minutes on each side. Serve with your favorite sauce and vegetables.

Soy Garlic Tri-Tip Steak

Prep + Cook Time: 2 hours 5 minutes | Servings: 2

Ingredients

1 ½ lb tri-ip steak
Salt and black pepper to taste

2 tbsp soy sauce
6 cloves garlic, roasted and crushed

Directions

Make a water bath, place Sous Vide in it, and set to130 F. Season the steak with pepper and salt and place it in a vacuum-sealable bag. Add in the soy sauce. Release air by the water displacement method and seal the bag. Submerge in the water bath and set the timer for 2 hours.

Once the timer has stopped, remove and unseal the bag. Heat a pan over high heat, place the steak in and sear on both sides for 2 minutes each. Slice and serve in a salad.

Greek Meatballs with Yogurt Sauce

Prep + Cook Time: 1 hour 10 minutes | Servings: 4

Ingredients

1 pound lean ground beef
¼ cup bread crumbs

1 large egg, beaten
2 tsp fresh parsley

Sea salt and black pepper to taste
3 tbsp extra-virgin olive oil

Yogurt Sauce:

6 ounces Greek yogurt
1 tbsp extra-virgin olive oil

Fresh dill
Lemon juice from 1 lemon

1 garlic clove, minced
Salt to taste

Directions

Start with the preparation of yogurt sauce. Whisk together all sauce ingredients in a medium bowl, cover and refrigerate for 1 hour. Prepare a water bath, place Sous Vide in it, and set to 141 F. Place the meat in a large bowl. Add the beaten egg, bread crumbs, fresh parsley, salt, and pepper. Thoroughly combine the ingredients together. Shape bite-sized balls and place in a large vacuum-sealable bag in a single layer.

Seal the bag and cook in a water bath for 1 hour. With a slotted spoon, carefully remove from the bag and discard the cooking liquid. Sear the meatballs in a medium-hot skillet with olive oil until they are browned, 2-3 minutes per side. Top with yogurt sauce and serve.

Dijon & Curry Ketchup Beef Sausages

Prep + Cook Time: 1 hour 45 minutes | Servings: 4

Ingredients

½ cup Dijon mustard

4 beef sausages

½ cup curry ketchup

Directions

Prepare a water bath and place the Sous Vide in it. Set to 134 F.

Place the sausages in a vacuum-sealable bag. Release air by the water displacement method, seal, and submerge the bag in the water bath. Cook for 90 minutes. Once the timer has stopped, remove the sausages and transfer to a high heat grill. Cook for 1-3 minutes until the grill marks appear. Serve with mustard and curry ketchup.

Jalapeno–Tomato Rib Roast

Prep + Cook Time: 1 hour 40 minutes | Servings: 4

Ingredients

3 lb racks beef ribs, cut into 2
Salt and black pepper to taste

½ cup jalapeno-tomato blend
½ cup barbecue sauce

Directions

Make a water bath, place Sous Vide in it, and set to 140 F. Season rib rack with salt and pepper. Put in a vacuum-sealable bag, release air and seal it. Put into the water bath and set the time to 1 hour.

Once the timer has stopped, unseal the bag. Mix the remaining ingredients. Let cool for 30 minutes. Preheat a grill on medium heat. Coat ribs with the jalapeno sauce and place it on the grill. Sear for 2 minutes on all sides.

Baked Korean-Style Marinated Beef Ribs

Prep + Cook Time: 5 hours 20 minutes | Servings: 5

Ingredients

2 tbsp canola oil
3 pounds beef ribs
Salt and black pepper to taste
½ cup sugar

½ cup soy sauce
¼ cup apple cider vinegar
¼ cup orange juice
2 tbsp minced garlic

1 tsp red pepper flakes
¼ cup chopped chives
¼ cup sesame seeds

Directions

Prepare a water bath and place the Sous Vide in it. Set to 141 F Season the ribs with salt and pepper. Combine the brown sugar, soy sauce, vinegar, orange juice, canola oil, garlic, and red pepper flakes. Place the ribs in two vacuum-sealable bags with the orange sauce. Release air by the water displacement method. Refrigerate for 2 hours. Seal and submerge the bags in the water bath. Cook for 3 hours.

Chili Beef Meatballs

Prep + Cook Time: 55 minutes | Servings: 3

Ingredients

1 pound lean ground beef
2 tbsp all-purpose flour
¼ cup milk

½ tsp freshly ground black pepper
¼ tsp chili pepper
3 garlic cloves, crushed

1 tsp olive oil
1 tsp salt
½ cup celery leaves, finely chopped

Directions

Prepare a water bath, place Sous Vide in it, and set to 136 F. In a large bowl, combine the ground beef with flour, milk, black pepper, chili pepper, garlic, salt, and celery. Mix with your hands until all of the ingredients are thoroughly combined. Shape bite-sized balls and place in a large vacuum-sealable bag in a single layer.

Submerge the sealed bag in the water bath and cook for 50 minutes. Take the meatballs out of the bag, and pat dry. Sear the meatballs in a medium-hot skillet with the olive oil, turning to brown on all sides.

Sirloin Steak with Mashed Turnips

Prep + Cook Time: 1 hour 20 minutes | Servings: 4

Ingredients

4 sirloin steaks
2 lbs of turnips, diced

Salt and black pepper to taste
4 tbsp butter

Olive oil for searing

Directions

Make a water bath, place Sous Vide in it, and set it to 128 F. Season steaks with pepper and salt and place in a vacuum-sealable bag. Release air by the water displacement method, seal, and submerge the bag in the water bath. Set the timer for 1 hour.

Place turnips in boiling water and cook until tender for about 10 minutes. Strain turnips and place in a mixing bowl. Add in butter and mash them. Season with pepper and salt. Once the timer has stopped, remove and unseal the bags. Remove the steaks from the bag and pat dry. Season to taste. Sear the steaks in a pan with oil over medium heat for about 2 minutes on each side. Serve steaks with mashed turnips.

Stuffed Bell Peppers

Prep + Cook Time: 2 hours 35 minutes | Servings: 6

Ingredients

6 medium-sized bell peppers
1 pound lean ground beef
1 medium-sized onion, finely chopped

1 medium-sized tomato, chopped
½ tsp cayenne pepper, ground
3 tbsp extra-virgin olive oil

Salt and black pepper to taste

Directions

Prepare a water bath, place Sous Vide in it, and set to 180 F. Cut the stem end of each pepper and remove the seeds. Rinse and set aside. In a large bowl, combine ground beef, onion, tomato, cayenne pepper, olive oil, salt, and pepper. Spoon the beef mixture into the peppers.

Gently place 1-2 peppers to each vacuum-sealable bag and seal the bag. Submerge the bags in the water bath and cook for 1 hour and 20 minutes. Once done, remove the bags and chill for 10 minutes before serving.

Chili Seared Tenderloin

Prep + Cook Time: 2 hours 45 minutes | Servings: 5

Ingredients

2 tbsp honey
3 pounds tenderloin
2 tbsp olive oil
Salt and black pepper to taste

2 tbsp onion powder
2 tbsp garlic powder
1 tbsp paprika
2 tsp smoked serrano chili powder

1 tsp dried sage
1 tsp nutmeg
1 tsp ground cumin
2 tbsp butter

Directions

Prepare a water bath and place the Sous Vide in it. Set to 130 F. Brush the tenderloin with olive oil. Combine salt, pepper, honey, onion powder, garlic powder, smoked paprika, smoked serrano chili powder, sage, nutmeg, and cumin. Rub the tenderloin with the mixture.

Place in a large vacuum-sealable bag. Release air by the water displacement method, seal, and submerge the bag in the water bath. Cook for 2 hours and 30 minutes. Once the timer has stopped, remove the steak and pat dry with a kitchen towel. Heat butter in a skillet over high heat and sear steak for 2-3 minutes on all sides. Allow to rest for 5 minutes and cut to serve.

BBQ Beef Brisket

Prep + Cook Time: 48 hours 15 minutes | Servings: 6

Ingredients

2 pounds beef brisket
Salt and black pepper to taste

1 tbsp olive oil
1 tbsp garlic powder

Directions

Prepare a water bath and place the Sous Vide in it. Set to 150 F. Rub the salt, pepper and garlic powder over the meat and place it in a vacuum-sealable bag. Release air by the water displacement method, seal and submerge in the water bath. Set the timer for 48 hours. After 2 days, heat the olive oil in a pan over medium heat. Remove the beef from the bag and sear all sides.

Garlicky Prime Ribs

Prep + Cook Time: 10 hours 15 minutes | Servings: 8

Ingredients

3 pounds prime rib, trimmed
1 rosemary sprig

1 thyme sprig
Salt and black pepper to taste

6 garlic cloves
1 tbsp olive oil

Directions

Prepare a water bath and place the Sous Vide in it. Set to 140 F. Season the rib with salt and pepper and place it in a vacuum-sealable bag with thyme and rosemary. Release air by the water displacement method, seal, and submerge the bag in the water bath. Set the timer for 10 hours.

Once the timer has stopped, remove the bag. Crush the garlic cloves into a paste, spread the paste over the meat. Heat the olive oil in a pan and sear the meat on all sides, for a few minutes.

Flank Steak with Tomato Roast

Prep + Cook Time: 3 hours 30 minutes | Servings: 3

Ingredients

1 lb flank steak	Salt and black pepper to taste	1 cup cherry tomatoes
4 tbsp olive oil, divided into two	2 garlic cloves, minced	1 tbsp balsamic vinegar
1 tbsp + 1 tsp italian seasoning	2 whole garlic cloves	3 tbsp Parmesan cheese, grated

Directions

Prepare a water bath, place Sous Vide in it, and set to 129 F. Place the steak in a vacuum-sealable bag. Add half olive oil, Italian seasoning, black pepper, salt, and crushed garlic and rub gently.

Release air by the water displacement method and seal the bag. Submerge in the water bath. Set the timer for 3 hours and cook 10 minutes. Before the timer has stopped, preheat an oven to 400 F.

In a bowl, toss tomatoes with the remaining ingredients, except for the Parmesan cheese. Pour into a baking dish and place in the oven on the farthest rack from the fire. Bake for 15 minutes.

Once the timer has stopped, unseal and remove the steak. Transfer to a flat surface and sear both sides with a torch until golden brown. Let cool and slice thinly. Serve steak with tomato roast. Garnish with Parmesan cheese.

Shredded BBQ Roast

Prep + Cook Time: 14 hours 20 minutes | Servings: 3

Ingredients

1 pound beef chuck roast	2 tbsp BBQ seasoning

Directions

Make a water bath, place the Sous Vide in it, and set to 165 F.

Preheat a grill. Pat dry the meat using a paper towel and rub with BBQ seasoning. Set aside for 15 minutes. Place meat in vacuum-sealable bag, release air by water displacement method and seal bag. Submerge in the water bath. Set the timer for 14 hours and cook. Once done, remove the meat and shred it. Serve and enjoy!

Beef Steak with Shallots and Parsley

Prep + Cook Time: 1 hour 15 minutes | Servings: 4

Ingredients

2 pounds beef steak, sliced	1 tbsp fresh parsley leaves, finely chopped	1 tbsp shallot, finely chopped
2 tbsp Dijon mustard		½ tsp dried thyme
3 tbsp olive oil	1 tsp fresh rosemary, finely chopped	1 garlic clove, crushed

Directions

Prepare a water bath and place Sous Vide in it. Set to 136 F.

In a small bowl, combine Dijon mustard, olive oil, parsley, rosemary, shallot, thyme, and garlic. Rub the meat with this mixture and place in a vacuum-sealable bag. Release air by the water displacement method, seal, and submerge the bag in the water bath. Set the timer for 1 hour. Serve with salad.

Prime Rib with Celery Herb Crust

Prep + Cook Time: 5 hours 15 minutes | Servings: 3

Ingredients

1 ½ lb rib eye steak, bone in
Salt and black pepper to taste
½ tsp pink pepper

½ tbsp celery seeds, dried
1 tbsp garlic powder
2 sprigs rosemary, minced

2 cups beef stock
1 egg white

Directions

Rub salt on the meat and marinate for 1 hour. Make a water bath, place Sous Vide in it, and set to 130 F. Place beef in a vacuum-sealable bag, release air by the water displacement method and seal the bag. Submerge the bag in the water bath. Set the timer for 4 hours and cook. Once ready, remove the beef and pat dry; set aside.

Mix the black pepper powder, pink pepper powder, celery seeds, garlic powder, and rosemary. Brush the beef with the egg white. Dip the beef in the celery seed mixture to coat graciously. Place in a baking sheet and bake in an oven for 15 minutes. Remove and allow to cool on a cutting board.

Gently slice the beef, cutting against the bone. Pour liquid in a vacuum bag and beef broth in a pan and bring to boil over medium heat. Discard floating fat or solids. Place beef slices on a plate and drizzle sauce over it. Serve with a side of steamed green vegetables.

Sirloin Steaks with Mushroom Cream Sauce

Prep + Cook Time: 1 hour 20 minutes | Servings: 3

Ingredients

3 (6-oz) boneless sirloin steaks
Salt and black pepper to taste
4 tsp unsalted butter
1 tbsp olive oil

6 oz white mushrooms, quartered
2 large shallots, minced
2 cloves garlic, minced
½ cup beef stock

½ cup heavy cream
2 tsp mustard sauce
Thinly sliced scallions for garnishing

Directions

Prepare a water bath, place Sous Vide in it, and set to 135 F. Season the beef with pepper and salt and place them in a 3 separate vacuum-sealable bag. Add 1 teaspoon of butter to each bag. Release air by the water displacement method, seal, and submerge the bag in the water bath. Set to 45 minutes.

Ten minutes before the timer stops, heat oil and the remaining butter in a skillet over medium heat. Once the timer has stopped, remove and unseal the bag. Remove the beef, pat dry, and place in the skillet. Reserve the juices in the bags. Sear on each side for 1 minute and transfer to cutting board. Slice and set aside.

In the same skillet, add the shallots and mushrooms. Cook for 10 minutes and add the garlic. Cook for 1 minute. Add the stock and reserved juices. Simmer for 3 minutes. Add in heavy cream, bring to a boil on high heat and reduce to lower heat after 5 minutes. Turn the heat off and stir in the mustard sauce. Place the steak on a plate, top with mushroom sauce and garnish with scallions.

Beef Pear Steak

Prep + Cook Time: 3 hours 10 minutes | Servings: 3

Ingredients

3 (6 oz) beef pear steaks
2 tbsp olive oil

4 tbsp unsalted butter
4 cloves garlic, crushed

4 sprigs fresh thyme

Directions

Make a water bath, place the Sous Vide in it, and set it to 135F. Season the beef with salt and place in 3 vacuum-sealable bags. Release air by the water displacement method and seal bags. Submerge in the water bath. Set the timer for 3 hours and cook.

Once the timer has stopped, remove the beef, pat dry, and season with pepper and salt. Warm oil in a skillet over medium heat until it starts to smoke. Add the steaks, butter, garlic, and thyme. Sear for 3 minutes on both sides. Baste with some more butter as you cook. Slice steaks into desired slices.

Tomato Stuffed Mushrooms

Prep + Cook Time: 60 minutes | Servings: 4

Ingredients

2 pounds Cremini mushrooms
1 yellow bell pepper, finely chopped
2 medium-sized tomatoes, peeled and

finely chopped
2 spring onions, finely chopped
1 ¾ cup lean ground beef

3 tbsp olive oil
Salt and black pepper to taste

Directions

Prepare a water bath and place the Sous Vide in it. Set to 131 F. Steam the mushrooms and set caps aside. Chop up the mushroom stems. Heat 2 tablespoons of olive oil in a large skillet. Add onions and sauté for 1 minute.

Now, add in ground beef and sauté for an additional minute, stirring constantly. Stir in mushroom stems, tomatoes, bell pepper, salt, and black pepper, and continue to sauté for a further 3 minutes.

Arrange mushroom caps on a clean work surface and drizzle with the remaining oil. Scoop the beef mixture into each cap and place in a large vacuum-sealable bag in a single layer. Release air by the water displacement method, seal, and submerge the bag in the water bath. Set the timer for 50 minutes.

Once the timer has stopped, remove the mushrooms from the bag. Transfer to a serving dish. Pour over any of the mushroom juices that are left in bag. Serve with salad.

Simple Corned Beef

Prep + Cook Time: 5 hours 10 minutes | Servings: 4

Ingredients

15 ounces beef brisket
1 tbsp salt
¼ cup beef stock

1 tsp paprika
1 cup beer
2 onions, sliced

½ tsp oregano
1 tsp cayenne pepper

Directions

Prepare a water bath and place Sous Vide in it. Set to 138 F. Cut the beef into 4 pieces. Place in separate vacuum-sealable bags. Whisk beer, stock and spices in a bowl. Stir in the onions. Divide the mixture between the bags. Release air by the water displacement method, seal, and submerge the bag in the water bath. Set the timer for 5 hours. Once the timer has stopped, remove the bag and transfer to a plate.

Beef with Onions

Prep + Cook Time: 1 hour 15 minutes | Servings: 3

Ingredients

¾ cup lean beef, chopped into bite-sized pieces
2 large onions, finely chopped
3 tbsp mustard

1 tsp soy sauce
1 tsp dried thyme

2 tbsp vegetable oil
2 tbsp sesame oil

Directions

Prepare a water bath and place the Sous Vide in it. Set to 136 F. Pat dry the meat with kitchen paper. Using a kitchen brush, spread the mustard over meat and sprinkle with dried thyme. Place in a vacuum-sealable bag along with soy sauce, chopped onions, and sesame oil. Seal the bag and submerge in the bath and cook for 1 hour.

Remove from the water bath. Pat the meat dry with a paper towel and set aside. Heat the vegetable oil in a skillet over medium heat. Add beef and stir-fry for 5 minutes, stirring constantly. Remove from the heat and serve.

Beef Sirloin in Tomato Sauce

Prep + Cook Time: 2 hours 5 minutes | Servings: 3

Ingredients

1 pound beef sirloin medallions
1 cup fire-roasted tomatoes
1 tsp hot pepper sauce
3 garlic cloves, crushed

2 tsp chili pepper
2 tsp garlic powder
2 tsp fresh lime juice
1 bay leaf

2 tsp vegetable oil
Salt and black pepper to taste

Directions

Prepare a water bath, place Sous Vide in it, and set to 129 F. Season beef with salt and black pepper.

In a bowl, combine the fire-roasted tomatoes with hot pepper sauce, crushed garlic, chili pepper, garlic powder, and lime juice. Add the sirloin to the mixture and toss to coat. Place in the vacuum-sealable bag in a single layer and seal it. Submerge in the water bath and cook for 2 hours.

Once the timer has stopped, remove the medallions and pat them dry. Discard the bay leaf. Reserve cooking juices. Sear in a high hot skillet for about 1 minute. Serve with the sauce and mashed potatoes.

Beef Chuck Shoulder with Mushrooms

Prep + Cook Time: 6 hours 15 minutes | Servings: 3

Ingredients

1 pound beef chuck shoulder
1 medium-sized carrot, sliced
1 large onion, chopped

¾ cup button mushrooms, sliced
1 cup beef stock
2 tbsp olive oil

4 garlic cloves, finely chopped
Salt and black pepper to taste

Directions

Prepare a water bath and place the Sous Vide in it. Set to 136 F. Place beef chuck shoulder in a large vacuum-sealable bag along with sliced carrot, and half of the broth. Submerge the sealed bag in the water bath and cook for 6 hours. Once the timer has stopped, remove the meat from bag and pat dry.

In a pot, heat the olive oil and put in onion and garlic. Stir-fry until translucent, for 3-4 minutes. Add beef shoulder, the remaining broth, 2 cups of water, mushrooms, salt, and pepper. Bring it to a boil and reduce the heat to a minimum. Cook for an additional 5 minutes, stirring constantly.

Honey-Dijon Brisket

Prep + Cook Time: 48 hours 20 minutes | Servings: 12

Ingredients

6 pounds beef brisket
2 tbsp olive oil
4 large shallots, sliced
4 garlic cloves, peeled and smashed

¼ cup apple cider vinegar
½ cup tomato paste
½ cup honey
¼ cup Dijon mustard

2 cups water
1 tbsp whole black peppercorns
2 dried allspice berries
Salt to taste

Directions

Prepare a water bath and place the Sous Vide in it. Set to 155 F.

Heat the olive oil in a skillet over high heat and sear the brisket until golden brown on both sides. Set aside. In the same skillet on medium heat, sauté shallots and garlic for 10 minutes.

Combine vinegar, honey, tomato paste, mustard, peppercorn, water, allspice, and cloves. Add in the shallot mixture. Mix well. Place the brisket and the mixture in a vacuum-sealable bag. Release air by the water displacement method, seal, and submerge the bag in the water bath. Cook for 48 hours.

Once the timer has stopped, remove the bag and pat the meat dry. Pour the cooking juices in a saucepan over high heat and cook until the sauce has reduced by half, 10 minutes. Serve with the brisket.

Classic Beef Stew

Prep + Cook Time: 3 hours 15 minutes | Servings: 4

Ingredients

1 pound beef neck, chopped into bite-sized pieces

½ large eggplant, sliced	5 peppercorns, whole	¼ tsp chili pepper (optional)
1 cup fire-roasted tomatoes	2 tbsp butter, unsalted	1 tsp salt
1 cup beef broth	1 bay leaf, whole	Fresh parsley to garnish
½ cup burgundy	1 tbsp tomato paste	
¼ cup vegetable oil	½ tbsp cayenne pepper	

Directions

Prepare a water bath and place the Sous Vide in it. Set to 135 F. Rinse the meat under cold running water. Pat dry with kitchen paper and place on a clean working surface. Using a sharp knife, cut into bite-sized pieces.

In a large bowl, combine burgundy with oil, peppercorns, bay leaf, cayenne pepper, chili pepper, and salt. Dip meat in this mixture and refrigerate for 2 hours. Remove the meat from the marinade and pat dry with kitchen paper. Reserve the liquid. Place in a large vacuum-sealable bag. Seal the bag.

Submerge the sealed bag in the water bath and cook for 1 hour. Remove from the water bath, discard the bay leaf, and transfer to a deep, heavy-bottomed pot. Add butter and gently melt over medium heat. Put in eggplants, tomatoes, and ¼ cup of the marinade. Cook for a further 5 minutes, stirring constantly. Taste, adjust the seasonings and serve garnished with chopped fresh parsley.

Red Wine Beef Ribs

Prep + Cook Time: 6 hours 15 minutes | Servings: 3

Ingredients

1 pound beef short ribs	2 tbsp olive oil	1 tsp Paprika
¼ cup red wine	½ cup beef stock	Salt and black pepper to taste
1 tsp honey	¼ cup apple cider vinegar	
½ cup tomato paste	1 garlic clove, minced	

Directions

Prepare a water bath and place the Sous Vide in it. Set to 140 F. Rinse and drain the ribs. Season with salt, pepper, and paprika. Place in a vacuum-sealable bag in a single layer along with wine, tomato paste, beef broth, honey, and apple cider. Release air by the water displacement method, seal, and submerge the bag in the water bath.

Set the timer for 6 hours. Pat the ribs dry. Discard cooking liquids. In a large skillet, heat the olive oil over medium heat. Add garlic and stir-fry until translucent. Put in ribs and brown for 5 minutes per side.

Beef Pepper Meat

Prep + Cook Time: 6 hours 10 minutes | Servings: 2

Ingredients

1 pound beef tenderloin, cut into bite-sized pieces

1 large onion finely chopped	1 tsp dried thyme, ground	Salt and black pepper to taste
1 tbsp butter, melted	1 tbsp lemon juice, freshly squeezed	
1 tbsp fresh parsley, finely chopped	1 tbsp tomato paste	

Directions

Prepare a water bath and place the Sous Vide in it. Set to 158 F. Thoroughly combine all the ingredients, except for the parsley, in a large vacuum-sealable bag. Release air by the water displacement method and seal.

Submerge the bag in the water bath. Set the timer for 6 hours. Once the timer has stopped, remove from the water bath and open the bag. Serve immediately garnished with chopped fresh parsley.

Beef Stroganoff

Prep + Cook Time: 24 hours 15 minutes | Servings: 4

Ingredients

1 pound chuck roast, cut into chunks
½ onion, chopped
1 pound mushrooms, sliced
1 garlic cloves, minced

¼ cup white wine
4 tbsp Greek yogurt
½ cup beef stock
1 tbsp butter

1 sprig of fresh flat-leaf parsley
Salt and black pepper to taste

Directions

Prepare a water bath and place the Sous Vide in it. Set to 140 F. Season the beef with salt and pepper. Place in a vacuum-sealable bag and seal. Immerse in the preheated water and cook for 24 hours.

The next day, melt the butter in a pan over medium heat. Put in onions and garlic and sauté until softened, about 3 minutes. Add in mushrooms and cook for an additional 5 minutes. Pour in wine and stock and cook until the mixture is reduced by half. Stir in the beef and cook for another minute. Taste and adjust the seasonings. Serve warm with minced fresh parsley.

Garlic Burgers

Prep + Cook Time: 70 minutes | Servings: 4

Ingredients

1 pound lean ground beef
3 garlic cloves, crushed
2 tbsp breadcrumbs
3 eggs, beaten

4 burger buns
4 crisphead lettuce leaves
4 tomato slices
¼ cup lentils, soaked

¼ cup oil, divided in half
1 tbsp cilantro, finely chopped
Salt and black pepper to taste

Directions

Prepare a water bath, place Sous Vide in it, and set to 139 F.

Meanwhile, in a bowl, combine lentils with beef, garlic, cilantro, breadcrumbs, eggs, and three tablespoons of oil. Season with salt and black pepper. Using your hands, shape burgers and lay on a lightly floured working surface. Place each burger in a vacuum-sealable bag and seal. Submerge in the water bath and cook for 1 hour.

Once the timer has stopped, remove the burgers from the bag and pat them dry with paper towel. Set aside. Heat the remaining oil in a large skillet. Brown burgers for 2-3 minutes on each side for extra crispiness. Drizzle burgers with your favorite sauce and transfer to buns. Garnish as with lettuce and tomato and serve immediately.

Beef Fillet with Baby Carrots

Prep + Cook Time: 2 hours 15 minutes | Servings: 5

Ingredients

2 pounds beef fillet
7 baby carrots, sliced
1 onion, chopped

1 cup tomato paste
2 tbsp vegetable oil
2 tbsp fresh parsley, finely chopped

Salt and black pepper to taste

Directions

Prepare a water bath and place the Sous Vide in it. Set to 133 F. Wash and pat dry the meat with kitchen paper. Using a sharp knife, cut into bite-sized pieces and season with salt and pepper.

In a skillet, brown beef in oil over medium heat, turning to brown equally for 5 minutes. Add the carrots and onion and cook until softened, about 2 minutes. Stir in tomato paste, salt, and pepper. Pour in ½ cup of water.

Remove from the heat and transfer to a large vacuum-sealable bag in a single layer. Release air by the water displacement method, seal, and submerge the bag in the water bath. Set the timer for 2 hours. Remove the bag from the bath and transfer contents to serving plate. Serve garnished with fresh parsley.

Ground Beef Stew

Prep + Cook Time: 60 minutes | Servings: 3

Ingredients

4 medium-sized eggplants, halved
½ cup lean ground beef
2 medium-size tomatoes, chopped

¼ cup extra virgin olive oil
2 tbsp toasted almonds, finely chopped
1 tbsp fresh celery leaves, chopped

Salt and black pepper to taste
1 tsp thyme

Directions

Prepare a water bath and place the Sous Vide in it. Set to 180 F. Slice eggplants in half, lengthwise. Scoop the flesh and transfer to a bowl. Generously sprinkle with salt and let sit for ten minutes. Heat 3 tablespoons of oil over medium heat. Briefly fry the eggplants, for 3 minutes on each side and remove from the frying pan. Use some kitchen paper to soak up the excess oil. Set aside.

Put the ground beef in the same frying pan. Stir-fry for 5 minutes, stir in tomatoes and simmer until the tomatoes have softened. Add in eggplants, almonds and celery leaves and cook for 5 minutes. Turn off heat and stir in thyme. Transfer everything to a large vacuum-sealable bag. Release air by the water displacement method, seal, and submerge the bag in the water bath. Set the timer for 40 minutes.

Once the timer has stopped, remove the bag and pour the contents over a large bowl. Taste and adjust the seasonings. Serve garnished with parsley, if desired.

Beef Bites with Teriyaki Sauce & Seeds

Prep + Cook Time: 70 minutes | Servings: 2

Ingredients

2 beef steaks
½ cup teriyaki sauce
2 tbsp soy sauce

2 tsp fresh chilis, chopped
1 ½ tbsp sesame seeds, toasted
2 tbsp poppy seeds, toasted

8 oz rice noodles
2 tbsp sesame oil
1 tbsp scallion, finely chopped

Directions

Prepare a water bath and place the Sous Vide in it. Set to 134 F. Chop the beef in cubes and place in a vacuum-sealable bag. Add 1/2 cup of teriyaki sauce. Release air by the water displacement method, seal, and submerge the bag in the water bath. Cook for 60 minutes.

In a bowl, mix the soy sauce and chilis. In another bowl, put the poppy seeds. After 50 minutes, start cooking the noodles. Drain them and transfer to a bowl. Once the timer has stopped, remove the beef and discard cooking juices. Heat the sesame oil in a skillet over high heat and add the beef with 6 tbsp of teriyaki sauce. Cook for 5 seconds. Serve in a bowl and garnish with toasted seeds.

Delicious Cheesy Steak Roll

Prep + Cook Time: 2 hours 75 minutes | Servings: 4

Ingredients

2 bell peppers, thinly sliced
½ red onion, thinly sliced
2 tbsp olive oil

Salt and black pepper to taste
1 pound skirt steak, thinly sliced
4 soft hoagie rolls

8 slices cheddar cheese

Directions

Prepare a water bath and place the Sous Vide in it. Set to 186 F. Place the beef in a vacuum-sealable bag. Season with salt and pepper. Release air by the water displacement method, seal, and submerge the bag in the water bath. Cook for 2 hours. Then, add in the bell peppers, onion, and olive oil inside and submerge it. Cook for 50more minutes. Once done, remove the bag and set aside. Preheat the oven over 400 F. Cut the hoagie rolls by the middle and top with cheese. Bake for 2 minutes. Transfer to a plate and top with peppers, steaks and onions.

Lemony & Peppery Flank Steak

Prep + Cook Time: 2 hours 15 minutes | Servings: 4

Ingredients

2 pounds flank steak
1 tbsp lime zest
1 lemon, sliced

½ tsp cayenne pepper
1 tsp garlic powder
Salt and black pepper to taste

¼ cup maple syrup
½ cup chicken stock

Directions

Prepare a water bath and place the Sous Vide in it. Set to 148 F. Combine the spices and zest and rub over the steak. Let sit for about 5 minutes. Whisk the stock and maple syrup. Place the steak in a vacuum-sealable bag and add the lemon slices. Release air by the water displacement method, seal and submerge the bag in water bath. Set timer for 2 hours. Once done, remove and transfer to a grill and cook for 30 seconds each side. Serve.

Beef & Veggie Stew

Prep + Cook Time: 4 hours 25 minutes | Servings: 12

Ingredients

16 ounces beef fillet, cubed
4 potatoes, chopped
3 carrots, sliced
5 ounces shallot, sliced
1 onion, chopped

2 garlic cloves, minced
¼ cup red wine
¼ cup heavy cream
2 tbsp butter
1 tsp paprika

½ cup chicken stock
½ tsp turmeric
Salt and black pepper to taste
1 tsp lemon juice

Directions

Prepare a water bath and place the Sous Vide in it. Set to 155 F. Place the beef along with salt, pepper, turmeric, paprika, and red wine in a vacuum-sealable bag. Massage to coat well. Release air by the water displacement method, seal, and submerge the bag in the water bath. Set the timer for 4 hours.

Meanwhile, combine the remaining ingredients in another vacuum-sealable bag. Seal and immerse it in the same bath 3 hours before the end of the cooking time of the meat. Once done, remove everything and place in a pot over medium heat and cook for 15 minutes.

Zesty Beef Steak

Prep + Cook Time: 2 hours 10 minutes | Servings: 5

Ingredients

2 pounds beef steak
3 tbsp olive oil
2 tsp lemon zest

½ tsp pepper
1 tsp oregano
1 tbsp butter

¼ tsp red pepper flakes

Directions

Prepare a water bath and place the Sous Vide in it. Set to 130 F. Combine all of the spices and rub into the meat. Place in a vacuum-sealable bag. Release air by the water displacement method, seal, and submerge the bag in the water bath. Set the timer for 2 hours. Once the timer has stopped, remove the bag and cut the steak into 5 equal pieces. Sear on all sides in a pan over medium heat for about 30 seconds.

Rosemary Ribeye Stew

Prep + Cook Time: 6 hours 35 minutes | Servings: 12

Ingredients

3 pounds bone-in beef ribeye roast
Salt and black pepper to taste
1 tbsp green pepper

1 tbsp dried celery seeds
2 tbsp garlic powder
4 sprigs rosemary

1 tbsp cumin
1 cup beef stock
1 egg white

Directions

Prepare a water bath and place the Sous Vide in it. Set to 132 F. Season the beef with salt and pepper and place it in a vacuum-sealable bag. Submerge the bag in the water bath. Cook for 6 hours.

Preheat the oven to 425 F. Once the timer has stopped, remove the beef. Combine peppers, celery seeds, garlic powder, cumin, and rosemary. Brush the roasted beef with white egg, celery mixture, and salt. Place the roast in a baking tray and bake for 10 minutes. Allow cooling for 10 minutes and slice. Serve the beef topped with sauce.

Worcestershire Meatloaf

Prep + Cook Time: 2 hours 15 minutes | Servings: 4

Ingredients

1 pound ground beef	1 egg	Salt and black pepper to taste
1 cup breadcrumbs	1 cup yogurt	
1 onion, minced	1 garlic clove, minced	

Glaze:

1 tbsp ketchup	2 tsp brown sugar	2 tbsp Worcestershire sauce

Directions

Prepare a water bath and place the Sous Vide in it. Set to 170 F. Combine all of the meatloaf ingredients in a bowl. Mix with your hands until fully incorporated. Place in a vacuum-sealable bag and shape into a log. Release air by the water displacement method, seal, and submerge the bag in the water bath. Set timer for 2 hours.

Once the timer has stopped, remove the bag and transfer to a baking dish. Whisk together the glaze ingredients and brush over the meatloaf. Cook under a broiler until it begins to bubble.

Drunken Beef Steak

Prep + Cook Time: 2 hours 15 minutes | Servings: 4

Ingredients

1 pound beef steak	2 tsp butter	Salt and black pepper to taste
1 cup red wine	1 tsp sugar	

Directions

Prepare a water bath and place the Sous Vide in it. Set to 131 F. Combine red wine with the spices and pour into a vacuum-sealable bag. Place the meat inside. Release air by the water displacement method, seal, and submerge the bag in the water bath. Set the timer for 2 hours. Once the timer has stopped, remove the bag. Melt butter in a pan and sear the meat on all sides for a few minutes.

Divine Sirloin with Sweet Potato Purée

Prep + Cook Time: 1 hour 20 minutes | Servings: 4

Ingredients

4 sirloin steaks	¼ cup steak seasoning	4 tbsp butter
2 pounds sweet potatoes, cubed	Salt and black pepper to taste	Canola oil for searing

Directions

Prepare a water bath and place the Sous Vide in it. Set to 129 F. Place the steaks in a vacuum-sealable bag. Release air by the water displacement method, seal, and submerge the bag in the water bath. Cook for 1 hour.

Boil the potatoes for 15 minutes. Drain it and transfer to a bowl with butter. Mash and season with salt and pepper. Once the timer has stopped, remove the steaks and pat dry. Heat the oil in a pot over medium heat. Sear for 1 minute. Serve with the potato puree.

Beef Pie with Mushrooms

Prep + Cook Time: 3 hours | Servings: 4

Ingredients

1 pound beef tenderloin
Salt and black pepper to taste
1 tbsp Dijon mustard
1 sheet puff pastry, thawed

8 oz cremini mushrooms
8 oz shiitake mushrooms
1 shallot, diced
3 garlic cloves, chopped

1 tbsp butter
6 slices bacon, chopped
1 egg yolk, beaten

Directions

Prepare a water bath and place the Sous Vide in it. Set to 124 F. Season the beef with salt and pepper and place in a vacuum-sealable bag. Release air by the water displacement method, seal, and submerge the bag in the water bath. Cook for 2 hours. Once the timer has stopped, remove the beef and pat dry and slice-it.

Melt the butter in a skillet over medium heat and cook shallot and garlic for 3 minutes. When tender, add in the mushrooms and bacon and cook until the water has evaporated, about 5 minutes.

Preheat the oven to 475 F. Brush the beef slices with Dijon mustard. Arrange them on a greased pie pan and cover with the bacon mixture. Top with the puff pastry and brush with egg yolk. Make a few slits in the surface and place in the oven. Bake for 25-30 minutes until golden brown on top. Let sit for 10 minutes. Slice and serve.

Classic Cheese Burgers

Prep + Cook Time: 1 hour 15 minutes | Servings: 4

Ingredients

1 pound ground beef
2 hamburger buns

2 slices cheddar cheese
Salt and black pepper to taste

Butter for toasting

Directions

Prepare a water bath and place the Sous Vide in it. Set to 137 F. Season beef with salt and pepper and shape into patties. Place in a vacuum-sealable bag. Release air by the water displacement method, seal, and submerge the bag in the water bath. Cook for 1 hour.

Meanwhile, heat a skillet and toast the buns with butter. Once the timer has stopped, remove the burgers and transfer to a skillet. Sear for 30 seconds per side. Top the burger with cheese and cook until melted. Put the burger between the buns and serve.

Creamy Veal Marsala

Prep + Cook Time: 1 hour 35 minutes | Servings: 4

Ingredients

1 pound veal steaks
Garlic salt and black pepper to taste
2 cups thinly sliced Enoki mushrooms

½ cup heavy cream
1 shallot, thinly sliced
3 tbsp Marsala

2 tbsp butter
2 sprigs fresh sage
2 tbsp chives, finely

Directions

Prepare a water bath and place the Sous Vide in it. Set to 138 F.

Season veal with salt and garlic and place it with the mushrooms, cream, marsala, pepper, butter, and thyme in a vacuum-sealable bag. Release air by the water displacement method, seal, and submerge the bag in the water bath. Cook for 90 minutes.

Once the timer has stopped, remove the bag and transfer to a serving plate. Discard the sage and reserve the cooking liquids. Heat a saucepan over medium heat, add in cooking liquids and simmer for 5 minutes. Lower the heat and add in the veal. Serve the veal with rice. Garnish with chives.

Rib Eye Noodles with Cauliflower

Prep + Cook Time: 2 hours 10 minutes | Servings: 2

Ingredients

2 rib-eye steaks
8 oz noodles, boiled and drained
2 cups oil

2 cups cauliflower, boiled and drained
1 onion, sliced
2 cups warm chicken stock

2 tbsp cornstarch
Salt and black pepper to taste

Directions

Prepare a water bath and place the Sous Vide in it. Set to 134 F. Place the rib eye in a vacuum-sealable bag. Release air by the water displacement method, seal, and submerge the bag in the water bath. Cook for 1-2 hours. In a bowl, combine chicken stock and cornstarch.

Heat oil in a frying pan and fry the noodles for 5 minutes; set aside. Add in onion and cauliflower and fry with the chicken mix. Cook until thick. Once done, pat the rib dry. Season with salt and pepper. Transfer to the frying pan and sear for 1 minute each side. In a bowl, put noodles, veggies and the steak. Season with salt and pepper.

Kimchi Rib Eye Tacos with Avocado

Prep + Cook Time: 2 hours 25 minutes | Servings: 4

Ingredients

2 pounds short rib, thinly sliced
½ cup soy sauce
3 green onion stalks, sliced
1 tbsp Tabasco sauce

6 cloves garlic, chopped
2 tbsp brown sugar
1-inch turmeric, grated
1 tbsp sesame oil

½ a tsp red pepper powder
8 corn tortillas
Kimchi for topping
1 Sliced avocado

Directions

Prepare a water bath and place the Sous Vide in it. Set to 138 F. Heat a saucepan over medium heat and combine soy sauce, green onion, garlic, tabasco sauce, brown sugar, turmeric, red pepper powder, and sesame oil. Cook until the sugar dissolved. Allow chilling. Place the sauce mixture in a vacuum-sealable bag. Release air by the water displacement method, seal, and submerge the bag in the water bath. Cook for 2 hours.

Once the timer has stopped, remove the sauce and transfer to a saucepan for reduced. In a grill, put the short ribs and cook until crispy. Chop the ribs in cubes. Create a taco with the tortilla, beef and avocado. Garnish with Kimchi and hot sauce. Serve and enjoy!

Liver with Garlic

Prep + Cook Time: 1 hour 25 minutes | Servings: 4

Ingredients

1 pound calf's liver, thinly sliced
3 tbsp olive oil
2 garlic cloves, crushed

1 tbsp fresh mint, finely chopped
2 tsps cayenne pepper, ground
1 tsp salt

1 tsp Italian seasoning mix

Directions

Make a water bath, place Sous Vide in it, and set to 129 F. Rinse the liver thoroughly under cold running water. Make sure to wash out all the blood traces. Pat dry with kitchen paper. Using a sharp paring knife, remove all though veins, if any. Cut crosswise into thin slices.

Next, in a small bowl, combine olive oil, garlic, mint, cayenne, salt, and Italian seasoning. Mix until well incorporated. Brush liver slices with this mixture and refrigerate for 30 minutes. Remove from the refrigerator and place in a large vacuum-sealable bag. Release air by the water displacement method and seal the bags.

Submerge them in the water bath and set the timer for 40 minutes. Once the timer has stopped, remove from the water bath and open the bag. Grease a large skillet with some oil and place in meat liver slices. Briefly, brown on both sides for 2 minutes. Drizzle with extra-virgin olive oil and serve with bread.

Easy-to-Make Tenderloin with Cayenne Sauce

Prep + Cook Time: 55 minutes | Servings: 2

Ingredients

16 beef tenderloin steaks
¼ tsp cayenne powder
Salt and black pepper to taste
½ tbsp butter
½ tbsp olive oil
2 tbsp onion, finely chopped

1 clove garlic, minced
¼ cup sherry
2 tbsp balsamic vinegar
1 chipotle pepper
¼ cup water
1 tbsp tomato paste

1 tsp soy sauce
1 tbsp molasses
1 tbsp vegetable oil
Cilantro, chopped, for garnish

Directions

Prepare a water bath and place the Sous Vide in it. Set to 125 F. Combine the steak with chipotle pepper, salt and pepper, and place in a vacuum-sealable bag. Release air by the water displacement method, seal, and submerge the bag in the water bath. Cook for 40 minutes.

Meanwhile, prepare the sauce by heating a skillet over medium heat. Add in butter and onion, and cook until softened. Stir in garlic and cook for 1 more minute. Pour in sherry and cook until reduced. Pour in balsamic vinegar, cayenne, water, tomato paste, soy sauce, and molasses. Stir. Broil until thick.

Once the timer has stopped, remove the steak and transfer to a heated skillet with butter over high heat and sear for 1 minute. Top with the sauce and garnish with cilantro to serve.

White Wine Veal & Mushroom Chops

Prep + Cook Time: 3 hours 20 minutes | Servings: 4

Ingredients

1 pound lean veal cuts, chopped into bite-sized pieces
4 cups button mushrooms, sliced
3 large carrots, sliced

1 cup celery root, finely chopped
2 tbsp butter, softened
1 tbsp extra-virgin olive oil
1 tbsp cayenne pepper

Salt and black pepper to taste
¼ cup white wine
A handful fresh celery leaves, chopped

Directions

Prepare a water bath, place Sous Vide in it, and set to 144 F. In a large bowl, combine meat with mushrooms, sliced carrots, celery root, olive oil, cayenne pepper, salt, and black pepper. Stir well and transfer to a large vacuum-sealable bag. Submerge the sealed bag in the water bath and cook for 3 hours.

Once done, remove the meat from the bag and pat dry. Reserve the cooking liquids. Melt the butter in a large saucepan. Simmer cooking liquids until slightly thickened. Pour in white wine and bring it to a boil for 1 minute. Sprinkle with finely chopped celery leaves and serve warm with the sauce on the side.

Peppercorn Veal Chops with Pine Mushrooms

Prep + Cook Time: 3 hours 15 minutes | Servings: 5

Ingredients

1 pound veal chops
1 pound Pine mushrooms, sliced
½ cup freshly squeezed lemon juice

1 tbsp bay leaves, crushed
5 peppercorns
3 tbsp vegetable oil

2 tbsp extra virgin olive oil
Salt and black pepper to taste

Directions

Prepare a water bath, place Sous Vide in it, and set to 154 F. Season the chops with salt and pepper. Place in a vacuum-sealable bag in a single layer along with lemon juice, bay leaves, peppercorns, and olive oil. Seal the bag. Submerge the bag in the water bath and cook for 3 hours. Remove from the water bath and set aside.

Heat the vegetable oil in a large skillet. Add pine mushrooms and stir-fry with a pinch of salt over medium heat until all the liquid evaporates. Add veal chops along with its marinade and continue to cook for 3 minutes. Serve.

Dijon Veal Liver

Prep + Cook Time: 85 minutes | Servings: 5

Ingredients

2 pounds veal liver, sliced
2 tbsp Dijon mustard
3 tbsp olive oil

1 tbsp cilantro, finely chopped
1 tsp fresh rosemary, finely chopped
1 garlic clove, crushed

½ tsp thyme

Directions

Make a water bath, place Sous Vide in it, and set to 129 F. Rinse the liver thoroughly under cold running water. Make sure to wash out all the blood traces. Pat dry with kitchen paper. Using a sharp paring knife remove all though veins, if any. Cut crosswise into thin slices.

In a small bowl, combine olive oil, garlic, cilantro, thyme, and rosemary. Mix until well incorporated. Generously brush liver slices with this mixture and refrigerate for 30 minutes.

Remove from the refrigerator and place in a large vacuum-sealable bag. Submerge the sealed bag in the water bath and set the timer for 40 minutes. Once done, open the bag. Grease a large skillet with some oil and place meat liver slices in it. Briefly, brown on both sides for 2 minutes. Serve with gherkins.

Saucy Veal with Port Wine

Prep + Cook Time: 2 hours 5 minutes | Servings: 6

Ingredients

3 tbsp butter
¾ cup vegetable broth
½ cup Port wine
¼ cup sliced shiitake mushrooms

3 tbsp olive oil
4 garlic cloves, minced
1 leek, white part only, chopped
Salt and black pepper to taste

8 veal cutlets
1 fresh rosemary sprig

Directions

Prepare a water bath and place the Sous Vide in it. Set to 141 F. Combine broth, Port wine, mushrooms, butter, olive oil, garlic, leek, salt, and pepper. Place the veal in a large vacuum-sealable bag. Add in rosemary and the mixture. Release air by the water displacement method, seal, and submerge the bag in the water bath.

Cook for 1 hour and 45 minutes. Once done, remove the veal and pat dry. Discard the rosemary and transfer the cooking juices to a saucepan. Cook for 5 minutes. Add the veal and cook for 1 minute. Top with sauce to serve.

Lamb Meatballs with a Yogurt Sauce

Prep + Cook Time: 2 hours 15 minutes | Servings: 2

Ingredients

½ pound ground lamb meat
¼ cup fresh parsley, chopped
¼ cup onion, minced
¼ cup toasted almond nuts, chopped
2 garlic cloves, minced

Salt to taste
2 tsp ground coriander
¼ tsp ground cinnamon
1 cup yogurt
½ cup diced cucumber

3 tbsp fresh mint, chopped
1 tsp lemon juice
¼ tsp cayenne pepper
Pitta bread

Directions

Prepare a water bath and place Sous Vide in it. Set to 134 F. Combine lamb, onion, almond, salt, garlic, cinnamon, and coriander. Make 20 balls and arrange them in a vacuum-sealable bag. Release air by the water displacement method, seal, and submerge the bag in the water bath. Cook for 120 minutes.

Meanwhile, prepare the sauce by mixing yogurt, mint, cucumber, cayenne, lemon juice, and 1 tbsp of salt. Once the timer has stopped, remove the balls and bake for 3-5 minutes. Top with the sauce and serve with pita bread.

Portobello Veal

Prep + Cook Time: 2 hours 10 minutes | Servings: 4

Ingredients

2 pounds veal cutlets
1 cup beef stock
4 Portobello mushrooms, sliced

1 tsp garlic powder
1 tbsp oregano, dried
3 tbsp balsamic vinegar

2 tbsp olive oil
Salt and black pepper to taste

Directions

Prepare a water bath, place Sous Vide in it, and set to 140 F. In a bowl, combine the beef stock with mushrooms, garlic powder, oregano, balsamic vinegar, olive oil, and salt. Rub well each cutlet with this mixture and place in a large vacuum-sealable bag in a single layer. Add the remaining marinade and seal.

Submerge in the water bath and cook for 2 hours. Once the timer has stopped, remove the cutlets from the bag and pat dry. Simmer cooking juices in a saucepan for about 4 minutes. Add in cutlets and cook for 1 minute. Transfer to plates. Spoon the sauce over the veal and serve.

Veal Chops

Prep + Cook Time: 2 hours 40 minutes | Servings: 4

Ingredients

2 (16 oz) veal steaks

Salt and black pepper to taste

2 tbsp olive oil

Directions

Prepare a water bath, place the Sous Vide in it, and set to 140 F. Rub the veal with pepper and salt and place in a vacuum-sealable bag. Release air by the water displacement method and seal the bag.

Submerge in the water bath. Set the timer for 2 hours 30 minutes. Once the timer has stopped, remove and unseal the bag. Remove the veal, pat dry using a paper towel, and rub with olive oil. Preheat a on high heat for 5 minutes. Place the steak in and sear to deeply brown on both sides. Remove to a serving board. Serve.

Veal Gravy

Prep + Cook Time: 1 hour 40 minutes | Servings: 3

Ingredients

½ lb veal cutlets
Salt and black pepper to taste
1 cup mushrooms, thinly sliced

⅓ cup heavy cream
2 shallots, thinly sliced
1 tbsp unsalted butter

1 sprig thyme leaves
1 tbsp chopped chives

Directions

Prepare a water bath and place the Sous Vide in it. Set to 129 F. Rub the cutlets with garlic and salt and place the veal with all the remaining listed ingredients except the chives in a vacuum-sealable bag. Release the air by the water displacement method and seal. Submerge in the water bath. Set the timer for 1 hour 30 minutes and cook.

Once done, remove the bag and take out the veal onto a plate. Transfer the sauce to a pan, discard the thyme and simmer for 5 minutes. Add the veal and cook for 3 minutes. Garnish with chives. Serve.

Minted Lamb Chops with Nuts

Prep + Cook Time: 2 hours 35 minutes | Servings: 4

Ingredients

1 pound lamb chops
Salt and black pepper to taste
1 cup fresh mint leaves

½ cup cashew nuts
½ cup packed fresh parsley
½ cup scallion, sliced

3 tbsp lemon juice
2 cloves garlic, minced
6 tbsp olive oil

Directions

Prepare a water bath and place the Sous Vide in it. Set to 125 F. Season the lamb with salt and pepper and place in a vacuum-sealable bag. Release air by the water displacement method, seal, and submerge the bag in the water bath. Cook for 2 hours.

In a food processor, blend the mint, parsley, cashews, scallions, garlic, and lemon juice. Pour 4 tbsp of olive oil. Season with salt and pepper. Once the timer has stopped, remove the lamb, brush with 2 tbsp of olive oil and transfer to a hot grill. Cook for 1 minute per side. Serve with nuts.

African-Style Lamb Chops with Apricots

Prep + Cook Time: 2 hours 15 minutes | Servings: 2

Ingredients

2 lamb loin chops	1 tsp spice blend	1 tbsp honey
Salt and black pepper to taste	4 apricots	1 tsp olive oil

Directions

Prepare a water bath and place the Sous Vide in it. Set to 134 F. Combine the lambs with salt and pepper. Brush lamb chops with the spice blend and place in a vacuum-sealable bag. Add in apricots and honey. Release air by the water displacement method, seal, and submerge the bag in the water bath. Cook for 2 hours.

Once the timer has stopped, remove the chops and pat dry. Reserve the apricots and cooking liquid. Heat a skillet over medium heat and sear the lamb for 30 seconds per side. Transfer to a plate and allow cooling for 5 minutes. Drizzle with cooking liquid. Garnish with apricots.

Spicy Shoulder Lamb Rice

Prep + Cook Time: 24 hours 10 minutes | Servings: 2

Ingredients

1 lamb shoulder roast, boneless	2 tsp garlic salt	1 tsp dried red chili flakes
1 tbsp olive oil	1 tsp coriander	1 cup brown rice, cooked
1 tbsp curry powder	1 tsp ground cumin	

Directions

Prepare a water bath and place the Sous Vide in it. Set to 158 F. Combine the olive oil, garlic, salt, cumin, coriander, and chili flakes. Marinate the lamb. Place in a vacuum-sealable bag. Release air by the water displacement method, seal, and submerge the bag in the water bath. Cook for 24 hours. Once done, remove the lamb and chop into slices. Serve with cooking juices over the rice.

Sweet Lamb with Mustard Sauce

Prep + Cook Time: 1 hour 10 minutes | Servings: 4

Ingredients

1 lamb of rack, trimmed	1 tsp sherry wine vinegar	1 tbsp thyme
3 tbsp runny honey	Salt to taste	Toasted mustard seeds for garnish
2 tbsp Dijon mustard	2 tbsp avocado oil	Chopped green onion

Directions

Prepare a water bath and place the Sous Vide in it. Set to 135 F. Combine all the ingredients, except the lamb. Place the lamb in a vacuum-sealable bag. Release air by the water displacement method, seal, and submerge the bag in the water bath. Cook for 1 hour. Once the timer has stopped, remove the lamb and transfer to a plate.

Heat the oil in a frying pan over high heat and sear the lamb for 2 minutes on each side. Chop and top with cooking juices. Garnish with green onion and toasted mustard seeds.

Mustard & Honey Marinated Rack of Lamb

Prep + Cook Time: 1 hour 10 minutes | Servings: 4

Ingredients

1 rack of lamb, trimmed
3 tbsp honey
2 tbsp Dijon mustard

1 tsp sherry vinegar
Salt to taste
2 tbsp avocado oil

1 small red onion, chopped

Directions

Prepare a water bath and place the Sous Vide in it. Set to 135 F. Combine well all the ingredients, except the lamb. Glaze the lamb with the mixture and place in a vacuum-sealable bag.

Release air by the water displacement method, seal, and submerge the bag in the water bath. Cook for 1 hour. Once the timer has stopped, remove the lamb and transfer to a plate. Reserve the cooking juices.

Heat the oil in a skillet over medium heat and sear the lamb for 2 minutes per side. Chop it and sprinkle with the cooking juices. Garnish with red onion. Serve and enjoy!

Lemon Mint Lamb

Prep + Cook Time: 2 hours 15 minutes | Servings: 2

Ingredients

1 rack of lamb
Salt and black pepper to taste
2 sprigs fresh rosemary
¼ cup olive oil

2 cups fresh lima beans, shelled,
blanched and peeled
1 tbsp lemon juice
1 tbsp fresh chives, minced

1 tbsp fresh parsley, minced
1 tbsp fresh mint
1 garlic clove, minced

Directions

Prepare a water bath and place the Sous Vide in it. Set to 125 F. Season the lamb with salt and pepper and place in a vacuum-sealable bag. Release air by the water displacement method, seal and submerge the bag in water bath.

Cook for 2 hours. Once the timer has stopped, remove the lamb and pat dry. Heat 1 tbsp of olive oil in a grill over high heat and sear the seasoned lamb for 3 minutes. Set aside and allow chilling.

For the salad, combine the lima beans, lemon juice, parsley, chives, mint, garlic, and 3 tbsp of olive oil. Season with salt and pepper. Cut the lamb into chops and serve with lima beans salad.

Lamb Shank with Veggies & Sweet Sauce

Prep + Cook Time: 48 hours 45 minutes | Servings: 4

Ingredients

4 lamb shanks
2 tbsp oil
2 cups all-purpose flour
1 red onion, sliced
4 garlic cloves, smashed and peeled

4 carrots, medium diced
4 stalks celery, medium diced
3 tbsp tomato paste
½ cup sherry wine vinegar
1 cup red wine

¾ cup honey
1 cup beef stock
4 sprigs fresh rosemary
2 bay leaves
Salt and black pepper to taste

Directions

Prepare a water bath and place the Sous Vide in it. Set to 155 F.

Heat oil in a skillet over high heat. Season the shanks with salt, pepper and flour. Sear until golden brown. Set aside. Reduce the heat and cook the onion, carrots, garlic, and celery for 10 minutes. Season with salt and pepper. Stir in tomato paste and cook for 1 more minute. Add in vinegar, stock, wine, honey, bay leaves.

Cook for 2 minutes. Place the veggies, sauce and lambs in a vacuum-sealable bag. Release air by the water displacement method, seal, and submerge the bag in the water bath. Cook for 48 hours.

Once the timer has stopped, remove the shanks and dry it. Reserve the cooking juices. Sear the shanks for 5 minutes until golden. Heat a saucepan over high and pour in cooking juices. Cook until reduced, for10 minutes. Transfer the shanks to a plate and drizzle with the sauce to serve.

Herb Crusted Lamb Rack

Prep + Cook Time: 3 hours 30 minutes | Servings: 6

Ingredients

Lamb Rack:

3 large racks of lamb
Salt and black pepper to taste

1 sprig rosemary
2 tbsp olive oil

Herb Crust:

2 tbsp fresh rosemary leaves
½ cup macadamia nuts
2 tbsp Dijon mustard

½ cup fresh parsley
2 tbsp fresh thyme leaves
2 tbsp lemon zest

2 cloves garlic
2 Egg whites

Directions

Make a water bath, place the Sous Vide in it, and set to 140 F.

Pat dry the lamb using a paper towel and rub the meat with salt and black pepper. Place a pan over medium heat and add the olive oil. Once heated, sear the lamb on both sides for 2 minutes; set aside. Place in garlic and rosemary, toast for 2 minutes and place the lamb over. Let lamb absorb the flavors for 5 minutes.

Place lamb, garlic, and rosemary in a vacuum-sealable bag, release air by the water displacement method and seal the bag. Submerge the bag in the water bath. Set the timer to cook for 3 hours. Once the timer has stopped, remove the bag, unseal it and take out the lamb. Whisk the egg whites and set aside.

Blend the remaining listed herb crust ingredients using a blender and set aside. Pat dry the lamb using a paper towel and brush with the egg whites. Dip into the herb mixture and coat graciously.

Place the lamb racks with crust side up on a baking sheet. Bake in an oven for 15 minutes. Gently slice each cutlet using a sharp knife. Serve with a side of pureed vegetables.

Pancetta & Lamb Stew

Prep + Cook Time: 24 hours 25 minutes | Servings: 6

Ingredients

2 pounds boneless lamb shoulder, cubed
1 pound fingerling potatoes, cut lengthwise

4 oz pancetta, cut into strips
1 cup red wine
2 tbsp tomato paste
1 cup beef stock

4 large shallots, quartered
4 baby carrots, chopped
4 stalks celery, chopped
3 cloves garlic, smashed

4 oz dried Portobello mushrooms
3 sprigs fresh rosemary
3 sprigs fresh thyme
Salt and black pepper to taste

Directions

Prepare a water bath and place the Sous Vide in it. Set to 146 F.

Heat a skillet over high heat and cook the pancetta until browned. Set aside. Season the lamb with salt and pepper and sear in the same skillet; set aside. Pour in wine and stock, and cook for 5 minutes.

Place wine mix, lamb, pancetta, searing juices, veggies and herbs in a vacuum-sealable bag. Release air by the water displacement method, seal, and submerge the bag in the water bath. Cook for 24 hours.

Once the timer has stopped, remove the bag and transfer cooking juices to a hot saucepan over medium heat and cook for 15 minutes Stir in the lamb to sear for a few minutes and serve.

Popular South African Lamb & Cherry Kebabs

Prep + Cook Time: 8 hours 40 minutes | Servings: 6

Ingredients

¾ cup white wine vinegar
½ cup dry red wine
2 onions, chopped
4 garlic cloves, minced
Zest of 2 lemons
6 tbsp brown sugar

2 tbsp caraway seeds, crushed
1 tbsp cherry jam
1 tbsp cornflour
1 tbsp curry powder
1 tbsp grated ginger
2 tsp salt

1 tsp allspice
1 tsp ground cinnamon
2 pounds lamb shoulder, cubed
1 tbsp butter
6 pearl onions, peeled and halved
12 dried cherries, halved

Directions

Prepare a water bath and place the Sous Vide in it. Set to 141 F. Combine well the vinegar, red wine, onions, garlic, lemon zest, brown sugar, caraway seeds, cherry jam, cornflour, curry, ginger, salt, allspice, and cinnamon.

Place the lamb in a large vacuum-sealable bag. Release air by the water displacement method, seal, and submerge the bag in the water bath. Cook for 8 hours. Before 20 minutes to the end, heat the butter in a saucepan and sauté the pearl onions for 8 minutes until softened. Set aside and allow to cool.

Once the timer has stopped, remove the lamb and pat dry with a kitchen towel. Reserve the cooking juices and transfer into a saucepan over medium heat and cook for 10 minutes until reduced by half. Fill the skewer with all kebab ingredients and roll them. Heat a grill over high heat and cook the kebabs for 45 seconds per side. Serve.

Lemon Lamb Chops with Chimichurri Sauce

Prep + Cook Time: 2 hours 15 minutes | Servings: 4

Ingredients

4 lamb shoulder chops
2 tbsp avocado oil
Salt and black pepper to taste
1 cup firmly packed fresh parsley,

chopped
2 tbsp fresh oregano
1 clove garlic, finely minced
1 tbsp champagne vinegar

1 tbsp lemon juice
1 tbsp smoked paprika
¼ tsp crushed red pepper flakes
1/3 cup salted butter, soft

Directions

Prepare a water bath and place Sous Vide in it. Set to 132 F. Season the lamb with salt and pepper and place in a vacuum-sealable bag. Release air by the water displacement method, seal, and submerge the bag in the water bath. Cook for 2 hours. Combine well in a bowl, the parsley, garlic, oregano, champagne vinegar, paprika, lemon juice, red pepper flakes, black pepper, salt, and soft butter. Allow chilling in the fridge.

Once the timer has stopped, remove the lamb and pat dry. Season with salt and pepper. Heat avocado oil in a skillet over high heat and sear the lamb for a few minutes on all sides. Top with butter dressing, and serve.

Spicy Lamb Kebabs

Prep + Cook Time: 2 hours 20 minutes | Servings: 4

Ingredients

1 pound leg lamb, boneless, cubed
2 tbsp chili paste
1 tbsp olive oil

Salt to taste
1 tsp cumin
1 tsp coriander

½ tsp black pepper
Greek yogurt
Fresh mint leaves for serving

Directions

Prepare a water bath and place the Sous Vide in it. Set to 134 F. Combine all the ingredients and place them in a vacuum-sealable bag. Release air by the water displacement method, seal, and submerge the bag in the water bath. Cook for 2 hours. Once the timer has stopped, remove the lamb and dry it. Transfer the lamb to a grill and cook for 5 minutes. Set aside and allow resting for 5 minutes. Serve with Greek yogurt and mint.

Bell Pepper & Lamb Curry

Prep + Cook Time: 30 hours 30 minutes | Servings: 4

Ingredients

2 tbsp butter
2 bell peppers, chopped
3 garlic cloves, minced
1 tsp turmeric
1 tsp ground cumin
1 tsp paprika

1 tsp grated fresh ginger
½ tsp salt
2 cardamom pods
2 fresh thyme sprigs
1 ¼ pounds boneless lamb meat, cubed
1 large onion, chopped

3 tomatoes, chopped
1 tsp allspice
2 tbsp Greek yogurt
1 tbsp chopped fresh cilantro

Directions

Prepare a water bath and place the Sous Vide in it. Set to 179 F. Combine 1 tbsp of butter, bell peppers, 2 garlic cloves, turmeric, cumin, paprika, ginger, salt, cardamom, and thyme. Place the lamb in a vacuum-sealable bag with the butter mixture. Release air by the water displacement method, seal, and submerge the bag in the water bath. Cook for 30 hours. Once the timer has stopped, remove the bag and set aside.

Heat the remaining butter in a saucepan over high heat. Add in onion and cook for 4 minutes. Add the remaining garlic and cook for 1 minute more. Reduce the heat and place in tomatoes and allspice. Cook for 2 minutes. Pour in yogurt, lamb and the cooking juices. Cook for 10-15 minutes. Garnish with cilantro. Serve and enjoy!

Peppery Lemon Lamb Chops with Papaya Chutney

Prep + Cook Time: 1 hour 15 minutes | Servings: 4

Ingredients

8 lamb chops
2 tbsp olive oil
½ tsp Garam Masala
¼ tsp lemon pepper

Dash of garlic pepper
Salt and black pepper to taste
½ cup yogurt
¼ cup fresh cilantro, chopped

2 tbsp papaya chutney
1 tbsp curry powder
1 tbsp onion, finely chopped
Chopped cilantro for garnish

Directions

Prepare the sauce by mixing yogurt, papaya chutney, cilantro, curry powder, and onion. Set aside until ready to serve. Prepare a water bath and place the Sous Vide in it. Set to 138 F. Brush the chops with olive oil and top with Garam Masala, lemon pepper, garlic powder, salt, and pepper. Place in a vacuum-sealable bag. Release air by the water displacement method, seal, and submerge the bag in the water bath. Cook for 1 hour.

Heat the remaining oil in a skillet over medium heat and sear the lamb for 30 seconds per side. Strain with a baking sheet. Serve the chops with the yogurt sauce. Garnish with cilantro.

Garlic Rack of Lamb

Prep + Cook Time: 1 hour 30 minutes | Servings: 4

Ingredients

2 tbsp butter
2 racks of lamb, frenched

2 tbsp sesame oil
4 garlic cloves, minced

4 fresh basil sprigs, halved
Salt and black pepper to taste

Directions

Prepare a water bath and place the Sous Vide in it. Set to 130 F. Season the rack lamb with salt and pepper. Place in a large vacuum-sealable bag. Release air by the water displacement method, seal, and submerge the bag in the water bath. Cook for 1 hour and 15 minutes. Once done, remove the rack and pat dry with kitchen towel.

Heat sesame oil in a skillet over high heat and sear the rack for 1 minute per side; reserve. Melt the butter in the skillet and cook the garlic and basil for 30 seconds. Return the lamb and toss to coat with the garlic mixture; cook for 1 minute. Cut into pieces and serve.

Goat Cheese Lamb Ribs

Prep + Cook Time: 4 hours 10 minutes | Servings: 2

Ingredients

Ribs:

2 half racks lamb ribs
2 tbsp vegetable oil
1 clove garlic, minced

2 tbsp rosemary leaves, chopped
1 tbsp fennel pollen
Salt and black pepper to taste

½ tsp cayenne pepper

To Garnish:

8 oz goat cheese, crumbled

2 oz roasted walnuts, chopped

3 tbsp parsley, chopped

Directions

Make a water bath, place the Sous Vide in it, and set to 134 F. Mix the listed lamb ingredients except for the lamb. Pat dry the lamb using a kitchen towel and rub with the spice mixture. Place the meat in a vacuum-sealable bag, release air by the water displacement method, seal, and submerge the bag in the water bath. Cook for 4 hours.

Once the timer has stopped, remove the lamb. Heat the oil in a pan over high heat. Sear the lamb until golden brown. Cut the ribs between the bones. Garnish with goat cheese, walnuts, and parsley. Serve and enjoy!

Herby Lamb with Veggies

Prep + Cook Time: 48 hours 30 minutes | Servings: 8

Ingredients

2 lb lamb shanks, bone-in
1 can diced tomatoes with juice
1 cup veal stock
1 cup onion, finely diced

½ cup celery, finely diced
½ cup carrot, finely diced
½ cup red wine
2 sprigs fresh rosemary

Salt and black pepper to taste
1 tsp ground coria
1 tsp ground cumin
1 teaspoon thyme

Directions

Prepare a water bath and place the Sous Vide in it. Set to 149 F.

Combine all the ingredients and place in a vacuum-sealable bag. Release air by the water displacement method, seal, and submerge the bag in the water bath. Cook for 48 hours.

Once the timer has stopped, remove the shanks and transfer them to a plate and allow cooling for 48 hours. Clean the lamb removing the bones and the fat, then chop into bites. Transfer the no-fat cooking juices and bites lambs to a saucepan. Cook for 10 minutes over high heat until the sauce thickens. Serve.

Thyme & Sage Grilled Lamb Chops

Prep + Cook Time: 3 hours 20 minutes | Servings: 6

Ingredients

6 tbsp butter
4 tbsp dry white wine
4 tbsp chicken broth
4 fresh thyme sprigs

2 garlic cloves, minced
1 ½ tsp chopped fresh sage
1 ½ tsp cumin
6 lamb chops

Salt and black pepper to taste
2 tbsp olive oil

Directions

Prepare a water bath and place the Sous Vide in it. Set to 134 F.

Heat a pot over medium heat and combine butter, white wine, broth, thyme, garlic, cumin, and sage. Cook for 5 minutes. Allow to cool. Season the lamb with salt and pepper. Place in three vacuum-sealable bags with the butter mixture. Release air by the water displacement method, seal and submerge the bags in the water bath.

Cook for 3 hours. Once done, remove the lamb and pat dry with kitchen towels. Brush the chops with olive oil. Heat a skillet over high heat and sear the lamb for 45 seconds per side. Allow resting for 5 minutes.

Lamb Shoulder

Prep + Cook Time: 4 hours 10 minutes | Servings: 3

Ingredients

1 pound lamb shoulder, deboned
Salt and black pepper to taste

2 tbsp olive oil
1 garlic clove, crushed

1 sprig thyme
1 sprig rosemary

Directions

Prepare a water bath and place the Sous Vide in it. Set to 145 F. Pat dry the lamb shoulders with a paper towel and rub with pepper and salt. Place the lamb and the remaining listed ingredients in a vacuum-sealable bag. Release air by the water displacement method, seal, and submerge the bag in the water bath. Set the timer for 4 hours.

Once done, remove the bag and transfer the lamb shoulders to a baking dish. Strain the juices into a saucepan and cook over medium heat for 2 minutes. Preheat a grill for 10 minutes and grill the shoulder until golden brown and crispy. Serve the lamb shoulder and sauce with a side of buttered greens.

Jalapeño Lamb Roast

Prep + Cook Time: 3 hours | Servings: 6

Ingredients

1 ½ tbsp canola oil
1 tbsp black mustard seeds
1 tsp cumin seeds
Salt and black pepper to taste

4 lb butterflied lamb leg
½ cup mint leaves, chopped
½ cup cilantro leaves, chopped
1 shallot, minced

1 clove garlic, minced
2 red jalapenos, minced
1 tbsp red wine vinegar
1 ½ tbsp olive oil

Directions

Heat ½ tbsp of olive oil in a skillet over low heat. Add cumin and mustard seeds and cook for 1 minute. Turn off heat and transfer seeds to a bowl. Sprinkle with salt and black pepper. Mix. Spread half of the spice mixture inside the lamb leg and roll it. Secure with a butcher's twine at 1- inch intervals. Season with salt and pepper and massage. Spread half of the spice mixture evenly over of lamb leg, then carefully roll it back up.

Make a water bath and place Sous Vide in it. Set to 145 F. Place the lamb leg in vacuum-sealable bag, release air by the water displacement method, seal and submerge it in the water bath. Set the timer for 2 hours 45 minutes and cook. Make the sauce; add to the cumin mustard mixture shallot, cilantro, garlic, red wine vinegar, mint, and red chili. Mix and season with salt and pepper. Set aside.

Once the timer has stopped, remove and unseal the bag. Remove the lamb and pat dry using a paper towel. Add canola oil to a pan, preheat over high heat for 10 minutes. Place in lamb and sear to brown on both sides. Remove twine and slice lamb. Serve with sauce.

Chili Lamb Steaks with Sesame Seed Topping

Prep + Cook Time: 3 hours 10 minutes | Servings: 2

Ingredients

2 lamb steaks
2 tbsp olive oil

Salt and black pepper to taste
2 tbsp avocado oil

1 tsp sesame seeds
Pinch of red pepper flakes

Directions

Prepare a water bath and place the Sous Vide in it. Set to 138 F. Place the lamb with olive oil in a vacuum-sealable bag. Release air by the water displacement method, seal and submerge the bag in water bath. Cook for 3 hours.

Once done, pat the lamb dry. Season with salt and pepper. Heat avocado oil in a skillet over high heat and sear the lamb. Chop into bites. Garnish with sesame seeds and pepper flakes.

Lamb Chops with Basil Chimichurri

Prep + Cook Time: 3 hours 40 minutes | Servings: 4

Ingredients

Lamb Chops:

3 lamb racks, frenched	3 cloves garlic, crushed	Salt and black pepper to taste

Basil Chimichurri:

1 ½ cups fresh basil, finely chopped	3 cloves garlic, minced	½ cup olive oil
2 banana shallots, diced	1 tsp red pepper flakes	3 tbsp red wine vinegar

Directions

Prepare a water bath and place the Sous Vide in it. Set to 140 F. Pat dry the racks with a kitchen towel and rub with pepper and salt. Place meat and garlic in a vacuum-sealable bag, release air by water displacement method and seal the bag. Submerge the bag in the water bath. Set the timer for 2 hours and cook.

Make the basil chimichurri: mix all the listed ingredients in a bowl. Cover with cling film and refrigerate for 1 hour 30 minutes. Once the timer has stopped, remove the bag and open it. Remove the lamb and pat dry using a paper towel. Sear with a torch to a golden brown. Pour the basil chimichurri on the lamb. Serve and enjoy!

Harissa Lamb Kabobs

Prep + Cook Time: 2 hours 30 minutes | Servings: 4

Ingredients

3 tbsp olive oil	1 ½ tsp ground cumin	1 ½ lb boneless lamb shoulder, cubed
4 tsp red wine vinegar	1 ½ tsp ground coriander	1 cucumber, peeled and chopped
2 tbsp chili paste	1 tsp hot paprika	Zest and juice of ½ lemon
2 garlic cloves, minced	Salt to taste	1 cup Greek-style yogurt

Directions

Prepare a water bath and place the Sous Vide in it. Set to 134 F. Combine 2 tbsp of olive oil, vinegar, chili, garlic, cumin, coriander, paprika, and salt. Place the lamb and sauce in a vacuum-sealable bag. Release air by water displacement method, seal and submerge the bag in the bath. Cook for 2 hours.

Once the timer has stopped, remove the lamb and pat dry with a kitchen towel. Discard cooking juices. Mix the cucumber, lemon zest and juice, yogurt, and pressed garlic in a small bowl. Set aside. Fill the skewer with the lamb and roll it. Heat the oil in a skillet over high heat and cook the skewer for 1-2 minutes per side. Top with the lemon-garlic sauce and serve.

Lamb & Bean Stew

Prep + Cook Time: 7 hours 20 minutes | Servings: 4

Ingredients

2 tbsp vegetable oil	2 cups frozen pearl onions	1 cup dry white wine
1 tbsp butter	2 large parsnips, chopped	2 cups chicken stock
1 lb trimmed lamb meat, cubed	2 minced cloves garlic	1 can white beans, drained and rinsed
Salt and black pepper to taste	2 tbsp all-purpose flour	4 fresh rosemary sprigs

Directions

Prepare a water bath and place the Sous Vide in it. Set to 138 F. Heat a non-stick pan over high heat with butter and oil. Add the lamb. Season with pepper and salt. Cook for 7 minutes. Put in onions and cook for 5 minutes. Mix the garlic and wine until bubble. Stir in beans, rosemary, and stock. Remove from the heat.

Place the lamb in a vacuum-sealable bag. Release air by the water displacement method, seal, and submerge the bag in the water bath. Cook for 7 hours. Once the timer has stopped, remove the bag and transfer into a bowl. Garnish with rosemary.

PORK

Sweet Mustard Pork with Crispy Onions

Prep + Cook Time: 48 hours 40 minutes | Servings: 6

Ingredients

1 tbsp ketchup
4 tbsp honey mustard
2 tbsp soy sauce
2 ¼ pounds pork shoulder

1 large sweet onion, cut into thin rings
2 cups milk
1 ½ cups all-purpose flour
2 tsp granulated onion powder

1 tsp paprika
Salt and black pepper to taste
4 cups vegetable oil, for frying

Directions

Prepare a water bath and place the Sous Vide in it. Set to 159 F. Combine well the mustard, soy sauce and ketchup to make a paste. Brush the pork with the sauce and place in a vacuum-sealable bag. Release air by the water displacement method, seal, and submerge the bag in the water bath. Cook for 48 hours.

To make the onions: separate the onion rings in a bowl. Pour the milk over them and allow to chill for 1 hour. Combine the flour, onion powder, paprika, salt, and pepper. Heat the oil in a skillet over medium heat. Drain the onions and deepen in the flour mix. Shake well and transfer into the skillet. Fry them for 2 minutes or until gets crispy. Transfer to a baking sheet and pat dry with kitchen towel. Repeat the process with the remaining onions.

Once the timer has stopped, remove the pork and transfer to a cutting board and pull the pork until it is shredded. Reserve cooking juices and transfer into a saucepan hot over medium heat and cook for 5 minutes until reduced. Top the pork with the sauce and garnish with crispy onions to serve.

Delicious Basil & Lemon Pork Chops

Prep + Cook Time: 1 hour 15 minutes | Servings: 4

Ingredients

4 tbsp butter
4 boneless pork rib chops
Salt and black pepper to taste

Zest and juice of 1 lemon
2 garlic cloves, smashed
2 bay leaves

1 fresh basil sprig

Directions

Prepare a water bath and place the Sous Vide in it. Set to 141 F Season the chops with salt and pepper. Place the chops with the lemon zest and juice, garlic, bay leaves, basil, and 2 tbsp of butter in a vacuum-sealable bag. Release air by the water displacement method, seal, and submerge the bag in the water bath. Cook for 1 hour.

Once the timer has stopped, remove the chops and pat dry with kitchen towel. Reserve the herbs. Heat the remaining butter in a skillet over medium heat and sear for 1-2 minutes per side.

Boneless Pork Ribs with Coconut-Peanut Sauce

Prep + Cook Time: 8 hours 30 minutes | Servings: 3

Ingredients

½ cup coconut milk
2 ½ tbsp peanut butter
2 tbsp soy sauce
1 tbsp sugar

3 inches fresh lemongrass
1 ½ tbsp pepper sauce
1 ½ inch ginger, peeled
3 cloves garlic

2 ½ tsp sesame oil
13 oz boneless pork ribs

Directions

Prepare a water bath and place Sous Vide in it. Set to 135 F. Blend all listed ingredients in a blender, except for the ribs and cilantro, until a smooth paste is obtained. Place the ribs and the mixture in a vacuum-sealable bag. Release air by the water displacement method and seal the bag. Place in the water bath. Set the timer to 8 hours.

Baby Ribs with Chinese Sauce

Prep + Cook Time: 4 hours 25 minutes | Servings: 4

Ingredients

1/3 cup hoisin sauce
1/3 cup dark soy sauce
1/3 cup sugar
3 tbsp honey
3 tbsp white vinegar

1 tbsp fermented bean paste
2 tsp sesame oil
2 crushed garlic cloves
1-inch piece fresh grated ginger
1 ½ tsp five-spice powder

Salt to taste
½ tsp fresh ground black pepper
3 pounds baby back ribs
Cilantro leaves for serving

Directions

Prepare a water bath and place the Sous Vide in it. Set to 168 F. In a bowl, mix hoisin sauce, dark soy sauce, sugar, white vinegar, honey, bean paste, sesame oil, five-spice powder, salt, ginger, white and black pepper. Reserve 1/3 of the mixture and allow chilling. Brush the ribs with the mixture and share among 3 vacuum-sealable bag. Release air by the water displacement method, seal and submerge the bags in the water bath. Cook for 4 hours.

Preheat the oven to 400 F. Once the timer has stopped, remove the ribs and brush with the remaining mixture. Transfer to a baking tray and put in the oven. Bake for 3 minutes. Take out and allow resting for 5 minutes. Cut the rack and top with cilantro. Serve and enjoy!

Jerk Pork Ribs

Prep + Cook Time: 20 hours 10 minutes | Servings: 6

Ingredients

5 lb (2) baby back pork ribs, full racks   ½ cup jerk seasoning mix

Directions

Make a water bath, place Sous Vide in it, and set to 145 F. Cut the racks into halves and season them with half of jerk seasoning. Place the racks in separate vacuum-sealable racks. Release air by the water displacement method, seal and submerge the bags in the water bath. Set the timer to 20 hours.

Cover the water bath with a bag to reduce evaporation and add water every 3 hours to avoid the water drying out. Once the timer has stopped, remove and unseal the bag. Transfer the ribs to a foiled baking sheet and preheat a broiler to high. Rub the ribs with the remaining jerk seasoning and place them in the broiler. Broil for 5 minutes. Slice into single ribs. Serve and enjoy!

Maple Tenderloin with Sautéed Apple

Prep + Cook Time: 2 hours 20 minutes | Servings: 4

Ingredients

1 pound pork tenderloin
1 tbsp fresh rosemary, chopped
1 tbsp maple syrup
1 tsp black pepper

Salt to taste
1 tbsp olive oil
1 apple, diced
1 thinly sliced small shallot

¼ cup vegetable broth
½ tsp apple cider

Directions

Prepare a water bath and place the Sous Vide in it. Set to 135 F. Remove the skin from the tenderloin and cut by the half. Combine the rosemary, maple syrup, pepper, and salt. Sprinkle over the tenderloin. Place in a vacuum-sealable bag. Release air by the water displacement method, seal, and submerge the bag in the water bath.

Cook for 2 hours. Once the timer has stopped, remove the bag and dry it. Reserve the cooking juices. Heat olive oil in a skillet over medium heat and sear the tenderloin for 5 minutes. Set aside. Low the heat and put in apple, rosemary springs, and shallot. Season with salt and sauté for 2-3 minutes until golden. Add in vinegar, broth, and cooking juices. Simmer for 3-5 minutes more. Cut the tenderloin into medallions and serve with the apple mix.

Balsamic Pork Chops

Prep + Cook Time: 1 hour 15 minutes | Servings: 5

Ingredients

2 pounds pork chops
3 garlic cloves, crushed
½ tsp dried basil

½ tsp dried thyme
¼ cup balsamic vinegar
Salt and black pepper to taste

3 tbsp extra virgin olive oil

Directions

Prepare a water bath, place Sous Vide in it, and set to 158 F. Season the pork chops generously with salt and pepper; set aside. In a small bowl, combine vinegar with 1 tbsp of olive oil, thyme, basil, and garlic. Stir well and spread the mixture evenly over meat. Place in a large vacuum-sealable bag and seal it.

Submerge the sealed bag in the water bath. Cook for for 1 hour. Once the timer has stopped, take the pork chops out of the bag, and pat them dry. Heat the remaining olive oil in a pan over high heat. Sear the chops for one minute per side, or until golden brown. Add in cooking juices and simmer for 3-4 minutes or until thickened.

Once the timer has stopped, take the bag out, unseal it and remove the ribs. Transfer to a plate and keep it warm. Put a skillet over medium heat and pour in the sauce of the bag. Bring to boil for 5 minutes, reduce the heat, and simmer for 12 minutes. Add the ribs and coat with the sauce. Simmer for 6 minutes. Serve with steamed greens.

Lime and Garlic Pork Tenderloin

Prep + Cook Time: 2 hours 15 minutes | Servings: 2

Ingredients

2 tbsp garlic powder
2 tbsp ground cumin
2 tbsp dried thyme

2 tbsp dried rosemary
1 pinch lime sea salt
2 (3-lb) pork tenderloin, silver skin

removed
2 tbsp olive oil
3 tbsp unsalted butter

Directions

Make a water bath, place Sous Vide in it, and set to 140 F. Add the cumin, garlic powder, thyme, lime salt, rosemary, and lime salt to a bowl and mix evenly. Brush the pork with olive oil and rub with salt and cumin herb mixture. Put the pork into two separate vacuum-sealable bags. Release air by the water displacement method and seal the bags. Submerge in the water bath and set the timer for 2 hours.

Once the timer has stopped, remove and unseal the bag. Remove the pork and pat dry using a paper towel. Discard the juice in the bag. Preheat a pan over high heat and add in butter. Place in pork and sear until golden brown, about 4-5 minut. Let the pork rest on a cutting board. Cut them into 2-inch medallions.

Flavorful Pork with Mustard & Molasses Glaze

Prep + Cook Time: 4 hours 15 minutes | Servings: 6

Ingredients

2 pounds pork loin roast
1 bay leaf
3 oz molasses
½ oz soy sauce

½ oz honey
Juice of 2 lemons
2 strips lemon peel
4 chopped scallions

½ tsp garlic powder
¼ tsp Dijon mustard
¼ tsp ground allspice
1 oz crushed corn chips

Directions

Prepare a water bath and place the Sous Vide in it. Set to 142 F. Place the pork loin and bay leaf in a vacuum-sealable bag. Add in molasses, soy sauce, lemon peel, honey, scallions, garlic powder, mustard, and allspice; shake well. Release air by the water displacement method, seal, and submerge the bag in the water bath.

Cook for 4 hours. Once the timer has stopped, remove the bag. Pour the remaining mixture into a saucepan and boil until reduced. Serve the pork with the sauce and top with crushed corn chips. Garnish with green onion.

Spicy Tenderloin with Sweet Papaya Sauce

Prep + Cook Time: 2 hours 45 minutes | Servings: 4

Ingredients

¼ cup light broth sugar
1 tbsp ground allspice
½ tsp cayenne pepper
¼ tsp ground cinnamon
¼ tsp ground cloves
Salt and black pepper to taste

2 pounds pork tenderloin
2 tbsp canola oil
2 pitted and peeled papayas, finely diced
¼ cup fresh cilantro, chopped
1 red bell pepper, seeded, stemmed and

finely diced
3 tbsp red onion, finely diced
2 tbsp lime juice
1 small jalapeno pepper, seeded and diced

Directions

Prepare a water bath and place the Sous Vide in it. Set to 135 F. Combine the sugar, allspice, cinnamon, cayenne, cloves, cumin, salt, and pepper. Sprinkle over the tenderloin.

Heat oil in a skillet over medium heat and sear the tenderloin for 5 minutes. Transfer to a plate and allow resting for 10 minutes. Place in a vacuum-sealable bag. Release air by the water displacement method.

Seal and submerge the bag in the water bath. Cook for 2 hours. Once the timer has stopped, remove the tenderloin and allow resting for 10 minutes. Slice them. For the sauce, mix the papaya, cilantro, bell pepper, onion, lime juice, and jalapeño. Serve the tenderloin and top with the sauce. Sprinkle with salt and pepper and serve.

Roasted Pork Neck

Prep + Cook Time: 1 hour 20 minutes | Servings: 6

Ingredients

2 lb pork neck, sliced into 2 pieces
4 tbsp olive oil
2 tsp soy sauce
2 tbsp barbecue sauce

½ tbsp sugar
4 sprigs rosemary, leaves removed
4 sprigs thyme, leaves removed
2 cloves garlic, minced

Salt and white pepper to taste
¼ tsp red pepper flakes

Directions

Make a water bath, place Sous Vide in it, and set to 140 F. Rub salt and pepper on the pork. Put the meat in 2 separate vacuum-sealable bags, release air and seal them. Put in the water bath and set the timer for 1 hour.

Once the timer has stopped, remove and unseal the bags. Mix the remaining listed ingredients. Preheat oven to 425 F. Put the pork on a roasting pan and rub soy sauce mixture generously into the pork. Roast in the oven for 15 minutes. Let the pork cool before slicing it. Serve with a side of steamed greens.

Herby Tenderloin with Spicy Pineapple Sauce

Prep + Cook Time: 2 hours 45 minutes | Servings: 4

Ingredients

¼ cup light brown sugar
1 tbsp ground allspice
½ tsp cayenne pepper
¼ tsp ground cloves
¼ tsp ground cumin

Salt to taste
1 pound pork tenderloin
2 tbsp canola oil
2 finely diced pineapple
1 seeded red bell pepper

¼ cup chopped fresh cilantro
3 tbsp finely chopped red onion
2 tbsp lime juice
1 small seeded and finely diced jalapeno

Directions

Prepare a water bath and place the Sous Vide in it. Set to 135 F. Combine brown sugar, cayenne, allspice, cloves, salt, cumin, and pepper. Brush the mixture over the pork. Heat oil in a skillet over medium heat and sear the pork for 5 minutes. Place in a vacuum-sealable bag. Release air by the water displacement method and seal.

Submerge the bag in the water bath. Cook for 2 hours. Once done, remove the pork and let it sit for 10 minutes. Mix the pineapple, bell pepper, onion, cilantro, lime juice, and jalapeño. Slice the pork and top with the sauce.

Smoked Paprika Pork Belly

Prep + Cook Time: 24 hours 15 minutes | Servings: 8

Ingredients

1 pound pork belly
½ tbsp smoked paprika

½ tsp garlic powder
1 tsp cilantro

½ tsp chili flakes
Salt and black pepper to taste

Directions

Prepare a water bath and place Sous Vide in it. Set to 175 F. Combine all of the spices in a small bowl and rub this mixture into the pork belly. Place the mixture in a vacuum-sealable bag. Release air by the water displacement method, seal, and submerge the bag in the water bath. Set the timer for 24 hours.

Once done, remove the bag and transfer the cooking liquid to a saucepan and place the pork belly on a plate. Simmer the cooking liquid until reduced by half. Drizzle over the pork and serve.

Pork Tacos Carnitas

Prep + Cook Time: 3 hours 10 minutes | Servings: 4

Ingredients

2 pounds pork shoulder
3 garlic cloves, minced

2 Bay leaves
1 onion, chopped

Salt and black pepper to taste
Corn tortillas

Directions

Prepare a water bath and place the Sous Vide in it. Set to 185 F.

Meanwhile, combine all of the spices and the rub them onto the pork. Place it in a vacuum-sealable bag with bay leaves, onion, and garlic. Release air by the water displacement method, seal, and submerge the bag in the water bath. Set the timer for 3 hours. Once done, transfer to a cutting board and shred with 2 forks. Divide between corn tortillas and serve.

Pork Ribs

Prep + Cook Time: 12 hours 10 minutes | Servings: 4

Ingredients

1 rack of pork ribs
2 tbsp brown sugar
½ cup barbecue sauce

1 tbsp garlic powder
2 tbsp paprika
Salt and black pepper to taste

1 tbsp onion powder

Directions

Prepare a water bath and place the Sous Vide in it. Set to 165 F. Place the pork along with the spices in a vacuum-sealable bag. Release air by the water displacement method, seal, and submerge the bag in the water bath. Set the timer for 12 hours. Once the timer has stopped, remove the ribs from the bag and bush with barbecue sauce. Wrap in aluminum foil and place under broiler for a few minutes. Serve immediately.

Thyme Pork Chops

Prep + Cook Time: 70 minutes | Servings: 4

Ingredients

4 pork chops
2 tsp fresh thyme

1 tbsp olive oil
Salt and black pepper to taste

Directions

Prepare a water bath and place the Sous Vide in it. Set to 145 F. Combine the pork with the remaining ingredients in a vacuum-sealable bag. Release air by the water displacement method, seal, and submerge the bag in the water bath. Set the timer for 60 minutes. Once done, remove the bag and sear it in a pan for a few seconds. Serve.

Pork Cutlets

Prep + Cook Time: 75 minutes | Servings: 6

Ingredients

2 pounds ground pork
½ cup breadcrumbs
1 egg

1 tsp paprika
Salt and black pepper to taste
1 tbsp flour

2 tbsp butter

Directions

Prepare a water bath and place the Sous Vide in it. Set to 140 F. Combine the pork, egg, paprika, flour, and salt. Shape into cutlets and place each in a small vacuum-sealable bag. Release air by the water displacement method.

Seal and submerge the bag in the water bath. Set the timer for 60 minutes. Once the timer has stopped, remove the bag. Melt the butter in a pan over medium heat. Coat the cutlets with the breadcrumbs and cook until golden on all sides. Serve and enjoy.

BBQ Pork Ribs

Prep + Cook Time: 1 hour 10 minutes | Servings: 4

Ingredients

1 lb pork ribs
1 tsp garlic powder

Salt and black pepper to taste
1 cup BBQ sauce

Directions

Make a water bath, place Sous Vide in it, and set to 140 F. Rub salt and pepper on the pork ribs, place in a vacuum-sealable bag, release air and seal it. Put in the water and set the timer to 1 hour.

Once the timer has stopped, remove and unseal the bag. Remove ribs and coat with BBQ sauce. Set aside. Preheat a grill. Once it is hot, sear the ribs all around for 5 minutes. Serve with a dip of choice.

Sage & Cider Chops

Prep + Cook Time: 70 minutes | Servings: 2

Ingredients

2 pork chops
1 sprig chopped rosemary
Salt and black pepper to taste

1 chopped garlic clove
1 cup hard cider, divided
1 teaspoon sage

1 tbsp vegetable oil
1 tbsp sugar

Directions

Prepare a water bath and place the Sous Vide in it. Set to 138 F. In a bowl, combine salt, pepper, sage, rosemary, and garlic. Rub the chops with this mixture and place in a vacuum-sealable bag. Add 1/4 cup of hard cider. Release air by the water displacement method, seal, and submerge the bag in the water bath. Cook for 45 minutes.

Once done, remove the bag. Heat oil in a skillet over medium heat and cook the veggies. Add in the chops and sear until golden. Allow resting for 5 minutes. Pour cooking juices into the skillet along with 1 cup of cider and sugar. Keep stirring until melted. To serve, top the chops with the sauce.

Sweet Pork Chops with Pear & Carrots

Prep + Cook Time: 4 hours 15 minutes | Servings: 2

Ingredients

2 boneless pork chops
Salt and black pepper to taste
10 sage leaves
2 cups shredded carrots

1 pear, shredded
1 tbsp apple cider vinegar
1 tsp olive oil
1 tsp honey

Juice of ½ lemon
2 tbsp chopped fresh parsley
1 tbsp butter

Directions

Season the chops with salt and pepper. Put sage leaves over the chops and allow resting. Prepare a water bath and place Sous Vide in it. Set to 134 F. Place the chops in a vacuum-sealable bag. Release air by the water displacement method, seal, and submerge the bag in the water bath. Cook for 2 hours.

Meanwhile, in a bowl mix well the carrots, pear, vinegar, olive oil, honey, and lemon juice. Season with salt and pepper. Top with parsley and allow chilling for 1 hour and 30 minutes. Melt the butter in a skillet over medium. Once the timer has stopped, remove the chops and dry it. Transfer to the skillet and sear for 1 minute per side. Serve with the carrot mix and garnish with sage.

Tomato Pork Chops with Potato Puree

Prep + Cook Time: 5 hours 40 minutes | Servings: 4

Ingredients

1 pound skinless pork chops
Salt and black pepper to taste
1 cup beef stock

½ cup tomato sauce
1 stalk celery, cut up into 1-inch dice
1 quartered shallot

3 sprigs fresh thyme
1 oz red mashed potatoes

Directions

Prepare a water bath and place the Sous Vide in it. Set to 182 F. Sprinkle the chops with salt and pepper, then place in a vacuum-sealable bag. Add in stock, tomato sauce, shallot, whiskey, celery, and thyme. Release air by the water displacement method, seal, and submerge the bag in the water bath. Cook for 5 hours.

Once the timer has stopped, remove the chops and transfer to a plate. Reserve the cooking liquids. Heat a saucepan over high heat and pour the drained juices; let simmer. Reduce the heat and stir for 20 minutes. Then add in chops and cook for 2-3 more minutes. Serve with potato puree.

Rosemary Pork Tenderloin

Prep + Cook Time: 2 hours 15 minutes | Servings: 4

Ingredients

1 pound pork tenderloin
2 garlic cloves

2 sprigs rosemary
1 tbsp dried rosemary

Salt and black pepper to taste
1 tbsp olive oil

Directions

Prepare a water bath and place the Sous Vide in it. Set to 140 F. Season the meat with salt, rosemary and pepper and place in a vacuum-sealable bag with the garlic and rosemary spring inside. Release air by the water displacement method, seal, and submerge the bag in the water bath. Set the timer for 2 hours. Once the timer has stopped, remove the bag. Heat oil in a pan over medium heat. Sear the meat on all sides for about 2 minutes.

Paprika Tenderloin with Herbs

Prep + Cook Time: 2 hours 20 minutes | Servings: 4

Ingredients

1 pound pork tenderloin, trimmed
Salt and black pepper to taste

1 tbsp chopped fresh basil
1 tbsp chopped fresh parsley

1 tablespoon paprika
2 tbsp butter, melted

Directions

Prepare a water bath and place the Sous Vide in it. Set to 134 F. Combine the basil, paprika, and parsley. Rub the tenderloin with salt, pepper, and herb mixture. Place in a vacuum-sealable bag. Add in 1 tbsp of butter. Release air by the water displacement method, seal, and submerge the bag in the water bath. Cook for 2 hours.

Once done, remove the tenderloin and transfer to a heated with the remaining butter skillet. Sear the for 1-2 minutes on each side. Remove and allow resting for 5 minutes. Cut the tenderloin into medallions. Serve.

Paprika Pancetta with Pearl Onions

Prep + Cook Time: 1 hour 50 minutes | Servings: 4

Ingredients

1 pound pearl onions, peeled   1 tbsp thyme
4 pancetta slices, crumbled and cooked   1 tsp paprika

Directions

Prepare a water bath and place Sous Vide in it. Set to 186 F. Place pancetta, pearl onions, thyme, and paprika in a vacuum-sealable bag. Release air by the water displacement method, seal and submerge the bag in the bath. Cook for 90 minutes. Once done, remove the bag and discard the cooking juices.

Toasts with Eggs & Crispy Pancetta

Prep + Cook Time: 70 minutes | Servings: 2

Ingredients

4 large egg yolks   2 slices pancetta   4 slices toasted bread

Directions

Prepare a water bath and place the Sous Vide in it. Set to 143 F. Place the egg yolks in a vacuum-sealable bag. Release air by the water displacement method, seal, and submerge the bag in the water bath. Cook for 60 minutes.

Meanwhile, cut the pancetta in slices and fry until crisp. Transfer to a baking sheet. Once the timer has stopped, remove the yolks and place them over the toasted bread. Top with pancetta and serve.

Tasty Potato & Bacon with Scallions

Prep + Cook Time: 1 hour 50 minutes | Servings: 6

Ingredients

1 ½ pounds Russet potatoes, sliced   4 oz bacon cut into thick strips   4 thinly sliced scallions
½ cup chicken stock   ½ cup chopped onion
Salt and black pepper to taste   1/3 cup apple cider vinegar

Directions

Prepare a water bath and place the Sous Vide in it. Set to 186 F. Place the potatoes in a vacuum-sealable bag. Season with salt and pepper. Release air by the water displacement method, seal, and submerge the bag in the water bath. Cook for 1 hour and 30 minutes. Once done, remove potatoes to a plate.

Heat a skillet over medium heat and cook the bacon for 5 minutes. Transfer to a baking sheet. In the same skillet cook onion for 1 minute. Add in potatoes, cooked bacon and vinegar. Cook until simmer. Put in scallions and season with salt and pepper. Serve and enjoy!

Bell Pepper & Carrot Pork Chops

Prep + Cook Time: 1 hour 15 minutes | Servings: 3

Ingredients

4 pork chops   1 yellow onion, diced   Salt and black pepper to taste
1 red bell pepper, diced   1 carrot, chopped   2 tbsp vegetable oil

Directions

Prepare a water bath and place the Sous Vide in it. Set to 138 F. Salt the pork and place it in a vacuum-sealable bag. Release air by the water displacement method, seal, and submerge the bag in the water bath. Cook for 1 hour.

Heat oil in a skillet over medium heat and sauté onion, carrot and bell peppers; set aside. Once the timer has stopped, remove the pork and transfer to the skillet and sear 1 minute per side. Slice and serve with the veggies.

Sweet Chops & Zucchini with Almonds

Prep + Cook Time: 3 hours 15 minutes | Servings: 2

Ingredients

2 pork loin chops
Salt and black pepper to taste
3 tbsp olive oil

1 tbsp freshly squeezed lemon juice
2 tsp red wine vinegar
2 tsp honey

2 tbsp olive oil
2 medium zucchini, sliced into ribbons
2 tbsp almonds, toasted

Directions

Prepare a water bath and place the Sous Vide in it. Set to 138 F. Place the seasoned pork in a vacuum-sealable bag. Add in 1 tbsp of olive oil. Release air by the water displacement method, seal, and submerge the bag in the water bath. Cook for 3 hours.

Mix lemon juice, honey, vinegar, and 2 tbsp of olive oil. Season with salt and pepper. Once the timer has stopped, remove the bag and discard the cooking juices. Heat rice oil in a skillet over high heat and sear the pork for 1 minute per side. Remove from the heat and allow resting for 5 minutes.

For the salad, in a bowl, mix zucchini with the dressing mix. Season with salt and pepper. Transfer the pork to a plate and serve with the zucchini. Garnish with almonds.

Pleasing Pork in Salsa Verde

Prep + Cook Time: 24 hours 25 minutes | Servings: 8

Ingredients

2 lb boneless pork shoulder, cubed
Salt and black pepper to taste
1 tbsp ground cumin
1 tbsp olive oil
1 pound tomatillos

3 poblano pepper, minced
½ white onion finely diced
1 serrano seeded and diced
3 crushed garlic cloves
1 bunch roughly chopped cilantro

1 cup chicken broth
½ cup lime juice
1 tbsp oregano

Directions

Prepare a water bath and place the Sous Vide in it. Set to 149 F. Season the pork with salt, cumin and pepper. Heat oil in a skillet over high heat and sear the pork for 5-7 minutes. Set aside. In the same skillet, cook tomatillos, poblano, onion, serrano, and garlic for 5 minutes. Transfer to a food processor and add in cilantro, lime juice, chicken broth, and oregano. Blend for 1 minute.

Place the pork and sauce in a vacuum-sealable bag. Release air by the water displacement method, seal, and submerge the bag in the water bath. Cook for 24 hours. Once the timer has stopped, remove the bag and transfer into serving bowls. Sprinkle with salt and pepper. Serve with rice.

Asian-Style Pork with Rice & Ginger

Prep + Cook Time: 2 hours 40 minutes | Servings: 4

Ingredients

1 cup brown rice
8 cups chicken stock
1 pound ground pork

1 tbsp minced fresh ginger
1 tsp minced fresh garlic
1 tbsp coconut oil

1 cup basil chiffonade
Salt and black pepper to taste

Directions

Prepare a water bath and place the Sous Vide in it. Set to 192 F. Place the rice in a vacuum-sealable bag. Release air by the water displacement method, seal, and submerge the bag in the water bath. Cook for 2 hours.

Once the timer has stopped, remove the rice and season with salt and pepper. Heat a skillet over medium heat and cook the pork, garlic and ginger. Remove from the heat and put basil. Season with salt and pepper. Serve the rice in bowls with the ginger pork mix.

Spicy Coconut Pork Ribs

Prep + Cook Time: 8 hours 30 minutes | Servings: 4

Ingredients

1/3 cup coconut milk
2 tbsp coconut butter
2 tbsp soy sauce
2 tbsp brown sugar
2 tbsp dry white wine

1 lemongrass stalk, finely chopped
1 tbsp Sriracha sauce
1 tbsp fresh ginger, grated
2 cloves garlic, sliced
2 tsp sesame oil

1 pound boneless pork ribs
Chopped up fresh cilantro
Cooked basmati rice for serving

Directions

Prepare a water bath and place the Sous Vide in it. Set to 134 F.

In a food processor, blend the coconut milk, coconut butter, soy sauce, brown sugar, wine, lemongrass, ginger, sriracha sauce, garlic, and sesame oil, until smooth. Place the ribs and brush with the mixture in a vacuum-sealable bag. Release air by the water displacement method, seal, and submerge the bag in the water bath.

Cook for 8 hours. Once the timer has stopped, remove the ribs and transfer them to a plate. Heat a saucepan over medium heat and pour in the cooking juices. Cook for 10-15 minutes to simmer. Add the ribs into the sauce and stir well. Cook for 5 minutes. Garnish with cilantro and serve with rice.

Crispy Pork Chops

Prep + Cook Time: 1 hour 15 minutes | Servings: 3

Ingredients

3 pork loin chops
Salt and black pepper to taste

1 cup flour
1 tsp sage

2 whole eggs
1 cup panko breadcrumbs

Directions

Prepare a water bath and place the Sous Vide in it. Set to 138 F. Cut the loin in slices without fat. Season with sage, salt and pepper. Place in a vacuum-sealable bag. Release air by the water displacement method, seal, and submerge the bag in the water bath. Cook for 1 hour.

Once the timer has stopped, remove the chops and dry it. Dip the chops in the flour, then in the eggs, and lastly, roll in the panko breadcrumbs. Heat the oil in a frying pan over medium heat and fry the chops for 1 minute. Allow cooling and slice. Serve with rice and vegetables.

Savory Pork Chops with Mushrooms

Prep + Cook Time: 65 minutes | Servings: 2

Ingredients

2 thick-cut bone-in pork chops
Salt and black pepper to taste
2 tbsp butter, cold

4 oz mixed wild mushrooms
¼ cup sherry
½ cup beef stock

1 tsp sage
1 tbsp steak marinade
Chopped garlic for garnish

Directions

Prepare a water bath and place the Sous Vide in it. Set to 138 F.

Combine the pork with salt and pepper and place in a vacuum-sealable bag. Release air by the water displacement method, seal, and submerge the bag in the water bath. Cook for 45 minutes. Once the timer has stopped, remove the pork and dry it. Discard cooking juices. Heat 1 tbsp of butter in a skillet over medium heat and sear the pork for 1 minute each side. Transfer to a plate and set aside.

In the same hot skillet, cook the mushrooms for 2-3 minutes. Stir in sherry, stock, sage and steak marinade until the sauce thickens. Add in remaining butter and season with salt and pepper; stir well. Top the pork with the sauce and garnish with garlic chives to serve.

Sweet Spare Ribs with Mango Soy Sauce

Prep + Cook Time: 36 hours 25 minutes | Servings: 4

Ingredients

4 pounds pork spare ribs
Salt and black pepper to taste
1 cup mango juice
¼ cup soy sauce

3 tbsp honey
1 tbsp chili garlic paste
1 tbsp ground ginger
2 tbsp coconut oil

1 tsp Chinese five-spice powder
1 tsp ground coriander

Directions

Prepare a water bath and place the Sous Vide in it. Set to 146 F. Season the ribs with salt and pepper and place in a vacuum-sealable bag. Release air by the water displacement method, seal, and submerge the bag in the water bath. Cook for 36 hours. Once the timer has stopped, remove the ribs and pat dry. Discard cooking juices.

Heat a saucepan over medium heat and boil mango juice, soy sauce, chili, garlic paste, honey, ginger, coconut oil, five-spices, and coriander for 10 minutes until reduced. Drizzle the ribs with the sauce. Transfer to a baking tray and cook for 5 minutes in the oven at 390 F.

Loin Pork with Almonds

Prep + Cook Time: 3 hours 20 minutes | Servings: 2

Ingredients

3 tbsp olive oil
3 tbsp mustard
2 tbsp honey
Salt and black pepper to taste

2 bone-in pork loin chops
1 tbsp lemon juice
2 tsp red wine vinegar
2 tbsp canola oil

2 cups mixed baby lettuce
2 tbsp thinly sliced sundried tomatoes
2 tsp almonds, toasted

Directions

Prepare a water bath and place the Sous Vide in it. Set to 138 F.

Combine 1 tbsp of olive oil, 1 tbsp of honey, and 1 tbsp of mustard and season with salt and pepper. Brush the loin with the mixture. Place in a vacuum-sealable bag. Release air by the water displacement method, seal, and submerge the bag in the water bath. Cook for 3 hours.

Prepare the dressing by mixing the lemon juice, vinegar, 2 tbsp of olive oil, 2 tbsp of mustard, and the remaining honey. Season with salt and pepper. Once the timer has stopped, remove the loin. Discard cooking juices. Heat canola oil in a skillet over high heat and sear the loin for 30 seconds per side. Allow resting for 5 minutes.

For the salad, combine in a bowl the lettuce, sun-dried tomatoes and almonds. Mix in 3/4 of the dressing. Top the loin with the dressing and serve with the salad.

Sweet Sausage & Grapes

Prep + Cook Time: 1 hour 20 minutes | Servings: 4

Ingredients

2 ½ cups seedless white grapes with stem removed
1 tbsp chopped fresh rosemary
2 tbsp butter

4 whole sweet Italian sausages
2 tbsp balsamic vinegar

Salt and black pepper to taste

Directions

Prepare a water bath and place the Sous Vide in it. Set to 160 F. Place grapes, rosemary, butter, and sausages in a vacuum-sealable bag. Release air by the water displacement method, seal, and submerge the bag in water bath.

Cook for 60 minutes. Once the timer has stopped, remove the sausages and transfer the cooking juices and grapes to a medium heat saucepan. Pour in balsamic vinegar and boil for 3 minutes. Season with salt and pepper. Heat a skillet over medium heat and sear the sausages for 3-4 minutes. Serve with the sauce and grapes.

Creamy Cognac Pork Loin

Prep + Cook Time: 4 hours 50 minutes | Servings: 4

Ingredients

3 pounds boneless pork loin roast
Salt to taste

2 thinly sliced onion
¼ cup cognac

1 cup milk
1 cup cheese cream

Directions

Prepare a water bath and place Sous Vide in it. Set to 146 F. Season the pork with salt and pepper. Heat a skillet over medium heat and sear the pork for 8 minutes. Set aside. Stir in onion and cook for 5 minutes. Add in cognac and cook until simmer. Allow cooling for 10 minutes.

Place the pork, onion, milk, and cream in a vacuum-sealable bag. Release air by the water displacement method, seal and submerge in the water bath. Cook for 4 hours. Once the timer has stopped, remove the pork. Set aside, keeping warm. Heat a saucepan and pour in cooking juices. Stir for 10 minutes until simmer. Season with salt and pepper. Cut the pork and top with cream sauce to serve.

Tasty Tenderloin with Avocado Dip

Prep + Cook Time: 2 hours 10 minutes | Servings: 3

Ingredients

1 pork tenderloin

2 tbsp avocado oil

Salt and black pepper to taste

Directions

Prepare a water bath and place Sous Vide in it. Set to 146 F. Season the tenderloin with salt and pepper. Brush with some avocado oil and place in a vacuum-sealable bag. Release air by the water displacement method, seal, and submerge the bag in the water bath. Cook for 2 hours. Once the timer has stopped, remove the tenderloin and dry it. Heat the remaining avocado oil and sear the pork for 4-5 minutes. Slice and serve.

Sweet Lemongrass Pork Chops

Prep + Cook Time: 2 hours 20 minutes | Servings: 2

Ingredients

2 tbsp coconut oil
1 stalk sliced lemongrass
1 tbsp minced shallot
1 tbsp Tamari sauce

1 tbsp mirin
1 tbsp rice wine vinegar
1 tbsp light brown sugar
1 tsp minced fresh ginger

1 tsp fish sauce
Salt to taste
2 pork chops
1 tsp minced garlic

Directions

Prepare a water bath and place the Sous Vide in it. Set to 138 F.

In a food processor, pour 1 tbsp of coconut oil, lemongrass, tamari sauce, shallot, vinegar, mirin, brown sugar, garlic, fish sauce, ginger, and salt. Blend for 1 minute. Place the pork in a vacuum-sealable bag. Add in the lemongrass mixture. Release air by the water displacement method, seal, and submerge the bag in the water bath.

Cook for 2 hours. Once the timer has stopped, remove the chops; dry it. Heat a tbsp of oil in a skillet over high heat and sear the chops until browned. Serve.

Pork Chops with Bell Pepper & Corn Stir-Fry

Prep + Cook Time: 1 hour 10 minutes | Servings: 4

Ingredients

4 pork chops
1 small red bell pepper, diced
1 small yellow onion, diced

2 cups frozen corn kernels
¼ cup cilantro
Salt and black pepper to taste

1 tablespoon thyme
4 tbsp vegetable oil

Directions

Prepare a water bath and place the Sous Vide in it. Set to 138 F. Salt the pork and place it in a vacuum-sealable bag. Release air by the water displacement method, seal and submerge the bag in the water bath. Cook for 1 hour

Heat oil in a skillet over medium heat and sauté onion, red pepper and corn. Season with salt and pepper. Stir in cilantro and thyme. Set aside. Once the timer has stopped, remove the pork and transfer to the hot skillet. Sear for 1 minute each side. Serve the pork with sautéed vegetables.

Pork & Mushroom Ramen Noodles

Prep + Cook Time: 24 hours 15 minutes | Servings: 2

Ingredients

8 oz cooked and drained ramen noodles	1 cup enoki mushrooms	2 tsp minced ginger
¾ pound pork shoulder	2 tsp soy sauce	2 tsp sesame oil
6 cups chicken stock	2 cloves minced garlic	2 sliced scallions

Directions

Prepare a water bath and put Sous Vide in it. Set to 158 F. Place pork in a vacuum-sealable bag. Release air by the water displacement method, seal and submerge the bag in the bath. Cook for 24 hours.

Once the timer has stopped, remove the pork and shred it. In a hot saucepan, add chicken stock, soy sauce, garlic, and mushrooms. Boil for 10 minutes. Pour the broth over the ramen noodles and top with pork. Drizzle with sesame oil and garnish with scallions to serve.

Tomato Pork Shanks with Carrots

Prep + Cook Time: 48 hours 30 minutes | Servings: 4

Ingredients

2 pork shanks	1 cup finely diced onion	Salt to taste
1 (14.5-oz) can diced tomatoes with juice	½ cup finely diced fennel bulb	½ cup red wine
1 cup beef stock	½ cup finely diced carrots	1 bay leaf

Directions

Prepare a water bath and place the Sous Vide in it. Set to 149 F. Remove the belly fat from the shanks and place it in a vacuum-sealable bag. Add the remaining ingredients Release air by the water displacement method, seal, and submerge the bag in the water bath. Cook for 48 hours.

Once the timer has stopped, remove the shank and discard the bay leaf. Reserve the cooking juices. Put the shank in a baking sheet and grill for 5 minutes until browned. Heat a saucepan over medium heat and stir in cooking juices. Cook for 10 minutes until thickens. Drizzle the pork with the sauce and serve.

Pork Chop with Spiced Coffee Sauce

Prep + Cook Time: 2 hours 20 minutes | Servings: 4

Ingredients

4 bone-in pork chops	1 tbsp ground coffee	1 tbsp garlic salt
1 tbsp paprika powder	1 tbsp brown sugar	1 tbsp olive oil

Directions

Prepare a water bath and place the Sous Vide in it. Set to 146 F. Place the pork in a vacuum-sealable bag. Release air by the water displacement method, seal, and submerge the bag in the water bath. Cook for 2 hours.

Meanwhile, prepare the sauce mixing well the paprika powder, ground coffee, brown sugar, and garlic salt. Once the timer has stopped, remove the pork and dry it. Drizzle the pork with the sauce. Heat oil in a skillet over high heat and sear the pork for 1-2 minutes per side. Allow resting for 5 minutes. Cut the pork in slices and serve.

Spicy Tenderloin

Prep + Cook Time: 3 hours 15 minutes | Servings: 4

Ingredients

1 pound pork tenderloin, trimmed
Salt to taste

½ tsp black pepper
3 tbsp chili paste

Directions

Prepare a water bath and place the Sous Vide in it. Set to 146 F.

Combine the tenderloin with salt and pepper and place in a vacuum-sealable bag. Release air by the water displacement method, seal, and submerge the bag in the water bath. Cook for 3 hours.

Once the timer has stopped, remove the pork and brush with chili paste. Heat a grill over high heat and sear the tenderloin for 5 minutes until browned. Allow resting. Cut the tenderloin into slices and serve.

Pancetta & Corn Cream Soup

Prep + Cook Time: 1 hour 15 minutes | Servings: 4

Ingredients

4 ears of corn, kernels shaved off
4 tbsp butter
1 cup milk

1 bay leaf
Salt and white pepper to taste
4 slices crispy cooked pancetta

2 tbsp minced chives

Directions

Prepare a water bath and place the Sous Vide in it. Set to 186 F. Combine the corn kernels, milk, corn cobs, 1 tbsp of salt, 1 tbsp of white pepper, and bay leaf. Place in a vacuum-sealable bag. Release air by the water displacement method, seal, and submerge the bag in the water bath. Cook for 1 hour.

Once the timer has stopped, take the bag out and remove corn cobs and bay leaf. Put the mixture into a blender in puree mode for 1 minute. If you want different consistency add some milk. Season with salt and pepper. Garnish with pancetta and chive to serve.

Cumin & Garlic Pork Kabobs

Prep + Cook Time: 4 hours 20 minutes | Servings: 4

Ingredients

1 pound boneless pork shoulder, cubed
Salt to taste
1 tbsp ground nutmeg
1 tbsp minced garlic

1 tsp cumin
1 tsp coriander
1 tsp garlic powder
1 tsp brown sugar

1 tsp fresh ground black pepper
1 tbsp olive oil

Directions

Prepare a water bath and place the Sous Vide in it. Set to 149 F. Brush the pork with salt, garlic, nutmeg, cumin, coriander, pepper, and brown sugar and place in a vacuum-sealable bag. Release air by the water displacement method, seal, and submerge the bag in the water bath. Cook for 4 hours.

Heat the grill over high heat. Once the timer has stopped, remove the pork and transfer to the grill. Sear for 3 minutes until browned.

Sweet Apple Sausages

Prep + Cook Time: 55 minutes | Servings: 4

Ingredients

¾ tsp olive oil

4 Italian sausages

4 tbsp apple juice

Directions

Prepare a water bath and place the Sous Vide in it. Set to 162 F.

Place the sausages and 1 tbsp of cider per sausage in a vacuum-sealable bag. Release air by the water displacement method, seal, and submerge the bag in the water bath. Cook for 45 minutes.

Heat oil in a skillet over medium heat. Once the timer has stopped, remove the sausages and transfer them to the skillet; cook for 3-4 minutes until browned. Serve and enjoy!

Awesome Pork Chops with Balsamic Glaze

Prep + Cook Time: 3 hours 20 minutes | Servings: 2

Ingredients

2 pork chops
Salt and black pepper to taste

1 tbsp olive oil
4 tbsp balsamic vinegar

2 tsp fresh rosemary, chopped

Directions

Prepare a water bath and place the Sous Vide in it. Set to 146 F. Combine the pork with salt and pepper and place in a vacuum-sealable bag. Release air by the water displacement method, seal and submerge in the water bath. Cook for 3 hours. Once the timer has stopped, remove the pork and dry it.

Heat olive oil in a frying pan and sauté the chops for 5 minutes until browned. Add in balsamic vinegar and simmer. Repeat the process for 1 minute. Plate and garnish with rosemary and balsamic sauce.

Red Cabbage & Potatoes with Sausage

Prep + Cook Time: 2 hours 20 minutes | Servings: 4

Ingredients

½ head red cabbage, sliced
1 apple, cut up into small dices
24 oz red potatoes, cut up into quarters
1 small onion, sliced

¼ tsp celery salt
2 tbsp cider vinegar
2 tbsp brown sugar
Black pepper to taste

1 pound smoked pork sausage, sliced
½ cup chicken broth
2 tbsp butter

Directions

Prepare a water bath and place the Sous Vide in it. Set to 186 F. Combine the cabbage, potatoes, onion, apple, cider, brown sugar, black pepper, celery, and salt. Place the sausages and the mixture in a vacuum-sealable bag. Release air by water displacement method, seal, and submerge the bag in the water bath. Cook for 2 hours.

Heat butter in a saucepan over medium heat. Once the timer has stopped, remove the bag and transfer the contents to a saucepan. Cook until the liquid evaporates. Add in cabbage, onion and potatoes and cook until browned. Divide the mixture into serving platters.

Garlic Pork Fillets

Prep + Cook Time: 2 hours 8 minutes | Servings: 3

Ingredients

1 pound pork tenderloin
1 cup vegetable broth

2 garlic cloves, minced
1 tsp garlic powder

3 tsp olive oil
Salt and black pepper to taste

Directions

Prepare a water bath, place Sous Vide in it, and set to 136 F. Rinse well the meat and pat dry with paper towels. Rub with garlic powder, salt and black pepper. Place in a large vacuum-sealable bag along with broth and minced garlic. Seal the bag and submerge in the water bath. Cook for 2 hours. Remove the tenderloin from the bag and pat dry with a paper towel. Heat oil in a large skillet. Brown the fillet for 2-3 minutes on each side. Slice the pork, arrange on a platter, then spoon pan juices on top.

Mexican Pork Carnitas with Salsa Roja

Prep + Cook Time: 49 hours 40 minutes | Servings: 8

Ingredients

3 tbsp olive oil
2 tbsp red pepper flakes
Salt to taste
2 tsp hot Mexican chili powder

2 tsp dried oregano
½ tsp ground cinnamon
2 ¼ pounds boneless pork shoulder
4 small ripe tomatoes, diced

¼ red onion, diced
¼ cup cilantro leaves, chopped
Freshly squeezed lemon juice
8 corn tortillas

Directions

Combine well the red pepper flakes, kosher salt, hot Mexican chili powder, oregano, and cinnamon. Brush chili mix over the pork and cover with aluminium foil. Allow chilling for 1 hour.

Prepare a water bath and place Sous Vide in it. Set to 159 F. Place the pork in a vacuum-sealable bag. Release air by the water displacement method, seal and submerge in the water bath. Cook for 48 hours. 15 minutes Before the end, mix together the tomatoes, onion and cilantro. Add in lemon juice and salt.

Once the timer has stopped, remove the bag and transfer the pork to a cutting board. Discard cooking juices. Pull the meat until it is shredded. Heat vegetable oil in a skillet over medium heat and cook the shredded pork until it gets crispy and crusty parts. Fill the tortilla with pork. Top with salsa roja and serve.

Juicy BBQ Baby Ribs

Prep + Cook Time: 16 hours 50 minutes | Servings: 5

Ingredients

4 pounds pork baby back ribs
3 ½ cups BBQ sauce

⅓ cup tomato puree
4 scallions, chopped

2 tbsp fresh parsley, chopped

Directions

Prepare a water bath and place the Sous Vide in it. Set to 162 F. Place the separate ribs in a vacuum-sealable bag with 3 cups of BBQ Sauce. Release air by the water displacement method, seal, and submerge the bag in the water bath. Cook for 16 hours. In a bowl, mix the remaining BBQ sauce and tomato puree. Keep in the fridge.

Once the timer has stopped, remove the ribs and pat dry with kitchen towel. Discard cooking juices. Preheat the oven to 300 F. Brush the ribs with the BBQ sauce on both sides and transfer to the oven. Bake for 10 minutes. Brush again with the sauce and bake for another 30 minutes. Garnish with scallions and parsley, and serve.

Pork Chops with Mushroom Sauce

Prep + Cook Time: 1 hour 10 minutes | Servings: 3

Ingredients

3 (8 oz) pork chops
Salt and black pepper to taste
3 tbsp butter, unsalted

6 oz mushrooms
½ cup beef stock
2 tbsp Worcestershire sauce

3 tbsp garlic chives, chopped for garnishing

Directions

Make a water bath, place Sous Vide in it, and set to 140 F. Rub pork chops with salt and pepper and place in a vacuum-sealable bag. Release air by the water displacement method, seal, and submerge the bag in the water bath. Set the timer for 55 minutes. Once the timer has stopped, remove and unseal the bag.

Remove the pork and pat dry using a paper towel. Discard the juices. Place a skillet over medium heat and add 1 tablespoon butter. Sear pork for 2 minutes on both sides. Set aside. With the skillet still over the heat, add the mushrooms and cook for 5 minutes. Turn heat off, add in the remaining butter and swirl until butter melts. Season with pepper and salt. Serve pork chops with mushroom sauce over it.

Savory Thyme & Garlic Pork Tenderloin

Prep + Cook Time: 2 hours 25 minutes | Servings: 8

Ingredients

2 tbsp butter
1 tbsp onion powder
1 tbsp ground cumin

1 tbsp cilantro
1 tbsp dried rosemary
Salt to taste

1 (3-pound) pork tenderloin, skinless
1 tbsp olive oil

Directions

Prepare a water bath and place the Sous Vide in it. Set to 140 F. Combine the onion powder, cumin, garlic powder, rosemary, and lime salt. Brush the pork first with olive oil and salt, then with onion mix. Place in a vacuum-sealable bag. Release air by the water displacement method, seal, and submerge the bag in a water bath.

Cook for 2 hours. Once the timer has stopped, remove the pork and pat dry with kitchen towel. Discard cooking juices. Heat butter in a skillet over high heat and sear the pork for 3-4 minutes until browned on all sides. Allow to cool for 5 minutes and cut into medallions.

Sweet Orange Pork Tacos

Prep + Cook Time: 7 hours 10 minutes | Servings: 8

Ingredients

½ cup orange juice
4 tbsp honey
2 tbsp fresh garlic, minced
2 tbsp fresh ginger, minced

2 tbsp Worcestershire sauce
2 tsp hoisin sauce
2 tsp sriracha sauce
Zest of ½ orange

1 pound pork shoulder
8 flour tortillas, warmed
½ cup chopped fresh cilantro
1 lime, cut into wedges

Directions

Prepare a water bath and place the Sous Vide in it. Set to 175 F. Combine well the orange juice, 3 tbsp honey, garlic, ginger, Worcestershire sauce, hoisin sauce, sriracha, and orange zest. Place the pork and orange sauce in a vacuum-sealable bag. Release air by the water displacement method, seal, and submerge the bag in the water bath. Cook for 7 hours. Once done, remove the pork and transfer to a baking sheet. Reserve cooking juices.

Heat a saucepan over medium heat and pour in juices with the remaining honey. Cook for 5 minutes until bubbling and reduced by half. Brush the pork with the sauce. Fill the tortillas with the pork. Garnish with cilantro and top with the remaining sauce to serve.

Pork with Vegetables

Prep + Cook Time: 2 hours 15 minutes | Servings: 3

Ingredients

1 pound pork tenderloin
1 cup red bell pepper, sliced
1 cup green bell pepper, sliced
1 cup zucchini, sliced

½ cup onion, finely chopped
1 cup cauliflower florets
½ cup freshly squeezed lemon juice
½ cup chicken stock

2 tsp olive oil
½ tsp ground ginger
1 tsp pink Himalayan salt

Directions

Prepare a water bath and place the Sous Vide in it. Set to 167 F.

Rinse the pork under cold running water. Using a sharp paring knife, cut the meat into bite-sized pieces. Combine with other ingredients and stir well. Transfer to a large vacuum-sealable bag and seal. Cook for 2 hours.

In a bowl, combine lemon juice with chicken stock, ginger, and salt. Stir well and add sliced vegetables. Heat the olive oil in a pan over medium heat and add the veggie mixture. Stir-fry for 5-6 minutes; set aside.

Once the timer has stopped, remove the pork and pat dry with kitchen towels. Add to the preheated pan and sear for 2-3 minutes on all sides. Slice and top with the sauteed vegetables. Serve and enjoy!

POULTRY

Chili Chicken & Chorizo Tacos with Cheese

Prep + Cook Time: 3 hours 25 minutes | Servings: 6

Ingredients

2 pork sausages, casings removed	3 garlic cloves	1 tbsp vegetable oil
1 poblano pepper, stemmed and seeded	2 tbsp lime juice	½ yellow onion, sliced thinly
½ jalapeño pepper, stemmed	1 tsp salt	8 corn taco shells
4 scallions, chopped	¾ tsp ground coriander	3 tbsp Provolone cheese
1 bunch fresh cilantro leaves	¾ tsp ground cumin	1 tomato
½ cup chopped fresh parsley	4 chicken breasts, sliced	1 Iceberg lettuce, shredded

Directions

Put the ½ cup water, poblano pepper, jalapeño pepper, scallions, cilantro, parsley, garlic, lime juice, salt, coriander, and cumin in a blender and mix until smooth. Place the chicken strips and pepper mixture in a vacuum-sealable bag. Transfer to the fridge and allow to chill for 1 hour.

Prepare a water bath and place Sous Vide in it. Set to 141 F. Place the chicken mix in the bath. Cook for 1 hour and 30 minutes. Heat oil in a skillet over medium heat and sauté onion for 3 minutes. Add in chorizo and cook for 5-7 minutes. Once the timer has stopped, remove the chicken. Discard cooking juices. Add in chicken and mix well. Fill the tortillas with the chicken-chorizo mixture. Top with cheese, tomato and lettuce. Serve.

Easy Spicy-Honey Chicken

Prep + Cook Time: 1 hour 45 minutes | Servings: 4

Ingredients

8 tbsp butter	1 tsp cumin	Salt and black pepper to taste
8 garlic cloves, chopped	4 tbsp honey	4 boneless, skinless chicken breasts
6 tbsp chili sauce	Juice of 1 lime	

Directions

Prepare a water bath and place the Sous Vide in it. Set to 141 F. Heat a saucepan over medium heat and put the butter, garlic, cumin, chili sauce, sugar, lime juice, and a pinch of salt and pepper. Cook for 5 minutes.

Combine the chicken with salt and pepper and place it in 4 vacuum-sealable bag with the marinate. Release air by the water displacement method, seal and submerge the bags in the water bath. Cook for 1 hour and 30 minutes.

Once the timer has stopped, remove the chicken and pat dry with kitchen towels. Reserve the half of cooking juices from each bag and transfer into a pot over medium heat. Cook until the sauce simmer, then Put the chicken inside and cook for 4 minutes. Remove the chicken and cut into slices. Serve with rice.

Crunchy Homemade Fried Chicken

Prep + Cook Time: 3 hours 20 minutes | Servings: 8

Ingredients

½ tbsp dried basil	Salt and white pepper to taste	2 tbsp garlic powder
2 ¼ cups sour cream	½ cup vegetable oil	1 ½ tbsp Cayenne red pepper powder
8 chicken drumsticks	3 cups flour	1 tbsp dried mustard

Directions

Prepare a water bath and place the Sous Vide in it. Set to 156 F. Season the chicken salt and place in a vacuum-sealable bag. Release air by the water displacement method, seal and submerge in the water bath. Cook for 3 hours. Once the timer has stopped, remove the chicken and pat dry with kitchen towels.

Combine salt, flour, garlic powder, cayenne red pepper powders, mustard, white pepper, and basil in a bowl. Place sour cream in another bowl. Dip the chicken in the flour mixture, then in the sour cream and again in the flour mixture. Heat oil in a skillet over medium heat. Cook in the drumsticks for 3-4 minutes until crispy. Serve.

Classic Chicken Cordon Bleu

Prep + Cook Time: 1 hour 50 minutes + Cooling Time | Servings: 4

Ingredients

½ cup butter
4 boneless, skinless chicken breasts
Salt and black pepper to taste

1 tsp cayenne pepper
4 garlic cloves, minced
8 ham slices

8 slices Emmental cheese

Directions

Prepare a water bath and place the Sous Vide in it. Set to 141 F. Season the chicken with salt and pepper. Cover with plastic wrap and rolled. Set aside and allow to chill.

Heat a saucepan over medium heat and add some black pepper, cayenne pepper, 1/4 cup of butter, and garlic. Cook until the butter melts. Transfer to a bowl. Rub the chicken on one side with the butter mixture. Then place 2 slices of ham and 2 slices of cheese and cover it. Roll each breast with plastic wrap and transfer to the fridge for 2-3 hours or in the freezer for 20-30 minutes.

Place the breast in two vacuum-sealable bags. Release air by the water displacement method, seal and submerge the bags in the water bath. Cook for 1 hour and 30 minutes. Once done, remove the breasts and take off the plastic. Heat the remaining butter in a skillet over medium heat and sear the chicken for 1-2 minutes per side.

Spicy Chicken Breasts

Prep + Cook Time: 1 hour 40 minutes | Servings: 4

Ingredients

½ cup chili sauce
2 tbsp butter

1 tbsp white vinegar
1 tbsp champagne vinegar

4 chicken breasts, halved
Salt and black pepper to taste

Directions

Prepare a water bath and place the Sous Vide in it. Set to 141 F. Heat a saucepan over medium heat and combine the chili sauce, 1 tbsp of butter and vinegar. Cook until the butter melted. Set aside.

Season the chicken with salt and pepper and place in two vacuum-sealable bags with the chili mix. Release air by the water displacement method, seal and submerge the bags in the water bath. Cook for 1 hour and 30 minutes.

Once the timer has stopped, remove the chicken and transfer to a baking sheet. Discard cooking juices. Heat the remaining butter in a skillet over high heat and sear the chicken 1 minute per side. Cut into stripes. Serve.

Delicious Chicken Wings with Buffalo Sauce

Prep + Cook Time: 3 hours | Servings: 3

Ingredients

3 pounds capon chicken wings

2½ cups buffalo sauce

1 bunch fresh parsley

Directions

Prepare a water bath and place the Sous Vide in it. Set to 148 F.

Combine the capon wings with salt and pepper. Place it in a vacuum-sealable bag with 2 cups of buffalo sauce. Release air by the water displacement method, seal, and submerge the bag in the water bath. Cook for 2 hours.

Heat the oven to broil. Once the timer has stopped, remove the wings and transfer them into a bowl. Pour the remaining buffalo sauce and mix well. Transfer the wings to a baking tray with aluminium foil and cover with the remaining sauce. Bake for 10 minutes, turning at least once. Garnish with parsley.

Savory Lettuce Wraps with Ginger-Chili Chicken

Prep + Cook Time: 1 hour 45 minutes | Servings: 5

Ingredients

½ cup hoisin sauce
½ cup sweet chili sauce
3 tbsp soy sauce
2 tbsp grated ginger
2 tbsp ground ginger

1 tbsp brown sugar
2 garlic cloves, minced
Juice of 1 lime
4 chicken breasts, cubed
Salt and black pepper to taste

12 lettuce leaves, rinsed
⅛ cup poppy seeds
4 chives

Directions

Prepare a water bath and place Sous Vide in it. Set to 141 F. Combine chili sauce, ginger, soy sauce, brown sugar, garlic, and half of the lime juice. Heat a saucepan over medium heat and pour in the mixture. Cook for 5 minutes. Set aside.

Season the breasts with salt and pepper. Place them in an even layer in a vacuum-sealable bag with the chili sauce mixture. Release air by the water displacement method, seal, and submerge the bag in the water bath. Cook for 1 hour and 30 minutes.

Once the timer has stopped, remove the chicken and pat dry with kitchen towels. Discard cooking juices. Combine the hoisin sauce with the chicken cubes and mix well. Make piles of 6 lettuce leaves.

Share chicken among lettuce leaves and top with the poppy seeds and chives before wrapping.

Aromatic Lemon Chicken Breasts

Prep + Cook Time: 1 hour 50 minutes | Servings: 4

Ingredients

3 tbsp butter
4 boneless skinless chicken breasts
Salt and black pepper to taste
Zest and juice of 1 lemon

¼ cup heavy cream
2 tbsp chicken broth
1 tbsp chopped fresh sage leaves
1 tbsp olive oil

3 garlic cloves, minced
1/4 cup red onions, chopped
1 large lemon, thinly sliced

Directions

Prepare a water bath and place the Sous Vide in it. Set to 141 F. Season the breast with salt and pepper.

Heat a saucepan over medium heat and combine the lemon juice and zest, heavy cream, 2 tbsp of butter, chicken broth, sage, olive oil, garlic, and red onions. Cook until the butter has melted. Place the breasts in 2 vacuum-sealable bags with the lemon-butter mix. Add in lemon slices. Release air by the water displacement method, seal and submerge the bags in the bath. Cook for 90 minutes.

Once the timer has stopped, remove the breasts and pat dry with kitchen towels. Discard the cooking juices. Heat the remaining butter in a skillet and sear the breasts for 1 minute per side. Cut the breasts into strips. Serve.

Mustard & Garlic Chicken

Prep + Cook Time: 60 minutes | Servings: 5

Ingredients

17 ounces chicken breasts
1 tbsp Dijon mustard
2 tbsp mustard powder

2 tsp tomato sauce
3 tbsp butter
1 tsp salt

3 tsp minced garlic
¼ cup soy sauce

Directions

Prepare a water bath and place the Sous Vide in it. Set to 150 F. Place all the ingredients in a vacuum-sealable bag and shake to combine. Release air by the water displacement method, seal, and submerge the bag in the water bath. Set the timer to 50 minutes. Once the timer has stopped, remove the chicken and slice. Serve warm.

Yummy Chicken Legs with Lime-Sweet Sauce

Prep + Cook Time: 14 hours 30 minutes | Servings: 8

Ingredients

¼ cup olive oil
12 chicken legs
4 red bell peppers, chopped
6 spring onions, chopped
4 garlic cloves, minced

1 oz fresh ginger, chopped
½ cup Worcestershire sauce
¼ cup lime juice
2 tbsp lime zest
2 tbsp sugar

2 tbsp fresh thyme leaves
1 tbsp allspice
Salt and black pepper to taste
1 tsp ground nutmeg

Directions

Put in a food processor the peppers, onions, garlic, ginger, Worcestershire sauce, olive oil, lime juice and zest, sugar, thyme, allspice, salt, black pepper, and nutmeg. and blend. Reserve 1/4 cup of sauce. Place the chicken and lime sauce in a vacuum-sealable bag. Release air by the water displacement method. Chill for 12 hours.

Prepare a water bath and place the Sous Vide in it. Set to 152 F. Seal and submerge the bag in the water bath. Cook for 2 hours. Once the timer has stopped, remove the chicken and pat dry with kitchen towels. Discard the cooking juices. Brush the chicken with the reserved lime sauce. Heat a skillet over high heat and sear the chicken for 30 seconds per side. Serve and enjoy!

Pepper Chicken Salad

Prep + Cook Time: 1 hour 15 minutes | Servings: 4

Ingredients

4 chicken breasts, boneless and skinless
¼ cup + 3 tbsp vegetable oil
1 onion, peeled and finely chopped

6 cherry tomatoes, halved
Salt and black pepper to taste
1 cup lettuce, finely chopped

2 tbsp freshly squeezed lemon juice

Directions

Make a water bath, place Sous Vide in it, and set to 149 F.

Thoroughly rinse the meat under the cold water and pat dry using a kitchen paper. Cut the meat into bite-sized pieces and place in a vacuum-sealable bag along with ¼ cup of oil and seal. Submerge the bag in the water bath. Once the timer has stopped, remove the chicken from the bag, pat dry and chill at room temperature.

In a bowl, mix the onion, tomatoes, and lettuce. Finally, add the chicken breasts and season with three tablespoons of oil, lemon juice, and salt. Top with Greek yogurt and olives. However, it's optional. Serve cold.

Orange Chicken Thighs

Prep + Cook Time: 2 hours | Servings: 4

Ingredients

2 pounds chicken thighs
2 small chili peppers, finely chopped
1 cup chicken broths

1 onion, chopped
½ cup freshly squeezed orange juice
1 tsp orange extract, liquid

2 tbsp vegetable oil
1 tsp barbecue seasoning mix
Fresh parsley to garnish

Directions

Make a water bath, place Sous Vide in it, and set to 167 F. Heat olive oil in a large saucepan. Add in chopped onions and stir-fry for 3 minutes, over a medium temperature, until translucent.

In a food processor, combine the orange juice with chili pepper and orange extract. Pulse until well combined. Pour the mixture into a saucepan and reduce the heat. Simmer for 10 minutes. Coat chicken with barbecue seasoning mix and place in a saucepan. Add in chicken broth and cook until half of the liquid evaporates. Remove to a large vacuum-sealable bag and seal. Submerge the bag in the water bath and cook for 45 minutes. Once the timer has stopped, remove the bag and open it. Garnish with fresh parsley and serve.

Chicken Stew with Mushrooms

Prep + Cook Time: 1 hour 5 minutes | Servings: 2

Ingredients

2 chicken thighs, skinless
½ cup fire-roasted tomatoes, diced
½ cup chicken stock
1 tbsp tomato paste

½ cup button mushrooms, chopped
1 medium-sized celery stalk
1 small carrot, chopped
1 small onion, chopped

1 tbsp fresh basil, finely chopped
1 garlic clove, crushed
Salt and black pepper to taste

Directions

Make a water bath, place Sous Vide in it, and set to 129 F. Rub the thighs with salt and pepper. Set aside. Chop the celery stalk into half-inch long pieces. Place the meat, onion, carrot, mushrooms, celery stalk, and fire-roasted tomatoes in a vacuum-sealable bag. Submerge the sealed bag in the water bath and set the timer for 45 minutes.

Once the timer has stopped, remove the bag from the water bath and open it. The meat should be falling off the bone easily, so remove the bones. Heat some oil in a medium-sized saucepan and add garlic. Briefly fry for about 3 minutes, stirring constantly. Add the contents of the bag, chicken stock, and tomato paste. Bring it to a boil and reduce the heat to medium. Cook for 5 more minutes, stirring occasionally. Serve sprinkled with basil.

Chicken Thighs with Carrot Puree

Prep + Cook Time: 60 minutes | Servings: 5

Ingredients

2 pounds chicken thighs
1 cup carrots, pureed
2 tbsp olive oil

¼ cup finely chopped onion
2 cups chicken broth
2 tbsp fresh parsley, finely chopped

2 crushed garlic cloves
Salt and black pepper to taste

Directions

Make a water bath, place Sous Vide in it, and set to 167 F.

In a bowl, combine 1 tablespoon of olive oil, parsley, salt, and pepper. Stir well and generously brush the thighs with the mixture. Place in a large vacuum-sealable bag and add chicken broth. Press the bag to remove the air. Seal the bag, put it in the water bath, and set the timer to 45 minutes. Once the timer has stopped, remove the thighs from the bag and pat them dry. Reserve the cooking liquid.

Heat the remaining olive oil in a large skillet over medium heat. Add garlic and onion and stir-fry for about 1-2 minutes or until soft. Add chicken thighs and cook for 2-3 minutes, turning occasionally. Taste for doneness, adjust the seasonings and then add broth. Bring it to a boil and remove from the heat. Transfer the thighs to a serving plate. Top with carrot puree and sprinkle with parsley. Serve and enjoy!

Whole Chicken

Prep + Cook Time: 7 hours 15 minutes | Servings: 6

Ingredients

1 (5 lb) full chicken, trussed
5 cups chicken stock
3 cups mixed bell peppers, diced

3 cups celery, diced
3 cups leeks, diced
1 ¼ tsp salt

1 ¼ tsp black peppercorns
2 bay leaves

Directions

Make a water bath, place Sous Vide in it, and set to 150 F. Season the chicken with salt. Place all the listed ingredients and chicken in a sizable vacuum-sealable bag. Release air by the water displacement method and seal the vacuum bag. Drop in the water bath and set the timer for 7 hours.

Cover the water with a plastic bag to reduce evaporation and water every 2 hours to the bath. Once the timer has stopped, remove and unseal the bag. Preheat a broiler, carefully remove the chicken and pat dry. Place the chicken in the broiler and broil until the skin is golden brown. Rest the chicken for 8 minutes, slice and serve.

Simple Spicy Chicken Thighs

Prep + Cook Time: 2 hours 55 minutes | Servings: 6

Ingredients

1 lb chicken thighs, bone-in
3 tbsp butter

1 tbsp cayenne pepper
Salt to taste

Directions

Make a water bath, place Sous Vide in it, and set to 165 F. Season the chicken with pepper and salt. Place chicken with one tablespoon of butter in a vacuum-sealable bag. Release air by the water displacement method, seal, and submerge the bag in the water bath. Set the timer for 2 hours 30 minutes.

Once the timer has stopped, remove the bag and unseal it. Preheat a grill and melt the remaining butter in a microwave. Grease the grill grate with some of the butter and brush the chicken with the remaining butter. Sear until dark brown color is achieved. Serve as a snack.

Whole Chicken

Prep + Cook Time: 6 hours 40 minutes | Servings: 6

Ingredients

1 medium whole chicken
3 garlic cloves

3 ounces chopped celery stalk
3 tbsp mustard

Salt and black pepper to taste
1 tbsp butter

Directions

Prepare a water bath and place the Sous Vide in it. Set to 150 F. Combine all the ingredients in a vacuum-sealable bag. Release air by the water displacement method, seal, and submerge the bag in the bath. Set the timer for 6 hours and 30 minutes. Once done, leave the chicken to cool slightly before carving.

Chicken Breasts with Cajun Sauce

Prep + Cook Time: 1 hour 55 minutes | Servings: 4

Ingredients

2 tbsp butter
4 boneless skinless chicken breasts

Salt and black pepper to taste
1 tsp cumin

½ cup Cajun chicken marinade

Directions

Prepare a water bath and place the Sous Vide in it. Set to 141 F. Season the breasts with salt and pepper and place in two vacuum-sealable bags with the cajun sauce. Release air by the water displacement method, seal and submerge the bags in the water bath. Cook for 1 hour and 30 minutes.

Once the timer has stopped, remove the chicken and pat dry. Discard cooking juices. Heat butter in a skillet over high heat and cook the breast for 1 minute per side. Slice the breasts and serve.

Basic Chicken Breasts

Prep + Cook Time: 75 minutes | Servings: 3

Ingredients

1 lb chicken breasts, boneless

Salt and black pepper to taste

1 tsp garlic powder

Directions

Make a water bath, place Sous Vide in it, and set it to 150 F. Pat dry the chicken breasts and season with salt, garlic powder, and pepper. Put the chicken in a vacuum-sealable bag, release air by the water displacement method and seal it. Place in the water and set the timer to cook for 1 hour. Once the timer has stopped, remove and unseal the bag. Remove the chicken and let chill for later use.

Sriracha Chicken Breasts

Prep + Cook Time: 1 hour 55 minutes | Servings: 4

Ingredients

8 tbsp butter, cubed
1 pound chicken breasts

Salt and black pepper to taste
1 tsp nutmeg

1 ½ cups sriracha sauce

Directions

Prepare a water bath and place the Sous Vide in it. Set to 141 F. Season the breasts with salt, nutmeg and pepper and. place in two vacuum-sealable bags with sriracha sauce. Release air by the water displacement method.

Seal and submerge the bags in the water bath. Cook for 1 ½ hours. Once the timer has stopped, remove the chicken and pat dry with kitchen towels. Discard the cooking juices. Heat butter in a skillet over high heat and cook the breasts for 1 minute per side. Cut the breasts into tiny pieces.

Parsley Chicken with Curry Sauce

Prep + Cook Time: 2 hours 35 minutes | Servings: 4

Ingredients

4 boneless skinless chicken breasts
Salt and black pepper to taste

1 tbsp thyme
1 tbsp parsley

5 cups butter curry sauce

Directions

Prepare a water bath and place the Sous Vide in it. Set to 141 F. Season the chicken with salt, thyme, parsley, and pepper. Place in two vacuum-sealable bags with the sauce. Release air by the water displacement method, seal and submerge the bags in the water bath. Cook for 1 hour and 30 minutes.

Once the timer has stopped, remove the chicken and pat dry with kitchen towels. Reserve the cooking juices. Heat a saucepan over high heat and pour in juices. Cook for 10 minutes until reduced. Chop the chicken into chunks and add them to the sauce. Cook for 2-3 minutes. Serve immediately.

Parmesan Crusted Chicken Breast

Prep + Cook Time: 65 minutes | Servings: 4

Ingredients

2 chicken breast, skinless and boneless
1 ½ cups basil pesto

½ cup macadamia nuts, ground
¼ cup Parmesan cheese, grated

3 tbsp olive oil

Directions

Make a water bath, place Sous Vide in it, and set to 65 F. Cut chicken into bite-size pieces and coat with pesto. Place the chicken flat in two separate vacuum bags without overlapping them. Release air by the water displacement method and seal the bags. Submerge them in the water bath and set the timer for 50 minutes.

Once the timer has stopped, remove and unseal the bags. Transfer the chicken pieces to a plate without the juices. Sprinkle macadamia nuts and cheese over it and coat well. Set a skillet over high heat, add in olive oil. Once the oil has heated, quickly fry the coated chicken for 1 minute all around. Drain fat. Serve as a starter dish.

Ground Chicken with Tomatoes

Prep + Cook Time: 100 minutes | Servings: 4

Ingredients

1 pound ground chicken
2 tbsp tomato paste
¼ cup chicken stock

¼ cup tomato juice
1 tbsp white sugar
1 tsp thyme

1 tbsp onion powder
½ tsp oregano

Directions

Prepare a water bath and place the Sous Vide in it. Set to 147 F.

Whisk together all the ingredients except the chicken in a saucepan. Cook over medium heat for a 2 minutes. Transfer to a vacuum-sealable bag. Release air by the water displacement method, seal, and submerge the bag in the bath. Cook for 80 minutes. Once done, remove the bag and slice. Serve warm.

Thyme Chicken with Lemon

Prep + Cook Time: 2 hours 15 minutes | Servings: 3

Ingredients

3 chicken thighs
Salt and black pepper to taste

3 lemon slices
3 thyme sprigs

3 tbsp olive oil for searing

Directions

Make a water bath, place Sous Vide in it, and set to 165 F. Season the chicken with salt and pepper. Top with lemon slices and thyme sprigs. Place them in a vacuum-sealable bag, release air by the water displacement method and seal the bag. Submerge in the water bag and set the timer for 2 hours.

Once the timer has stopped, remove and unseal the bag. Heat olive oil in a pan over high heat. Place the chicken thighs, skin down in the skillet and sear until golden brown. Garnish with extra lemon wedges. Serve and enjoy!

Buffalo Chicken Wings

Prep + Cook Time: 1 hour and 20 minutes | Servings: 6

Ingredients

3 lb chicken wings
3 tsp salt
2 tsp minced garlic

2 tbsp smoked paprika
1 tsp sugar
½ cup hot sauce

5 tbsp butter
2 ½ cups almond flour
Olive oil for frying

Directions

Make a water bath, place Sous Vide in it, and set to 144 F. Combine the wings, garlic, salt, sugar and smoked paprika. Coat the chicken evenly. Place in a sizable vacuum-sealable bag, release air by the water displacement method and seal the bag. Submerge in the water. Set the timer to cook for 1 hour. Once the timer has stopped, remove and unseal the bag. Pour flour into a large bowl, add in chicken and toss to coat.

Heat oil in a pan over medium heat, fry the chicken until golden brown. Remove and set aside. In another pan, melt butter and add the hot sauce. Coat the wings with butter and hot sauce. Serve as an appetizer

Shredded Chicken Patties

Prep + Cook Time: 3 hours 15 minutes | Servings: 5

Ingredients

1 lb chicken breasts
½ cup macadamia nuts, ground
⅓ cup olive oil mayonnaise

3 green onions, finely chopped
2 tbsp lemon juice
Salt and black pepper to taste

3 tbsp olive oil

Directions

Make a water bath, place Sous Vide in it, and set to 165 F. Put the chicken in a vacuum-sealable bag, release air by the water displacement method and seal it. Put the bag in the water bath and set the timer for 3 hours.

Once the timer has stopped, remove and unseal the bag. Shred the chicken and add it to a bowl along with all the remaining ingredients except olive oil. Mix evenly and make patties. Heat olive oil in a skillet over medium heat. Add patties and fry to golden brown on both sides.

Lemon Chicken with Mint

Prep + Cook Time: 2 hours 40 minutes | Servings: 3

Ingredients

1 pound chicken thighs, boneless and skinless

¼ cup olive oil

1 tbsp freshly squeezed lemon juice

2 garlic cloves, crushed

1 tsp ginger

Salt and cayenne pepper to taste

1 tsp fresh mint, finely chopped

Directions

In a small bowl, combine olive oil with lemon juice, garlic, ground ginger, mint, cayenne pepper, and salt. Generously brush each thigh with this mixture and refrigerate for at least 30 minutes.

Remove thighs from the refrigerator. Place in a large vacuum-sealable bag and cook for 2 hours at 149 F. Remove from the vacuum-sealable bag and serve immediately with spring onions.

Chicken with Cherry Marmalade

Prep + Cook Time: 4 hours 25 minutes | Servings: 4

Ingredients

2 pounds bone-in skin-on chicken

4 tbsp cherry marmalade

2 tbsp ground nutmeg

Salt and black pepper to taste

Directions

Prepare a water bath and place the Sous Vide in it. Set to 172 F. Season the chicken with salt and pepper and combine with the remaining ingredients. Place in a vacuum-sealable bag. Release air by the water displacement method, seal, and submerge the bag in the water bath. Cook for 4 hours. Once the timer has stopped, remove the bag and move into a baking dish. Heat the oven to 450 F. and roast for 10 minutes until crispy. Serve and enjoy!

Sweet Spicy Chicken Drumsticks

Prep + Cook Time: 2 hours 20 minutes | Servings: 3

Ingredients

½ tbsp sugar

½ cup soy sauce

2 ½ tsp ginger, chopped

2 ½ tsp garlic, chopped

2 ½ tsp red chili puree

¼ lb small chicken drumsticks, skinless

2 tbsp olive oil

2 tbsp sesame seeds to garnish

1 scallion, chopped to garnish

Salt and black pepper to taste

Directions

Make a water bath, place Sous Vide in it, and set to 165 F. Rub chicken with salt and pepper. Put the chicken in a vacuum-sealable bag, release air by water displacement method and seal it.

Put the bag in the water bath and set the timer for 2 hours. Once the timer has stopped, remove and unseal the bag. In a bowl, mix the remaining listed ingredients except for olive oil. Set aside.

Heat oil in a skillet over medium heat, add chicken. Once they brown slightly on both sides, add the sauce and coat the chicken. Cook for 10 minutes. Garnish with sesame and scallions. Serve with a side of cauliflower rice.

Zesty Chicken

Prep + Cook Time: 2 hours 40 minutes | Servings: 8

Ingredients

1 five-pound chicken, whole

3 tbsp lemon juice

½ cup olive oil

6 bay leaves, dried

2 tbsp rosemary, crushed

3 tbsp thyme, dried

2 tbsp coconut oil

¼ cup lemon zest

3 garlic cloves, minced

Salt and black pepper to taste

Directions

Make a water bath, place Sous Vide in it, and set to 149 F. Rinse the chicken under cold running water and pat dry with a kitchen towel. Set aside. In a small bowl, combine olive oil with salt, lemon juice, dried bay leaves, rosemary, and thyme. Stuff the chicken's cavity with lemon slices and this mixture.

In another bowl, combine coconut oil with lemon zest and garlic. Loosen the skin of the chicken from the flesh. Rub this mixture under the skin and place in a large plastic bag. Refrigerate for 30 minutes. Remove from the refrigerator and place in a large vacuum-sealable bag. Put the bag in the water bath and set the timer for 2 hours.

Stuffed Chicken Breasts

Prep + Cook Time: 1 hour 15 minutes | Servings: 6

Ingredients

2 pounds chicken breasts
2 tbsp fresh parsley, finely chopped
2 tbsp fresh basil, finely chopped

1 large egg
½ cup spring onions, chopped
Salt and black pepper to taste

2 tbsp olive oil

Directions

Make a water bath, place Sous Vide in it, and set to 165 F. Wash the chicken breasts thoroughly and pat dry with kitchen paper. Rub some salt and pepper and set aside.

In a bowl, combine egg, parsley, basil, and spring onions. Stir until well incorporated. Place chicken breasts on a clean surface and spoon the egg mixture onto the middle. Fold the breasts over to seal. Place breasts in separate vacuum-sealable bags and press to remove the air. Seal the lid and place in the prepared water bath.

Cook en sous vide for 1 hour. Once the timer has stopped, remove the chicken breasts. Heat oil in a skillet over medium heat. Add chicken breasts and brown for 2 minutes per side.

Mediterranean Chicken Thighs

Prep + Cook Time: 1 hour 40 minutes | Servings: 3

Ingredients

1 pound chicken thighs
1 cup olive oil
½ cup freshly squeezed lime juice

½ cup parsley leaves, finely chopped
3 garlic cloves, crushed
1 tbsp cayenne pepper

1 tsp dried oregano
1 tsp sea salt

Directions

Rinse the meat under cold running water and drain in a large colander. In a bowl, combine olive oil with lime juice, chopped parsley, crushed garlic, cayenne pepper, oregano, and salt. Submerge filets in this mixture and cover. Refrigerate for 30 minutes. Remove the meat from the refrigerator and drain. Place in a large vacuum-sealable and cook en Sous Vide for 1 hour at 167 F.

Paprika Chicken Lunch

Prep + Cook Time: 1 hour 15 minutes | Servings: 2

Ingredients

1 boneless chicken breast, halved
Salt and black pepper to taste

Pepper to taste
1 tbsp paprika

1 tbsp garlic powder

Directions

Prepare a water bath and place the Sous Vide in it. Set to 149 F. Drain the chicken and pat dry with a baking sheet. Season with garlic powder, paprika, pepper, and salt. Place in a vacuum-sealable bag. Release air by the water displacement method, seal and submerge in the water bath. Cook for 1 hour. Once the timer has stopped, remove the chicken and serve.

Chicken Breasts with Harissa Sauce

Prep + Cook Time: 65 minutes | Servings: 4

Ingredients

1 pound chicken breasts, cubed	2 tbsp fish sauce	Salt to taste
1 stalk of fresh lemongrass, chopped	2 tbsp coconut sugar	1 tbsp harissa sauce

Directions

Prepare a water bath and place the Sous Vide in it. Set to 149 F. In a blender, pulse lemongrass, fish sauce, sugar, and salt. Marinade the chicken with the sauce and make brochettes. Place it in a vacuum-sealable bag. Release air by the water displacement method, seal, and submerge the bag in the water bath. Cook for 45 minutes.

Once the timer has stopped, remove the bag and transfer to a cold water bath. Remove the chicken and whisk with harissa sauce. Heat a skillet over medium heat and sear the chicken. Serve.

Garlic Chicken with Mushrooms

Prep + Cook Time: 2 hours 15 minutes | Servings: 6

Ingredients

2 pounds chicken thighs, skinless	1 garlic clove, crushed	½ tsp sage leaves, dried
1 pound cremini mushrooms, sliced	4 tbsp olive oil	¼ tsp cayenne pepper
1 cup chicken stock	½ tsp onion powder	Salt and black pepper to taste

Directions

Wash the thighs thoroughly under cold running water. Pat dry with kitchen paper and set aside. In a large skillet, heat the olive oil over medium heat. Brown both sides of the chicken thighs for 2 minutes. Set aside. Add garlic to the skillet and sauté until lightly brown. Stir in mushrooms, pour in stock, and cook until it reaches to a boil. Remove and set aside. Season the thighs with salt, pepper, cayenne pepper, and onion powder. Place in a large vacuum-sealable bag along with mushrooms and sage. Seal the bag and cook en Sous Vide for 2 hours at 149 F.

Chicken Thighs with Herbs

Prep + Cook Time: 4 hours 10 minutes | Servings: 4

Ingredients

1 pound chicken thighs	½ cup freshly squeezed lemon juice	1 tsp cayenne pepper
1 cup extra virgin olive oil	1 tbsp fresh basil, chopped	1 tsp salt
¼ cup apple cider vinegar	2 tbsp fresh thyme, chopped	
3 garlic cloves, crushed	1 tbsp fresh rosemary, chopped	

Directions

Rinse the meat under cold running water and place in a large colander to drain. Set aside. In a large bowl, combine olive oil with apple cider vinegar, garlic, lemon juice, basil, thyme, rosemary, salt, and cayenne pepper. Submerge thighs into this mixture and refrigerate for one hour. Remove the meat from the marinade and drain. Place in a large vacuum-sealable bag and cook en Sous Vide for 3 hours at 149 F.

Almond Butternut Squash & Chicken Salad

Prep + Cook Time: 1 hour 15 minutes | Servings: 2

Ingredients

4 cups butternut squash, cubed and roasted		
6 chicken tenderloins	2 tbsp olive oil	1 tbsp cumin
4 cups rocket tomatoes	4 tbsp red onion, chopped	Salt to taste
4 tbsp sliced almonds	1 tbsp paprika	
Juice of 1 lemon	1 tbsp turmeric	

Directions

Prepare a water bath and place the Sous Vide in it. Set to 138 F. Place the chicken and all the spices in a vacuum-sealable bag. Shake well. Release air by the water displacement method, seal, and submerge the bag in the water bath. Cook for 60 minutes. Once the timer has stopped, remove the chic and transfer to a heated skillet. Sear for 1 minute on each side. In a bowl, combine the remaining ingredients. Serve with chicken on top.

Chicken Pudding with Artichoke Hearts

Prep + Cook Time: 1 hour and 30 minutes | Servings: 3

Ingredients

1 pound chicken breasts
2 medium-sized artichokes
2 tbsp butter

2 tbsp extra virgin olive oil
1 lemon, juiced
2 tsp fresh parsley, finely chopped

Salt and black pepper to taste
½ tsp chili pepper

Directions

Thoroughly rinse the meat and pat dry with kitchen paper. Using a sharp paring knife, cut the meat into smaller pieces and remove the bones. Rub with olive oil and set aside.

Heat the sauté pan over medium heat. Turn the heat down slightly to medium and add in the meat. Cook for 3 minutes until golden on both sides. Remove from the heat and transfer to a large vacuum-sealable bag. Seal the bag and cook en Sous Vide for one hour at 149 F.

Meanwhile, prepare the artichoke. Cut the lemon onto halves and squeeze the juice into a small bowl. Divide the juice in half and set aside. Using a sharp paring knife, trim off the outer leaves until you reach the yellow and soft ones. Trim off the green outer skin around the artichoke base and steam. Make sure to remove the 'hairs' around the artichoke heart. They are inedible so simply throw them away.

Cut artichoke into half-inch pieces. Rub with half of lemon juice and place in a heavy-bottomed pot. Add enough water to cover and cook until completely fork-tender. Remove from the heat and drain. Chill for a while at room temperature. Cut each piece into thin strips.

Now combine artichoke with chicken meat in a large bowl. Stir in salt, pepper, and the remaining lemon juice. Melt butter over medium heat and drizzle over pudding. Sprinkle with chili pepper and serve.

Cilantro Chicken with Peanut Butter Sauce

Prep + Cook Time: 1 hour 40 minutes | Servings: 2

Ingredients

4 chicken breasts
1 bag mixed salad
1 bunch cilantro
2 cucumbers
2 carrots
1 pack wonton wrappers

2 tbsp vegetable oil
¼ cup peanut butter
Juice of 1 lime
2 tbsp chopped cilantro
3 cloves garlic
2 tbsp fresh ginger

½ cup water
2 tbsp white vinegar
1 tbsp soy sauce
1 tsp fish sauce
1 tsp sesame oil
3 tbsp canola oil

Directions

Prepare a water bath and place the Sous Vide in it. Set to 149 F. Season the chicken with salt and pepper and place in a vacuum-sealable bag. Release air by the water displacement method, seal, and submerge the bag in the water bath. Cook for 60 minutes. Chop the cucumber, cilantro and carrots and combine with the salad. Heat the oil in a pot over medium heat. Slice the wonton wrappers in pieces and fry until crispy.

In a food processor, put peanut butter, lime juice, fresh ginger, cilantro, water, white vinegar, fish sauce, soy sauce, sesame, and canola oil. Blend until smooth. Once the timer ends, remove the chicken and transfer to a hot skillet. Sear for 30 seconds per side. Mix the wonton strips with the salad. Slice the chicken. Serve on top of the salad. Drizzle with the dressing.

Chicken & Walnut Salad

Prep + Cook Time: 2 hours 20 minutes | Servings: 4

Ingredients

2 skinless chicken breasts, boneless
Salt and black pepper to taste
1 tbsp corn oil
1 apple, cored and diced

1 tsp lime juice
½ cup white grapes, cut in half
1 stick rib celery, diced
1/3 cup mayonnaise

2 tsp Chardonnay wine
1 tsp Dijon mustard
1 head Romaine lettuce
½ cup walnuts, toasted and chopped

Directions

Prepare a water bath and place the Sous Vide in it. Set to 146 F. Place the chicken in a vacuum-sealable bag and season with salt and pepper. Release air by the water displacement method, seal, and submerge the bag in the water bath. Cook for 2 hours. Once the timer has stopped, remove the bag and discard cooking juices. In a large bowl, toss apple slices with lime juice. Add in celery and white grapes. Mix well.

In another bowl, stir the mayonnaise, Dijon mustard and Chardonnay wine. Pour the mixture over the fruit and mix well. Chop the chicken and put in a medium bowl, season with salt and combine well. Put the chicken in the salad bowl. Colocate the romaine lettuce in salad bowls and place salad on top. Garnish with walnuts.

Sweet & Sour Chicken Wings

Prep + Cook Time: 2 hours 15 minutes | Servings: 2

Ingredients

Cornstarch slurry (mixed 1 tbsp cornstarch and 2 tbsp water)
12 chicken wings
Salt and black pepper to taste
1 cup chicken fry mix
½ cup water

½ cup tamari sauce
½ minced onion
5 garlic cloves, minced
2 tsp ginger powder

2 tbsp brown sugar
¼ cup mirin
Sesame seeds for garnish
Olive oil for frying

Directions

Prepare a water bath and place the Sous Vide in it. Set to 147 F. Place the chicken wings in a vacuum-sealable bag and season with salt and pepper. Release air by the water displacement method, seal, and submerge the bag in the water bath. Cook for 2 hours. Once the timer has stopped, remove the bag. Heat a frying pan with oil.

In a bowl, combine 1/2 cup of dry mix and 1/2 cup of water. Pour the remaining fry mix into another bowl. Soak the wings in the wet mix, then in the dry mix. Fry for 1-2 minutes until crispy and golden brown. For the sauce, heat a saucepan and pour all the ingredients; cook until bubbly. Stir in the wings. Top with sesame seeds and serve.

Crispy Chicken with Mushrooms

Prep + Cook Time: 1 hour 15 minutes | Servings: 4

Ingredients

4 boneless chicken breasts
1 cup panko bread crumbs
1 pound sliced Portobello mushrooms

Small bunch of thyme
2 eggs
Salt and black pepper to taste

Canola oil to taste

Directions

Prepare a water bath and place the Sous Vide in it. Set to 149 F. Place the chicken in a vacuum-sealable bag. Season with salt and thyme. Release air by the water displacement method, seal and submerge in the water bath. Cook for 60 minutes. Heat a skillet over medium heat. Cook the mushrooms until the water has evaporated. Add in 3-4 sprigs of thyme. Season with salt and pepper. Once the timer has stopped, remove the bag.

Heat a frying pan with oil over medium heat. Mix the panko with salt and pepper. Layer the chicken in panko mix. Fry for 1-2 minutes per side. Serve with mushrooms.

Citrus Chicken Breasts

Prep + Cook Time: 3 hours | Servings: 2

Ingredients

1 ½ tbsp freshly squeezed orange juice
1 ½ tbsp freshly squeezed lemon juice
1 ½ tbsp brown sugar
1 tbsp Pernod
1 tbsp olive oil

1 tbsp whole grain
1 tsp celery seeds
Salt to taste
¾ tsp black pepper
2 chicken breasts, bone-in, skin on

1 fennel, trimmed, sliced
2 clementines, unpeeled and sliced
Chopped dill

Directions

Prepare a water bath and place the Sous Vide in it. Set to 146 F. Combine in a bowl the lemon juice, orange juice, Pernod, olive oil, celery seeds, brown sugar, mustard, salt, and pepper. Mix well. Place the chicken breast, sliced clementine and sliced fennel in a vacuum-sealable bag. Add the orange mixture. Release air by the water displacement method, seal, and submerge the bag in the water bath. Cook for 2 hours and 30 minutes.

Once the timer has stopped, remove the bag and transfer the contents to a bowl. Drain the chicken and put the cooking juices in a heated saucepan. Cook for 5 minutes until bubbly. Remove and place in the chicken. Cook for 6 minutes until brown. Serve the chicken on a platter and top with the sauce. Garnish with dill and fennel fronds.

Vegetable Chicken with Soy Sauce.

Prep + Cook Time: 6 hours 25 minutes | Servings: 4

Ingredients

1 whole bone-in chicken, trussed
1-quart low sodium chicken stock
2 tbsp soy sauce

5 sprigs fresh sage
2 dried bay leaves
2 cups sliced carrots

2 cups sliced celery
½ oz dried mushrooms
3 tbsp butter

Directions

Prepare a water bath and place the Sous Vide in it. Set to 149 F. Combine the soy sauce, chicken stock, herbs, veggies, and chicken. Place in a vacuum-sealable bag. Release air by the water displacement method, seal, and submerge the bag in the water bath. Cook for 6 hours.

Once the timer has stopped, remove the chicken and drain the veggies. Dry with a baking sheet. Season with olive oil, salt and pepper. Heat the oven to 450 F. and roast for 10 minutes. In a saucepan, stir the cooking juices. Remove from the heat and mix with butter. Slice the chicken without the skin and season with kosher salt and ground black pepper. Top with the sauce. Serve and enjoy!

Layered Cheese Chicken

Prep + Cook Time: 60 minutes | Servings: 2

Ingredients

2 chicken breasts, boneless, skinless
Salt and black pepper to taste
2 tsp butter
4 cups lettuce

1 large tomato, sliced
1 oz cheddar cheese cheese, sliced
2 tbsp red onion, diced
Fresh basil leaves

1 tbsp olive oil
2 lemon wedges for serving

Directions

Prepare a water bath and place the Sous Vide in it. Set to 146 F. Place the chicken in a vacuum-sealable bag. Season with salt and pepper. Release air by the water displacement method, seal, and submerge the bag in the water bath. Cook for 45 minutes.

Once the timer has stopped, remove the chicken and discard cooking juices. Heat a skillet over high heat with butter. Sear the chicken until browned. Transfer to a serving plate. Put the lettuce among the chicken and top with tomato, red onion, cheddar cheese, and basil. Sprinkle with olive oil, salt and pepper. Serve with lemon wedges.

Mustardy Chicken Legs

Prep + Cook Time: 2 hours 30 minutes | Servings: 4

Ingredients

4 whole chicken legs
Salt and black pepper to taste
2 tbsp olive oil
2 shallots, thinly sliced

3 garlic cloves, thinly sliced
½ cup dry white wine
1 cup chicken stock
¼ cup whole grain mustard

1 cup half-and-half cream
1 tsp turmeric
2 tbsp fresh tarragon, minced
1 tbsp fresh thyme, minced

Directions

Prepare a water bath and place the Sous Vide in it. Set to 172 F. Season the chicken with salt and pepper. Heat olive oil in a skillet over high heat and sear the chicken legs for 5-7 minutes. Set aside.

In the same skillet, add the shallots and garlic. Cook for 5 minutes. Add in white wine and cook for 2 minutes until bubble. Remove and pour in chicken stock and mustard.

Combine the mustard sauce with the chicken and place in a vacuum-sealable bag. Release air by the water displacement method, seal and submerge in the water bath. Cook for 2 hours.

Once the timer has stopped, remove the bag, reserve the chicken and separate the cooking liquids. In a preheated saucepan, put the cooking liquids and half-and-half cream. Cook until bubbly and half evaporated. Remove from the heat and combine tarragon, turmeric, thyme, and chicken legs. Mix well. Season and serve.

Chinese-Style Chicken Salad with Hazelnuts

Prep + Cook Time: 1 hour 50 minutes | Servings: 4

Ingredients

4 skinless, boneless chicken breasts
Salt and black pepper to taste
¼ cup honey
¼ cup soy sauce
3 tbsp peanut butter, melted

3 tbsp sesame oil
2 tbsp vegetable oil
4 tsp vinegar
½ tsp smoked paprika
1 head iceberg lettuce, torn

3 scallions, chopped
¼ cup slivered hazelnuts, toasted
¼ cup sesame seeds, toasted
2 cups wonton strips

Directions

Prepare a water bath and place the Sous Vide in it. Set to 152 F. Combine the chicken with salt and pepper and place it in a vacuum-sealable bag. Submerge the bag in the water bath. Cook for 90 minutes.

Meantime, combine the honey, soy sauce, peanut butter, sesame oil, vegetable oil, vinegar, and paprika. Stir until smooth. Allow to chill in the fridge. Once the timer has stopped, remove the chicken and pat dry with kitchen towels. Discard cooking juices. Cut the chicken into tiny slices and transfer into a salad bowl. Add the lettuce, scallions and hazelnuts. Top with the dressing. Garnish with sesame seeds and wonton strips.

Artichoke Stuffed Chicken

Prep + Cook Time: 3hours 15 minutes | Servings: 6

Ingredients

2 pounds chicken breast fillets, butterfly cut
½ cup baby spinach
8 garlic cloves, crushed

10 artichoke hearts
Salt and white pepper to taste

4 tbsp olive oil

Directions

Combine artichoke, pepper, and garlic in a food processor. Blend until completely smooth. Pulse again and gradually add oil until well incorporated. Stuff each breast with equal amounts of artichoke mixture and spinach. Fold the breast fillet back together and secure the edge with a wooden skewer. Season with salt and white pepper and transfer to separate vacuum-sealable bags. Seal the bags and cook en Sous Vide for 3 hours at 149 F.

Rosemary Chicken Stew

Prep + Cook Time: 4 hours 15 minutes | Servings: 2

Ingredients

2 chicken thighs
6 garlic cloves, crushed
¼ tsp whole black pepper

2 bay leaves
¼ cup dark soy sauce
¼ cup white vinegar

1 tbsp rosemary

Directions

Prepare a water bath and place the Sous Vide in it. Set to 165 F. Combine the chicken thighs with all the ingredients. Place in a vacuum-sealable bag. Release air by the water displacement method, seal and submerge in the water bath. Cook for 4 hours.

Once the timer has stopped, remove the chicken, discard bay leaves and reserve the cooking juices. Heat canola oil in a skillet over medium heat and sear the chicken. Add in cooking juices and cook until you have reached the desired consistency. Filter the sauce and top the chicken.

Chicken & Leek Stew

Prep + Cook Time: 70 minutes | Servings: 4

Ingredients

6 skinless chicken breasts
Salt and black pepper to taste
3 tbsp butter

1 large leek, sliced crossways
½ cup panko
2 tbsp chopped parsley

1 oz Copoundy Jack cheese
1 tbsp olive oil

Directions

Prepare a water bath and place the Sous Vide in it. Set to 146 F.

Place the chicken breasts in a vacuum-sealable bag. Season with salt and pepper. Release air by the water displacement method, seal and submerge in the water bath. Cook for 45 minutes.

Meanwhile, heat a skillet over high heat with butter and cook the leeks. Season with salt and pepper. Mix well. Lower the heat and let cook for 10 minutes.

Heat a skillet over medium heat with butter and add the panko. Cook until toast. Transfer to a bowl and combine with cheddar cheese and chopped parsley. Once the timer has stopped, remove the breasts. Heat a pan over high heat with olive oil and sear the chicken 1 minute per side. Serve over leeks and garnish with panko mix.

Cheesy Chicken Salad with Chickpeas

Prep + Cook Time: 1 hour 30 minutes | Servings: 2

Ingredients

6 chicken breast tenderloins
4 tbsp olive oil
2 tbsp hot sauce
1 tsp ground cumin
1 tsp light brown sugar

1 tsp ground cinnamon
Salt and black pepper to taste
1 can drained chickpeas
½ cup crumbled feta cheese
½ cup crumbled queso fresco cheese

½ cup torn basil
½ cup freshly torn mint
4 tsp pine nuts, toasted
2 tsp honey
2 tsp freshly squeezed lemon juice

Directions

Prepare a water bath and place the Sous Vide in it. Set to 138 F. Place the chicken breasts, 2 tbsp of olive oil, hot sauce, brown sugar, cumin, and cinnamon in a vacuum-sealable bag. Season with salt and pepper. Release air by the water displacement method, seal, and submerge the bag in the water bath. Cook for 75 minutes.

Meanwhile, combine in a bowl the chickpeas, basil, queso fresco, mint, and pine nuts. Pour in honey, lemon juice and 2 tbsp of olive oil. Season with salt and pepper. Once the timer has stopped, remove the chicken and chop in bites. Discard cooking juices. Stir the salad and chicken, mix well and serve.

Oregano Chicken Meatballs

Prep + Cook Time: 2 hours 20 minutes | Servings: 4

Ingredients

1 pound ground chicken
1 tbsp olive oil
2 garlic cloves, minced
1 tsp fresh oregano, minced

Salt to taste
1 tbsp cumin
½ tsp grated lemon zest
½ tsp black pepper

¼ cup panko breadcrumbs
Lemon wedges

Directions

Prepare a water bath and place Sous Vide in it. Set to 146 F. Combine in a bowl ground chicken, garlic, olive oil, oregano, lemon zest, cumin, salt, and pepper. Using your hands make at least 14 meatballs. Place the meatballs in a vacuum-sealable bag. Release air by the water displacement method, seal, and submerge the bag in the water bath. Cook for 2 hours. Once the timer has stopped, remove the bag and transfer the meatballs to a baking sheet, lined with foil. Heat a skillet over medium heat and sear the meatballs for 7 minutes. Top with lemon wedges.

Herbed Chicken with Mushroom Cream Sauce

Prep + Cook Time: 4 hours 15 minutes | Servings: 2

Ingredients

For Chicken

2 skinless boneless chicken breast
Salt to taste

1 tbsp dill
1 tbsp turmeric

1 tsp vegetable oil

For Sauce

3 chopped shallots
2 chopped garlic cloves
1 tsp olive oil

2 tbsp butter
1 cup sliced mushrooms
2 tbsp port wine

½ a cup chicken stock
1 cup goat cheese
¼ tsp cracked black pepper

Directions

Prepare a water bath and place the Sous Vide in it. Set to 138 F. Place the chicken seasoned with salt and pepper in a vacuum-sealable bag. Release air by the water displacement method, seal, and submerge the bag in the water bath. Cook for 4 hours. Once done, remove the bag and transfer to an ice bath. Let cool and dry off. Set aside.

Heat oil in a skillet over high heat, add in shallots and cook for 2-3 minutes. Put in butter, dill, turmeric, and garlic, cook for 1 minute more. Add in the mushrooms, wine and stock. Cook for 2 minutes, then pour the cream. Keep cooking until the sauce thickens. Season with salt and pepper. Heat a grill until smoked. Brush the chicken with oil and sear for 1 minute on each side. Top with the sauce.

Rice & Berry Loaded Cornish Hen

Prep + Cook Time: 4 hours 40 minutes | Servings: 2

Ingredients

2 whole Cornish game hens
4 tbsp butter plus 1 tbsp extra
2 cups shitake mushrooms, sliced

1 cup leeks, finely diced
¼ cup pecans, chopped
1 tbsp fresh thyme, minced

1 cup cooked wild rice
¼ cup dried cranberries
1 tbsp honey

Directions

Prepare a water bath and place the Sous Vide in it. Set to 149 F. Heat 4 tbsp of butter in a skillet over medium heat and add mushrooms, thyme, leek, and pecans. Cook for 5-10 minutes. Put in rice and cranberries. Remove from the heat. Allow cooling for 10 minutes.

Fill the hen cavities with the mixture. Truss the legs. Place hens in a vacuum-sealable bag. Release air by the water displacement method, seal and submerge the bag in the bath. Cook for 4 hours. Heat a pan over high heat. In a bowl, combine honey and 1 tbsp of melted butter. Pour over the hens. Sear the hens for 2 minutes and serve.

Crispy Fried Chicken

Prep + Cook Time: 2 hours | Servings: 4

Ingredients

8 chicken legs

Salt and black pepper to taste

2 tbsp olive oil

For Wet Mix

2 cups soy milk

1 tbsp lemon juice

For Dry Mix

1 cup flour

½ cup cornstarch

1 tbsp ginger

1 cup rice flour

2 tbsp paprika

Salt and black pepper to taste

Directions

Prepare a water bath and place the Sous Vide in it. Set to 154 F. Place the chicken seasoned with pepper and salt in a vacuum-sealable bag. Release air by the water displacement method, seal and submerge in the water bath. Cook for 1 hour. Once the timer has stopped, remove the bag. Allow cooling for 15 minutes.

Heat the olive oil in a skillet over medium heat. In a bowl, mix the soy milk and lemon juice. In another bowl, whisk the protein flour, rice flour, cornstarch, ginger, paprika, salt, and ground pepper to get the dry mix.

Dip the chicken into the dry mix then into the wet mix. Repeat 2-3 more times. Place in a baking rack. Repeat the process until the chicken is finished. Fry the chicken for 3-4 minutes. Top with lemon wedges and sauce. Serve.

Green Chicken Salad with Almonds

Prep + Cook Time: 95 minutes | Servings: 2

Ingredients

2 chicken breasts, skinless

4 red chilis, thinly sliced

1 scallion, thinly sliced

Salt and black pepper to taste

1 garlic clove, peeled

1 stalk lemongrass, white part only, sliced

1 cup almonds

3 tbsp fish sauce

1 piece 2-inch ginger, julienned

1 tbsp olive oil

2 tsp freshly squeezed lime juice

2 tbsp sugar

1 cup cilantro, chopped

Directions

Prepare a water bath and place the Sous Vide in it. Set to 138 F. Place the chicken seasoned with salt and pepper in a vacuum-sealable bag. Release air by the water displacement method, seal, and submerge the bag in the water bath. Cook for 75 minutes. After 60 minutes, heat olive oil in a saucepan to 350 F. Toast the almonds for 1 minute until dry. Batter the sugar, garlic and chili. Pour in fish sauce and lime juice.

Once ready, remove the bag and let cool. Cut the chicken in bites and place in a bowl. Pour the dressing and mix well. Add the cilantro, ginger, lemongrass and fried almonds. Garnish with chili and serve.

Crispy Chicken Bacon Wrap

Prep + Cook Time: 3 hours 15 minutes | Servings: 2

Ingredients

1 chicken breast

2 tbsp Dijon mustard

2 strips pancetta

1 tbsp grated Pecorino Romano cheese

Directions

Prepare a water bath and place the Sous Vide in it. Set to 146 F. Combine the chicken with salt. Marinade with Dijon mustard on both sides. Top with Pecorino Romano Cheese and wrap the pancetta around the chicken.

Place in a vacuum-sealable bag. Release air by the water displacement method, seal, and submerge the bag in the water bath. Cook for 3 hours. Once the timer has stopped, remove the chicken and pat dry. Heat a skillet over medium heat and sear until crispy.

Chessy Rolled Chicken

Prep + Cook Time: 1 hour 45 minutes | Servings: 2

Ingredients

1 chicken breast
¼ cup cream cheese
¼ cup julienned roasted red pepper

½ cup loosely packed arugula
6 slices prosciutto
Salt and black pepper to taste

1 tbsp oil

Directions

Prepare a water bath and place Sous Vide in it. Set to 155 F. Drain the chicken and beat it until getting tiny thicks. Then cut by half and season with salt and pepper. Spread 2 tbsp of cream cheese and add roasted red pepper and arugula on top. Roll the breasts like sushi and put 3 layers of prosciutto and roll the breasts. Place in a vacuum-sealable bag. Release air by the water displacement method, seal and submerge in the water bath. Cook for 90 minutes. Once the timer has stopped, remove the chicken from the bag and sear. Slice tiny and serve.

Green Chicken Curry with & Noodles

Prep + Cook Time: 3 hours | Servings: 2

Ingredients

1 chicken breast, boneless and skinless
Salt and black pepper to taste
1 can (13.5 oz) coconut milk
2 tbsp green curry paste
1¾ cups chicken stock

1 cup shiitake mushrooms
5 kaffir lime leaves, torn in half
2 tbsp fish sauce
1 ½ tbsp sugar
½ cup Thai basil leaves, chopped

2 oz cooked egg noodle nests
1 cup cilantro, roughly chopped
1 cup bean sprouts
2 tbsp fried noodles
2 red chilis, roughly chopped

Directions

Prepare a water bath and place the Sous Vide in it. Set to 138 F. Season the chicken with salt and pepper. Place it in a vacuum-sealable bag. Release air by the water displacement method, seal, and submerge the bag in the water bath. Cook for 90 minutes.

Passed 35 minutes, heat a saucepan over medium heat and stir in green curry paste and half coconut milk. Cook for 5-10 minutes until the coconut milk starts to thicken. Add in chicken stock and the rest of the coconut milk. Cook for 15 minutes. Lower the heat and add in kaffir lime leaves, shiitake mushrooms, sugar and fish sauce. Cook for at least 10 minutes. Remove from the heat and add the basil.

Once the timer has stopped, remove the bag and allow cooling for 5 minutes then chop in tiny slices. Serve in a soup bowl the curry sauce, cooked noodles and chicken. Top with bean sprouts, cilantro, chilis and fried noodles.

Herby Chicken with Butternut Squash Dish

Prep + Cook Time: 1 hour 15 minutes | Servings: 2

Ingredients

4 cups butternut squash, cubed and roasted
6 chicken tenderloins
4 cups rocket lettuce
4 tbsp sliced almonds
Juice of 1 lemon

2 tbsp olive oil
4 tbsp red onion, chopped
1 tbsp paprika
1 tbsp turmeric

1 tbsp cumin
Salt to taste

Directions

Prepare a water bath and place the Sous Vide in it. Set to 138 F.

Place the chicken and all seasonings in a vacuum-sealable bag. Release air by the water displacement method, seal and submerge in the water bath. Cook for 60 minutes. Once the timer has stopped, remove the bag and transfer the chicken to a hot skillet. Sear for 1 minute per side. In a bowl, combine the remaining ingredients. Serve the chicken with the salad.

Pesto Chicken Mini Bites with Avocado

Prep + Cook Time: 1 hour 40 minutes | Servings: 2

Ingredients

1 chicken breast, butterflied
Salt and black pepper to taste
1 tbsp sage

3 tbsp olive oil
1 tbsp pesto
1 zucchini, sliced

1 avocado
1 cup fresh basil leaves

Directions

Prepare a water bath and place the Sous Vide in it. Set to 138 F.

Pound the chicken breast until thin. Season with sage, pepper and salt. Place in a vacuum-sealable bag. Add 1 tbsp of oil and pesto. Release air by the water displacement method, seal, and submerge the bag in the water bath. Cook for 75 minutes. After 60 minutes, heat 1 tbsp of olive oil in a skillet over high heat, add the zucchini and ¼ cup water. Cook until the water has evaporated. Once the timer has stopped, remove the chicken.

Heat the remaining olive oil in a skillet over medium heat and sear the chicken for 2 minutes per side. Set aside and allow cooling. Cut the chicken in tiny slices just like the zucchini. Slice the avocado as well. Serve the chicken with slices of avocado on the top. Garnish with zucchini slices and basil.

Cheesy Chicken Balls

Prep + Cook Time: 1 hour 15 minutes | Servings: 6

Ingredients

1 pound ground chicken
2 tbsp onion, finely chopped
¼ tsp garlic powder
Salt and black pepper to taste

2 tbsp breadcrumbs
1 egg
32 small, diced mozzarella cubes
1 tbsp butter

3 tbsp panko
½ cup tomato sauce
½ oz grated Pecorino Romano cheese
Chopped parsley

Directions

Prepare a water bath and place the Sous Vide in it. Set to 146 F. In a bowl, mix the chicken, onion, salt, garlic powder, pepper, and breadcrumbs. Add in egg and combine well. Form 32 medium-size balls and fill with a cube of cheese, make sure the mix covers the cheese well. Place the balls in a vacuum-sealable bag and let chill for 20 minutes. Then, release air by the water displacement method, seal, and submerge the bag in the water bath.

Cook for 45 minutes. Once the timer has stopped, remove the balls. Melt butter in a skillet over high heat and add panko. Cook until toast. As well cook the tomato sauce. In a serving dish, place the balls and glaze with the tomato sauce. Top with the panko and cheese. Garnish with parsley.

Cherry Tomatoes, Avocado & Chicken Salad

Prep + Cook Time: 1 hour 30 minutes | Servings: 2

Ingredients

1 chicken breast
1 avocado, sliced
10 pieces of halved cherry tomatoes

2 cups chopped lettuce
2 tbsp olive oil
1 tbsp lime juice

1 garlic clove, crushed
Salt and black pepper to taste
2 tsp maple syrup

Directions

Prepare a water bath and place the Sous Vide in it. Set to 138 F. Place the chicken in a vacuum-sealable bag. Season with salt and pepper. Release air by the water displacement method, seal, and submerge the bag in the water bath. Cook for 75 minutes.

Once the timer has stopped, remove the chicken. Heat oil in a pan over medium heat. Sear the breasts for 30 seconds and slice. In a bowl, combine the garlic, lime juice, maple syrup, and olive oil. Add in lettuce, cherry tomatoes and avocado. Mix well. Plate the salad and top with chicken.

Milky Coconut Chicken

Prep + Cook Time: 75 minutes | Servings: 2

Ingredients

2 chicken breasts	4 tbsp coconut milk	Salt and black pepper to taste
For Sauce		
4 tbsp satay sauce	2 tbsp coconut milk	Dash of tamari sauce

Directions

Prepare a water bath and place the Sous Vide in it. Set to 138 F.

Place the chicken in a vacuum-sealable bag and season with salt and pepper. Add 4 tbsp of milk. Release air by the water displacement method, seal, and submerge the bag in the water bath. Cook for 60 minutes. Once the timer has stopped, remove the bag. Combine the sauce ingredients and microwave for 30 seconds. Slice the chicken. Place in a plate and glaze with the sauce. Serve and enjoy!

Chicken with Sun-Dried Tomatoes

Prep + Cook Time: 1 hour 15 minutes | Servings: 3

Ingredients

1 pound chicken breasts	2 tbsp fresh lemon juice	1 tbsp olive oil
½ cup sun-dried tomatoes	1 tbsp fresh mint, finely chopped	Salt and black pepper to taste
1 tsp raw honey	1 tbsp minced shallots	

Directions

Rinse the chicken breasts under cold running water and pat dry with kitchen paper. Set aside.

In a medium bowl, combine lemon juice, honey, mint, shallots, olive oil, salt, and pepper. Mix together until well incorporated. Add chicken breasts and sun-dried tomatoes. Shake to coat all well. Transfer all to a large vacuum-sealable bag. Press the bag to remove the air and seal the lid. Cook en Sous Vide for 1 hour at 167 F. Remove from the water bath and serve immediately.

Chinese-Style Chicken

Prep + Cook Time: 1 hour 35 minutes | Servings: 6

Ingredients

2 pounds chicken breasts	1 tbsp honey	¾ tsp Chinese five-spice powder
¼ cup onions, finely chopped	1 tsp sesame oil	
2 tbsp Worcestershire sauce	1 clove garlic, minced	

Directions

Prepare a water bath and place the Sous Vide in it. Set to 146 F. Place the chicken, onions, honey, Worcestershire sauce, sesame oil, garlic, and five-spice in a vacuum-sealable bag. Release air by the water displacement method, seal, and submerge the bag in the water bath. Cook for 75 minutes.

Heat a skillet over medium heat. Once the timer has stopped, remove the chicken and put it into the skillet. Sear for 5 minutes until golden brown. Chop the chicken in medallions.

Roman-Style Bacon & Chicken Dish

Prep + Cook Time: 1 hour 40 minutes | Servings: 4

Ingredients

4 chicken breasts, boneless, skinless	4 pieces of thinly sliced bacon	1 tbsp olive oil
8 sage leaves	Black pepper to taste	2 oz grated fontina cheese

Directions

Prepare a water bath and place the Sous Vide in it. Set to 146 F. Season the chicken with salt and pepper. Top with 2 sage leaves and 1 bacon slice. Place them in a vacuum-sealable bag. Release air by the water displacement method, seal, and submerge the bag in the water bath. Cook for 90 minutes.

Heat oil in a skillet over high heat and sear the chicken for 1 minute. Turn chicken and top with 1 tbsp of fontina cheese. Cover the skillet and allow the cheese to melt. Garnish with sage leaves. Serve and enjoy!

Minted Chicken & Pea Salad

Prep + Cook Time: 1 hour 30 minutes | Servings: 2

Ingredients

6 chicken breast tenderloins, boneless	2 cups snow peas, blanched	1 tbsp freshly squeezed lemon juice
4 tbsp olive oil	1 cup mint, freshly torn	2 tsp honey
Salt and black pepper to taste	½ cup crumbled queso fresco cheese	2 tsp red wine vinegar

Directions

Prepare a water bath and place the Sous Vide in it. Set to 138 F. Season the chicken with salt and pepper and drizzle with some olive oil; place it in a vacuum-sealable bag. Seal and submerge the bag in the water bath. Cook for 75 minutes. In a bowl, combine peas, queso fresco, and mint. Mix the lemon juice, vinegar, honey, remaining olive oil, salt, and pepper. Once ready, remove the chicken and slice in bites. Discard the cooking liquids. Serve.

Chili Chicken

Prep + Cook Time: 2 hours 15 minutes | Servings: 2

Ingredients

4 chicken thighs	3 tbsp fish sauce	3 tbsp cilantro, chopped
2 tbsp olive oil	¼ cup lime juice	2 red chilis (deseeded), chopped
Salt and black pepper to taste	1 tbsp sugar	1 tbsp sweet chili sauce
1 garlic clove, crushed	3 tbsp basil, chopped	1 tbsp green chili sauce

Directions

Prepare a water bath and place the Sous Vide in it. Set to 149 F. Mix the chicken, olive oil, salt, and pepper in a vacuum-sealable bag. Release air by the water displacement method, seal, and submerge the bag in water bath. Cook for 2 hours. Once ready, remove the chicken and chop into 4-5 pieces. Heat oil in a skillet over medium heat; sear the chicken until crispy. In a bowl, combine all the remaining ingredients and pour over the chicken.

Honey Flavored Chicken Wings

Prep + Cook Time: 135 minutes | Servings: 2

Ingredients

¾ tsp soy sauce	¼ tsp five-spice	½ inch ground mace
¾ tsp rice wine	6 chicken wings	1 clove garlic, minced
¾ tsp honey	½ inch fresh ginger	Sliced scallions for serving

Directions

Prepare a water bath and place the Sous Vide in it. Set to 160 F. In a bowl, combine the soy sauce, rice wine, honey, and five-spice. Place the chicken wings and garlic in a vacuum-sealable bag. Release air by the water displacement method, seal, and submerge the bag in the water bath. Cook for 2 hours.

Once the timer has stopped, remove the wings and transfer them to a baking tray. Bake in the oven for 5 minutes at 380 F. Serve on a platter and garnish with sliced scallions.

Cheesy Turkey Burgers

Prep + Cook Time: 1 hour 45 minutes | Servings: 6

Ingredients

6 tsp olive oil
1 ½ pounds ground turkey
16 cream crackers, crushed
2½ tbsp chopped fresh parsley
2 tbsp chopped fresh basil

½ tbsp Worcestershire sauce
½ tbsp soy sauce
½ tsp garlic powder
1 egg
6 buns, toasted

6 tomato slices
6 Romaine lettuce leaves
6 slices Monterey Jack cheese

Directions

Prepare a water bath and place the Sous Vide in it. Set to 148 F. Combine the turkey, crackers, parsley, basil, soy sauce and garlic powder. Add the egg and mix using your hands. In a baking sheet with wax pepper, with the mixture create 6 patties and place them. Cover and transfer to the fridge.

Remove the patties from the fridge and place in three vacuum-sealable bags. Release air by the water displacement method, seal and submerge the bags in the water bath. Cook for 1 hour and 15 minutes.

Once the timer has stopped, remove the patties. Discard cooking juices. Heat olive oil in a skillet over high heat and place the patties. Sear for 45 seconds per side. Place the patties over the toasted buns. Top with tomato, lettuce and cheese. Serve and enjoy!

Bacon & Nut Stuffed Turkey Wrapped in Ham

Prep + Cook Time: 3 hours 45 minutes | Servings: 6

Ingredients

1 white onion, chopped
3 tbsp butter
1 cup bacon cubes
4 tbsp pine nuts
2 tbsp chopped thyme

4 garlic cloves, minced
Zest of 2 lemons
4 tbsp chopped parsley
¾ cup bread crumbs
1 egg, beaten

4 lb boneless turkey breast, butterflied
Salt and black pepper to taste
16 slices ham

Directions

Prepare a water bath and place the Sous Vide in it. Set to 146 F.

Heat 2 tbsp of butter in a skillet over medium heat and sauté the onion for 10 minutes until softened. Set aside. In the same skillet, add the bacon and cook for 5 minutes until brown. Stir in pine nuts, thyme, garlic, and lemon zest and cook for 2 minutes more. Add in parsley and mix. Return the onion to the skillet, stir in crumbs and egg.

Take out the turkey and cover it with plastic wrap. With a meat hammer, pound it to the thickness. Place ham in an aluminium foil. Put the turkey on the ham and smash the center to create a strip. Roll the turkey tightly from one side to the other until it is completely wrapped. Cover with plastic wrap and place in a vacuum-sealable bag. Release air by the water displacement method, seal, and submerge the bag in the water bath. Cook for 3 hours.

Once the timer has stopped, remove the turkey and discard the plastic. Heat the remaining butter in a skillet over medium heat and put the breast. Sear the ham for 45 seconds per side. Roll the turkey and sear for 2-3 minutes more. Cut the breast into medallions and serve.

Caesar Salad Tortilla Rolls with Turkey

Prep + Cook Time: 1 hour 40 minutes | Servings: 4

Ingredients

2 garlic cloves, minced
2 skinless, boneless turkey breasts
Salt and black pepper to taste
1 cup mayonnaise

2 tbsp freshly squeezed lemon juice
1 tsp anchovy paste
1 tsp Dijon mustard
1 tsp soy sauce

4 cups iceberg lettuce
4 tortillas

Directions

Prepare a water bath and place the Sous Vide in it. Set to 152 F. Season the turkey breast with salt and pepper and put in a vacuum-sealable bag. Release air by the water displacement method, seal, and submerge the bag in the water bath. Cook for 1 hour and 30 minutes.

Combine the mayonnaise, garlic, lemon juice, anchovy paste, mustard, soy sauce, and remaining salt and pepper. Allow to rest in the fridge. Once the timer has stopped, remove the turkey and pat dry. Slice the turkey. Mix the lettuce with the cold dressing. Pour one-quarter of the turkey mixture into each tortilla and fold. Cut by the half and serve with the dressing.

Sage Turkey Roulade

Prep + Cook Time: 5 hours 15 minutes | Servings: 6

Ingredients

3 tbsp olive oil	3 tbsp ground sage	2 cups turkey or chicken stock
2 small yellow onions, diced	2 lemons' zest and juice	5 pounds halved turkey breast
2 stalks celery, diced	3 cups turkey stuffing mix	

Directions

Place a pan over medium heat, add olive oil, onion, and celery. Sauté for 2 minutes. Add the lemon juice, zest, and sage until the lemon juice reduce.

In a bowl, pour the stuffing mixture and add the cooked sage mixture. Mix with your hands. Add in stock, while mixing with your hand until ingredients hold together well and are not runny. Gently remove the turkey skin and lay it on a plastic wrap. Remove bones and discard.

Place the turkey breast on the skin and lay the second layer of plastic wrap on the turkey breast. Flatten it to 1 - inch of thickness using a rolling pin. Remove the plastic wrap on top and spread the stuffing on the flattened turkey, leaving ½ inch space around the edges.

Starting at the narrow side, roll the turkey like a pastry roll and drape the extra skin on the turkey. Secure the roll with butcher's twine. Wrap the turkey roll in the broader plastic wrap and twist the ends to secure the roll, which should form a tight cylinder.

Place the roll in a vacuum-sealable bag, release air and seal the bag. Refrigerate for 40 minutes. Make a water bath, place Sous Vide in it, and set to 155 F. Place the turkey roll in the water bath and set the timer for 4 hours.

Once the timer has stopped, remove the bag and unseal it. Preheat an oven to 400 F, remove the plastic wrap from the turkey and place on a baking dish with skin side up. Roast for 15 minutes. Slice in rounds. Serve with a creamy sauce and steamed low carb vegetables.

Thyme & Rosemary Turkey Legs

Prep + Cook Time: 8 hours 30 minutes | Servings: 4

Ingredients

5 tsp butter, melted	2 tbsp dried rosemary	1 tbsp thyme
10 garlic cloves, minced	1 tbsp cumin	2 turkey legs

Directions

Prepare a water bath and place the Sous Vide in it. Set to 134 F. Combine the garlic, rosemary, cumin, thyme, and butter. Rub the turkey with the mixture. Place the turkey in a vacuum-sealable bag. Release air by the water displacement method, seal, and submerge the bag in the water bath. Cook for 8 hours

Once the timer has stopped, remove the turkey. Reserve cooking juices. Heat a grill over high heat and put the turkey. Sprinkle with cooking juices. Turn around and sprinkle with some more juices. Allow to cool. Serve.

Thyme Turkey Breast

Prep + Cook Time: 3 hours 15 minutes | Servings: 6

Ingredients

1 turkey breast half, boneless with skin on
1 tbsp olive oil
1 tbsp garlic salt
1 tbsp thyme
1 tsp black pepper

Directions

Prepare a water bath and place the Sous Vide in it. Set to 146 F.

Combine the turkey breast, garlic, thyme, salt, and pepper. Place it in a vacuum-sealable bag. Release air by the water displacement method, seal, and submerge the bag in the water bath. Cook for 4 hours. Once the timer has stopped, remove the bag. Heat an iron skillet over high heat and sear the turkey for 5 minutes until golden.

Pesto Turkey Meatballs Burgers

Prep + Cook Time: 80 minutes | Servings: 4

Ingredients

1 pound ground turkey
3 scallions, finely chopped
1 large egg, beaten
1 tbsp breadcrumbs
1 tsp dried oregano
1 tbsp thyme
Salt and black pepper to taste
½ cup pesto
2 oz mozzarella cheese, torn into pieces
4 large hamburger buns

Directions

Prepare a water bath and place the Sous Vide in it. Set to 146 F. In a bowl, combine the turkey, egg, breadcrumbs, scallions, thyme, and oregano. Season with salt and pepper. Mix well. Make 4 balls and make a hole in the middle with the thumb. Fill each with some pesto and mozzarella cheese. Place them in a vacuum-sealable bag. Release air by the water displacement method, seal, and submerge the bag in the water bath. Cook for 60 minutes.

Once the timer has stopped, remove the balls and pat them dry. Heat a skillet over medium heat and add the remaining pesto and meatballs; stir for 2-3 minutes. Place the meatball and pesto in the buns and serve.

Turkey Breast with Pecans

Prep + Cook Time: 2 hours 15 minutes | Servings: 6

Ingredients

2 pounds turkey breast, thinly sliced
1 tbsp lemon zest
1 cup pecans, finely chopped
1 tbsp thyme, finely chopped
2 garlic cloves, crushed
2 tbsp fresh parsley, finely chopped
3 cups chicken broth
3 tbsp olive oil

Directions

Rinse the meat under cold running water and drain in a colander. Rub with lemon zest and transfer to a large vacuum-sealable bag along with chicken broth. Cook en Sous Vide for 2 hours at 149 F. Remove and set aside.

Heat olive oil in a medium-sized skillet and add garlic, pecan nuts, and thyme. Give it a good stir and cook for 4-5 minutes. Finally, add chicken breast to the frying pan and briefly brown on both sides. Serve immediately.

Turkey Breast with Cloves

Prep + Cook Time: 1 hour 45 minutes | Servings: 6

Ingredients

2 pounds turkey breast, sliced
2 garlic cloves, minced
1 cup olive oil
2 tbsp Dijon mustard
2 tbsp lemon juice
1 tsp fresh rosemary, finely chopped
1 tsp cloves, minced
Salt and black pepper to taste

Directions

In a large bowl, combine olive oil, with mustard, lemon juice, garlic, rosemary, cloves, salt, and pepper. Mix until well incorporated and add turkey slices. Soak and refrigerate for 30 minutes before cooking.

Remove from the refrigerator and transfer to 2 vacuum-sealable bags. Seal the bags and cook en Sous Vide for one hour at 149 F. Remove from the water bath and serve.

Spice Turkey Dish

Prep + Cook Time: 14 hours 15 minutes | Servings: 4

Ingredients

1 turkey leg	1 tbsp garlic salt	3 sprigs of thyme
1 tbsp olive oil	1 tsp black pepper	1 tbsp rosemary

Directions

Prepare a water bath and place the Sous Vide in it. Set to 146 F. Season the turkey with garlic, salt and pepper.

Place it in a vacuum-sealable bag. Release air by the water displacement method, seal and submerge the bag in the bath. Cook for 14 hours. Once done, remove the legs and pat dry.

Turkey in Orange Sauce

Prep + Cook Time: 75 minutes | Servings: 2

Ingredients

½ lb turkey breast, skinless and boneless	3 tbsp fresh orange juice	1 tsp Cayenne pepper
1 tbsp butter	½ cup chicken stock	Salt and black pepper to taste

Directions

In a medium bowl, combine orange juice, chicken stock, Cayenne pepper, salt, and pepper. Mix well and place the meat into this marinade. Refrigerate for 20 minutes. Place the meat along with marinade into a large vacuum-sealable bag and cook en Sous Vide for 40 minutes at 122 F.

In a saucepan, melt the butter over high heat. Remove the meat from the bag and add to the saucepan. Fry for 2 minutes and remove from the heat.

Dill & Rosemary Turkey Breast

Prep + Cook Time: 1 hour 50 minutes | Servings: 2

Ingredients

1 pound boneless turkey breasts	3 fresh dill sprigs	1 bay leaf
Salt and black pepper to taste	1 fresh rosemary sprig, chopped	

Directions

Prepare a water bath and place the Sous Vide in it. Set to 146 F.

Heat a skillet over medium heat, Put the turkey and sear for 5 minutes. Reserve the fat.

Season the turkey with salt and pepper. Place the turkey, dill, rosemary, bay leaf and reserved fat in a vacuum-sealable bag. Release air by the water displacement method, seal, and submerge the bag in the water bath. Cook for 1 ½ hours.

Heat a skillet over high heat. Once the timer has stopped, transfer the turkey to the skillet. Sear for 5 minutes. Serve and enjoy!

Roasted Sweet Duck

Prep + Cook Time: 3 hours 55 minutes | Servings: 4

Ingredients

6 oz boneless duck breast
¼ tsp cinnamon
¼ tsp smoked paprika

¼ tsp cayenne pepper
1 tbsp thyme
1 tsp honey

Salt and black pepper to taste

Directions

Prepare a water bath and place the Sous Vide in it. Set to 134 F. Pat dry the breast duck with a baking sheet and remove the skin, be careful not to cut the flesh. Season with salt.

Heat a frying pan over high heat. Sear the duck for 3-4 minutes. Remove and set aside.

In a bowl, combine the paprika, thyme, cayenne pepper, and cinnamon, mix well. Marinade the duck breast with the mixture. Place in a vacuum-sealable bag. Add 1 tbsp of honey. Release air by the water displacement method, seal, and submerge the bag in the water bath. Cook for 3 hours and 30 minutes.

Once the timer has stopped, remove the bag and dry. Heat a skillet over high heat and sear the duck for 2 minutes. Flip it and cook for 30 seconds more. Allow cooling and serve.

Thyme Duck Breast

Prep + Cook Time: 2 hours 10 minutes | Servings: 3

Ingredients

3 (6 oz) duck breast, skin on
3 tsp thyme leaves

2 tsp olive oil
Salt and black pepper to taste

Ingredients

Make crosswise strips on the breasts and without cutting into the meat. Season the skin with salt and the meat side with thyme, pepper, and salt. Place the duck breasts in 3 separate vacuum-sealable bags. Release air and seal the bags. Refrigerate for 1 hour.

Make a water bath, place Sous Vide in it, and set to 135 F. Remove the bags from the refrigerator and submerge in the water bath. Set the timer for 1 hour. Once the timer has stopped, remove and unseal the bags. Set a skillet over medium heat, add olive oil. Once it has heated, add duck and sear until skin renders and meat is golden brown. Remove and let sit for 3 minutes and then slice. Serve.

Orange Goose Confit

Prep + Cook Time: 12 hours 7 minutes + cooling Time | Servings: 6

Ingredients

3 bay leaves
6 goose legs
10 tsp salt

6 garlic cloves, smashed
1 fresh rosemary sprig, stemmed
1 ½ cups goose fat

1 tsp peppercorns
Zest of 1 orange

Directions

Brush the goose legs with garlic, salt, peppercorns and rosemary. Cover and allow to chill in the fridge for 12 to 24 hours. Prepare a water bath and place the Sous Vide in it. Set to 172 F. Remove the goose from the fridge.

Place the goose, goose fat, bay leaves, peppercorn, and orange zest in a vacuum-sealable bag. Release air by the water displacement method, seal, and submerge the bag in the water bath. Cook for 12 hours. Once the timer has stopped, remove the goose and transfer it to a preheated skillet over high heat; sear the goose for 5-7 minutes.

FISH & SEAFOOD

Halibut with Sweet Sherry & Miso Glaze

Prep + Cook Time: 50 minutes | Servings: 4

Ingredients

1 tbsp olive oil
2 tbsp butter
⅓ cup sweet sherry
⅓ cup red miso

¼ cup mirin
3 tbsp brown sugar
2½ tbsp soy sauce
4 fillets halibut

2 tbsp chopped scallions
2 tbsp chopped fresh parsley

Directions

Prepare a water bath and place the Sous Vide in it. Set to 134 F. Heat the butter in a saucepan over medium-low heat. Stir in sweet sherry, miso, mirin, brown sugar, and soy sauce for 1 minute. Set aside. Allow to cool. Place the halibut in 2 vacuum-sealable bags. Release air by the water displacement method, seal and submerge the bags in the water bath. Cook for 30 minutes.

Once the timer has stopped, remove the halibut from the bags and pat dry with kitchen towels. Reserve cooking juices. Heat a saucepan over high heat and pour in cooking juices. Cook until reduced by half.

Heat olive oil in a skillet over medium heat and transfer the fillets. Sear for 30 seconds on each side until crispy. Serve the fish and drizzle with Miso Glaze. Garnish with scallions and parsley.

Crispy Salmon with Sweet Ginger Glaze

Prep + Cook Time: 53 minutes | Servings: 4

Ingredients

½ cup Worcestershire sauce
6 tbsp white sugar
4 tbsp mirin
2 small garlic cloves, minced

½ tsp cornstarch
½ tsp grated fresh ginger
4 salmon fillets
4 tsp vegetable oil

2 cups cooked rice, for serving
1 tsp toasted poppy seeds

Directions

Prepare a water bath and place the Sous Vide in it. Set to 129 F. Combine the Worcestershire sauce, sugar, mirin, garlic, cornstarch, and ginger in a pot over medium heat. Cook for 1 minute until the sugar has dissolved. Reserve 1/4 cup of sauce. Allow to cool. Place the fillets salmon in 2 vacuum-sealable bags with the remaining sauce. Release air by the water displacement method, seal and submerge the bags in the bath. Cook for 40 minutes.

Once the timer has stopped, remove the fillets from the bags and pat dry with kitchen towels. Heat a saucepan over medium heat and cook the cup of sauce for 2 minutes until thickened. Heat oil in a skillet. Sear the salmon for 30 seconds per side. Serve salmon with sauce and poppy seeds.

Tasty Trout with Tamari Sauce

Prep + Cook Time: 35 minutes | Servings: 4

Ingredients

¼ cup olive oil
4 trout fillets, skinned and sliced

½ cup Tamari sauce
¼ cup light brown sugar

2 garlic cloves, minced
1 tbsp Coleman's mustard

Directions

Prepare a water bath and place Sous Vide in it. Set to 130 F. Combine the Tamari sauce, brown sugar, olive oil, and garlic. Place the trout in a vacuum-sealable bag with tamari mixture. Release air by the water displacement method, seal, and submerge the bag in the bath. Cook for 30 minutes. Once the timer has stopped, remove the trout and pat dry with kitchen towels. Discard the cooking juices. Garnish with tamari sauce and mustard to serve.

Citrus Fish with Coconut Sauce

Prep time: 1 hour 57 minutes | Servings: 6

Ingredients

2 tbsp vegetable oil
4 tomatoes, peeled and chopped
2 red bell peppers, diced
1 yellow onion, diced
½ cup orange juice

¼ cup lime juice
4 garlic cloves, minced
1 tsp caraway seeds, crushed
1 tsp cumin powder
1 tsp cayenne pepper

½ tsp salt
6 cod fillets, skin removed, cubed
14 ounces coconut milk
¼ cup shredded coconut
3 tbsp chopped fresh cilantro

Directions

Prepare a water bath and place the Sous Vide in it. Set to 137 F.

Combine in a bowl, the orange juice, lime juice, garlic, caraway seeds, cumin, cayenne pepper, and salt. Brush the fillets with the lime mixture. Cover and allow to chill in the fridge for 1 hour.

Meantime, heat oil in a saucepan over medium heat and put in tomatoes, bell peppers, onion, and salt. Cook for 4-5 minutes until softened. Pour the coconut milk over the tomato mixture and cook for 10 minutes. Let cool.

Take out the fillets from the fridge and place them in 2 vacuum-sealable bags with the coconut mixture. Release air by the water displacement method, seal and submerge the bags in the water bath. Cook for 40 minutes. Once the timer has stopped, remove the bags and transfer the contents into a serving bowl. Garnish with shredded coconut and cilantro. Serve with rice.

Lime-Parsley Poached Haddock

Prep + Cook Time: 75 minutes | Servings: 4

Ingredients

4 haddock fillets, skin on
½ tsp salt

6 tbsp butter
Zest and juice of 1 lime

2 tsp chopped fresh parsley
1 lime, quartered

Directions

Prepare a water bath and place the Sous Vide in it. Set to 137 F.

Season the fillets with salt and place in 2 vacuum-sealable bags. Add butter, half the lime zest and lime juice, and 1 tbsp of parsley. Release air by the water displacement method. Transfer into the fridge and allow to chill for 30 minutes. Seal and submerge the bags in the water bath. Cook for 30 minutes.

Once the timer has stopped, remove the fillets and pat dry with kitchen towels. Heat the remaining butter in a skillet over medium heat and sear the fillets for 45 seconds on each side, spooning the melted butter over the top. Pat dry with kitchen towel and transfer to a plate. Garnish with lime quarters and serve.

Crispy Tilapia with Mustard-Maple Sauce

Prep + Cook Time: 65 minutes | Servings: 4

Ingredients

2 tbsp maple syrup
6 tbsp butter
2 tbsp Dijon mustard

2 tbsp brown sugar
1 tablespoon parsley
1 tablespoon thyme

2 tbsp soy sauce
2 tbsp white wine vinegar
4 tilapia fillets, skin on

Directions

Prepare a water bath and place the Sous Vide in it. Set to 114 F. Melt 4 tbsp butter in a pan over medium heat and stir-fry in mustard, brown sugar, maple syrup, soy sauce, vinegar, parsley, and thyme for 2 minutes. Let cool.

Place tilapia fillets in a vacuum-sealable bag with maple sauce. Release air by the water displacement method, seal, and submerge the bag in the water bath. Cook for 45 minutes. Once ready, remove the fillets and place them in a preheated with the remaining butter skillet. Sear them for 2 minutes. Serve topped with mustard sauce.

Swordfish & Potato Salad with Kalamata Olives

Prep + Cook Time: 3 hours 5 minutes | Servings: 2

Ingredients

Potatoes

3 tbsp olive oil
1 pound sweet potatoes

2 tsp salt
3 fresh thyme sprigs

Fish

1 tbsp olive oil
1 swordfish steak

Salt and black pepper to taste
1 tsp canola oil

Salad

1 cup baby spinach leaves
1 cup cherry tomatoes, halved
¼ cup Kalamata olives, chopped

1 tbsp olive oil
1 tsp Dijon mustard
3 tbsp cider vinegar

¼ tsp salt

Directions

To make the potatoes: prepare a water bath and place the Sous Vide in it. Set to 192 F.

Place the potatoes, olive oil, sea salt and thyme in a vacuum-sealable bag. Release air by the water displacement method, seal, and submerge the bag in the water bath. Cook for 1 hour and 15 minutes. Once the timer has stopped, remove the bag and do not open. Set aside.

To make the fish: Make a water bath and place the Sous Vide in it. Set to 104 F. Season the swordfish with salt and pepper. Place in a vacuum-sealable bag with olive oil. Release air by the water displacement method, seal, and submerge the bag in the water bath. Cook for 30 minutes.

Heat canola oil in a skillet over high heat. Remove the swordfish and pat pat dry with kitchen towels. Discard the cooking juices. Transfer the swordfish into the skillet and cook for 30 seconds per side. Cut into slices and cover with plastic wrap. Set aside.

Finally, make the salad: to a salad bowl, add the cherry tomatoes, olives, olive oil, mustard, cider vinegar, and salt and mix well. Add in baby spinach. Remove the potatoes and cut them by the half. Discard cooking juices. Top the salad with potatoes and swordfish to serve.

Buttery Red Snapper with Citrus Saffron Sauce

Prep + Cook Time: 55 minutes | Servings: 4

Ingredients

4 pieces cleaned red snapper

2 tbsp butter

Salt and black pepper to taste

For Citrus Sauce

1 lemon
1 grapefruit
1 lime
3 oranges
1 tsp Dijon mustard

2 tbsp canola oil
1 yellow onion
1 diced zucchini
1 tsp saffron threads
1 tsp diced chili pepper

1 tbsp sugar
3 cups fish stock
3 tbsp chopped cilantro

Directions

Prepare a water bath and place the Sous Vide in it. Set to 132 F. Season the snapper fillets with salt and pepper and place in a vacuum-sealable bag. Release air by the water displacement method, seal, and submerge the bag in the water bath. Cook for 30 minutes.

Peel the fruits and chop in cubes. Heat oil in a skillet over medium heat and put the onion and zucchini. Sauté for 2-3 minutes. Add the fruits, saffron, pepper, mustard and sugar. Cook for 1 minute more. Stir the fish stock and simmer for 10 minutes. Garnish with cilantro, and set aside. Once the timer has stopped, remove the fish and transfer to a plate. Glaze with citrus-saffron sauce and serve.

Sous Vide Halibut

Prep + Cook Time: 1 hour 20 minutes | Servings: 4

Ingredients

1 pound halibut fillets
3 tbsp olive oil
¼ cup of shallots, finely chopped

1 tsp freshly grated lemon zest
½ tsp dried thyme, ground
1 tbsp fresh parsley, finely chopped

1 tsp fresh dill, finely chopped
Salt and black pepper to taste

Directions

Wash the fish under cold running water and pat dry with kitchen paper. Cut into thin slices generously sprinkle with salt and pepper. Place in a large vacuum-sealable bag and add two tablespoons of olive oil. Season with shallots, thyme, parsley, dill, salt, and pepper.

Press the bag to remove the air and seal the lid. Shake the bag to coat all fillets with spices and refrigerate for 30 minutes before cooking. Cook in sous vide for 40 minutes at 131 F. Remove the bag from water and set aside to cool for a while. Place on a kitchen paper and drain. Remove the herbs.

Preheat the remaining oil in a large skillet over high hest. Add fillets and cook for 2 minutes. Flip the fillets and cook for about 35-40 seconds and then remove from the heat. Transfer the fish again to a paper towel and remove excessive fat. Serve immediately.

Sesame Tuna with Ginger Sauce

Prep + Cook Time: 45 minutes | Servings: 6

Ingredients

Tuna:

3 tuna steaks
Salt and black pepper to taste

⅓ cup olive oil
2 tbsp canola oil

½ cup black sesame seeds
½ cup white sesame seeds

Ginger Sauce:

1-inch ginger, grated
2 shallots, minced
1 red chili, minced
3 tbsp water

2 ½ lime juice
1 ½ tbsp rice vinegar
2 ½ tbsp soy sauce
1 tbsp fish sauce

1 ½ tbsp sugar
1 bunch green lettuce leaves

Directions

Start with the sauce: place a small pan over low heat and add olive oil. Once it has heated, add ginger and chili. Cook for 3 minutes. Add sugar and vinegar, stir and cook until sugar dissolves. Add water and bring to a boil. Add in soy sauce, fish sauce, and lime juice and cook for 2 minutes. Set aside to cool.

Make a water bath, place Sous Vide in it, and set to 110 F. Season the tuna with salt and pepper and place in 3 separate vacuum-sealable bags. Add olive oil, release air from the bag by the water displacement method, seal, and submerge the bag in the water bath. Set the timer for 30 minutes.

Once the timer has stopped, remove and unseal the bag. Place tuna aside. Place a skillet over low heat and add canola oil. While heating, mix sesame seeds in a bowl. Pat dry tuna, coat them in sesame seeds and sear top and bottom in heated oil until seeds start to toast. Slice tuna into thin strips. Layer a serving platter with lettuce and arrange tuna on the bed of lettuce. Serve with ginger sauce as a starter.

Mustardy Swordfish

Prep + Cook Time: 55 minutes | Servings: 4

Ingredients

2 tbsp olive oil
2 swordfish steaks

Salt and black pepper to taste
½ tsp Coleman's mustard

2 tsp sesame oil

Directions

Prepare a water bath and place Sous Vide in it. Set to 104 F. Season swordfish with salt and pepper. Mix well the olive oil and mustard. Place the swordfish in a vacuum-sealable bag with the mustard mix. Release air by the water displacement method. Seal and submerge the bag in the water bath. Cook for 30 minutes.

Heat sesame oil in a skillet over high heat. Once the timer has stopped, remove the swordfish and pat dry with kitchen towels. Discard cooking juices. Transfer into the skillet and sear for 30 seconds per side. Cut the swordfish into slices and serve.

Spicy Fish Tortillas

Prep + Cook Time: 35 minutes | Servings: 6

Ingredients

⅓ cup whipping cream
4 halibut fillets, skinned
1 tsp chopped fresh cilantro
¼ tsp red pepper flakes

Salt and black pepper to taste
1 tbsp cider vinegar
½ sweet onion, chopped
6 tortillas

Shredded iceberg lettuce
1 large tomato, sliced
Guacamole for garnish
1 lime, quartered

Directions

Prepare a water bath and place the Sous Vide in it. Set to 134 F. Combine fillets with cilantro, red pepper flakes, salt, and pepper. Place in a vacuum-sealable bag. Release air by the water displacement method, submerge the bag in the bath. Cook for 25 minutes.

Meantime, mix the cider vinegar, onion, salt, and pepper. Set aside. Once the timer has stopped, remove the fillets and pat dry with kitchen towels. Using a blowtorch and sear the fillets. Chop into chunks. Put the fish over the tortilla, add lettuce, tomato, cream, onion mixture and guacamole. Garnish with lime.

Cilantro Trout

Prep + Cook Time: 60 minutes | Servings: 4

Ingredients

2 pounds trout, 4 pieces
5 garlic cloves
1 tbsp sea salt

4 tbsp olive oil
1 cup cilantro leaves, finely chopped
2 tbsp rosemary, finely chopped

¼ cup freshly squeezed lemon juice

Directions

Clean and rinse the fish. Pat dry with kitchen paper and rub with salt. Combine garlic with olive oil, cilantro, rosemary, and lemon juice. Use the mixture to fill each fish. Place in a vacuum-sealable bag and seal. Cook en Sous Vide for 45 minutes at 131 F. Serve and enjoy!

Tilapia Stew

Prep + Cook Time: 65 minutes | Servings: 3

Ingredients

1 pound tilapia fillets
½ cup onions, finely chopped
1 cup carrots, finely chopped
½ cup cilantro leaves, finely chopped

3 garlic cloves, finely chopped
1 cup green bell peppers, chopped
1 tsp Italian seasoning mix
1 tsp cayenne pepper

½ tsp chili pepper
1 cup fresh tomato juice
Salt and black pepper to taste
3 tbsp olive oil

Directions

Heat olive oil over medium heat. Add chopped onions and stir-fry until translucent. Now add bell pepper, carrots, garlic, cilantro, Italian seasoning mix, cayenne pepper, chili pepper, salt, and black pepper. Give it a good stir and cook for ten more minutes. Remove from the heat and transfer to a large vacuum-sealable bag along with tomato juice and tilapia fillets. Cook in sous vide for 50 minutes at 122 F. Remove from the water bath and serve.

Basil Tuna Steaks

Prep + Cook Time: 45 minutes | Servings: 5

Ingredients

6 tbsp olive oil

4 tuna steaks

Salt and black pepper to taste

Zest and juice of 1 lemon

2 garlic cloves, minced

1 tsp chopped fresh basil

Directions

Prepare a water bath and place Sous Vide in it. Set to 126 F. Season tuna with salt and pepper. Stir 4 tbsp of olive oil, lemon juice and zest, garlic, and basil. Place in two vacuum-sealable bags with the citrus marinate. Release air by the water displacement method, seal and submerge the bags in the water bath. Cook for 35 minutes.

Once the timer has stopped, remove the tuna and pat dry with kitchen towels. Reserve the cooking juices. Heat olive oil in a skillet over high heat and cook the tuna for 1 minute per side. Transfer into a plate and sprinkle with the cooking juices. Best served with rice.

Smoky Salmon

Prep + Cook Time: 1 hour 20 minutes | Servings: 3

Ingredients

3 salmon fillets, skinless

1 tbsp sugar

2 tsp smoked paprika

1 tsp mustard powder

Directions

Prepare a water bath, place Sous Vide in it, and set it to 115 F. Season the salmon with 1 teaspoon of salt and place in a zipper bag. Refrigerate for 30 minutes.

In a bowl, mix the sugar, smoked salt, remaining salt, and mustard powder and mix to combine. Remove the salmon from the fridge and rub with the monk powder mixture.

Place salmon in a vacuum-sealable bag, release air by the water displacement method and seal the bag. Submerge in the water bath and set the timer for 45 minutes. Once the timer has stopped, remove the bag and unseal it. Remove the salmon and pat dry using a kitchen towel. Place a non – stick skillet over medium heat, add the salmon and sear it for 30 seconds. Serve with a side of steamed greens.

Speedy North-Style Salmon

Prep + Cook Time: 30 minutes | Servings: 4

Ingredients

1 tbsp olive oil

4 salmon fillets, skin-on

Salt and black pepper to taste

Zest and juice of 1 lemon

2 tbsp yellow mustard

2 tsp sesame oil

Directions

Prepare a water bath and place Sous Vide in it. Set to 114 F. Combine lemon zest and juice, olive oil, salt, pepper, and mustard in a vacuum-sealable bag with the mustard mixture. Add the salmon and toss to coat. Release air by the water displacement method, seal and submerge the bags in the bath. Cook for 20 minutes. Heat sesame oil in a skillet. Once the timer has stopped, transfer the salmon to the skillet and sear for 30 seconds per side. Serve.

Curry Mackerel

Prep + Cook Time: 55 minutes | Servings: 3

Ingredients

3 mackerel fillets, heads removed

3 tbsp curry paste

1 tbsp olive oil

Salt and black pepper to taste

Directions

Make a water bath, place Sous Vide in it, and set to 120 F. Season the mackerel with pepper and salt and place in a vacuum-sealable bag. Release air by the water displacement method, seal and submerge it in the water bath, and set the timer for 40 minutes.

Once the timer has stopped, remove and unseal the bag. Set a skillet over medium heat, add olive oil to heat. Coat the mackerel with the curry powder (do not pat the mackerel dry). Add the mackerel and sear it until golden brown, about 2-3 minutes. Serve with a side of steamed green leafy vegetables.

Wild Salmon Steaks

Prep + Cook Time: 1 hour 25 minutes | Servings: 4

Ingredients

2 pounds wild salmon steaks
3 garlic cloves, crushed
1 tbsp fresh rosemary, finely chopped

1 tbsp freshly squeezed lemon juice
1 tbsp freshly squeezed orange juice
1 tsp orange zest

1 tsp pink Himalayan salt
1 cup fish stock

Directions

Combine orange juice with lemon juice, rosemary, garlic, orange zest, and salt. Brush the mixture over each steak and refrigerate for 20 minutes. Transfer to a large vacuum-sealable bag and add fish stock. Seal the bag and cook in sous vide for 50 minutes at 131 F. Preheat a large, non-stick grill pan. Remove the steaks from vacuum-sealable bag and grill for 3 minutes on each side, until lightly charred.

Halibut with Shallots & Tarragon

Prep + Cook Time: 50 minutes | Servings: 2

Ingredients

2 lb halibut fillets
3 sprigs tarragon leaves
1 tsp garlic powder

1 tsp onion powder
Salt and white pepper to taste
2 ½ tsp + 2 tsp butter

2 shallots, peeled and halved
2 sprigs thyme
Lemon wedges for garnishing

Directions

Make a water bath, place Sous Vide in it, and set to 124 F. Cut halibut fillets into 3 pieces each and rub with salt, garlic powder, onion powder, and pepper. Place the fillets, tarragon, and 2 ½ teaspoons of butter into 3 different vacuum-sealable bags. Release air by the water displacement method and seal the bags. Place them in the water bath and cook for 40 minutes.

Once the timer has stopped, remove and unseal the bags. Place a skillet over low heat and add the remaining butter. Once it is heated, remove the skin of the halibuts and pat dry. Add halibuts with shallots and thyme and sear bottom and top until crispy. Garnish with lemon wedges. Serve with a side of steamed vegetables.

Minty Sardines

Prep + Cook Time: 1 hour 20 minutes | Servings: 3

Ingredients

2 pounds sardines
¼ cup olive oil

3 garlic cloves, crushed
1 large lemon, freshly juiced

2 sprigs fresh mint
Salt and black pepper to taste

Directions

Wash and clean each fish but keep the skin. Pat dry with kitchen paper. In a large bowl, combine olive oil with garlic, lemon juice, fresh mint, salt, and pepper. Place the sardines in a large vacuum-sealable bag along with the marinade. Cook in a water bath for one hour at 104 F. Remove from the bath and drain but reserve the sauce. Drizzle fish with sauce and steamed leek.

Grouper with Beurre Nantais

Prep + Cook Time: 45 minutes | Servings: 6

Ingredients

Grouper:

2 lb grouper, cut into 3 pieces each
1 tsp cumin powder
½ tsp garlic powder

½ tsp onion powder
½ tsp coriander powder
¼ cup fish seasoning

¼ cup pecan oil
Salt and white pepper to taste

Beurre Blanc:

1 lb butter
2 tbsp apple cider vinegar
2 shallots, minced

1 tsp peppercorns, crushed
5 oz heavy cream,
Salt to taste

2 sprigs dill
1 tbsp lemon juice
1 tbsp saffron powder

Directions

Make a water bath, place Sous Vide in it, and set to 132 F. Season the grouper pieces with salt and white pepper. Place in a vacuum-sealable bag, release air by the water displacement method, seal, and submerge the bag in the water bath. Set the timer for 30 minutes. Mix the cumin, garlic, onion, coriander, and fish seasoning. Set aside.

Meanwhile, make the beurre blanc. Place a pan over medium heat and add, shallots, vinegar, and peppercorns. Cook to attain a syrup. Reduce heat to low and add butter, whisking continuously. Add dill, lemon juice, and saffron powder, stir continuously and cook for 2 minutes. Add cream and season with salt. Cook for 1 minute.

Once the timer has stopped, remove and unseal the bag. Set a skillet over medium heat, add pecan oil. Pat dry the grouper and seasoning with the spice mixture and sear them in the heated oil. Serve grouper and beurre nantais with a side of steamed spinach.

Herb-Marinated Tuna Steaks

Prep + Cook Time: 1 hour 25 minutes | Servings: 5

Ingredients

2 lb tuna steaks, about 1-inch thick
1 tsp dried thyme, ground
1 tsp fresh basil, finely chopped
¼ cup finely chopped shallots

2 tbsp fresh parsley, finely chopped
1 tbsp fresh dill, finely chopped
1 tsp freshly grated lemon zest
½ cup sesame seeds

4 tbsp olive oil
Salt and black pepper to taste

Directions

Wash the tuna fillets under cold running water and pat dry with kitchen paper. Set aside. In a large bowl, combine thyme, basil, shallots, parsley, dill, oil, salt, and pepper. Mix until well incorporated and then soak the steaks in this marinade. Coat well and refrigerate for 30 minutes. Place the steaks in a large vacuum-sealable bag along with marinade. Press the bag to remove the air and seal the lid. Cook en Sous Vide for 40 minutes at 131 F.

Remove the steaks from the bag and transfer them to kitchen paper. Gently pat dry and remove the herbs.

Preheat a skillet over high heat. Roll the steaks in sesame seeds and transfer them to the skillet. Cook for 1 minute on each side and remove from the heat.

Sea Bream in White Wine

Prep + Cook Time: 2 hours | Servings: 2

Ingredients

1 pound sea bream, about 1-inch thick, cleaned
1 cup of extra virgin olive oil
1 lemon, juiced
1 tbsp sugar

1 tbsp dried rosemary
½ tbsp dried oregano
2 garlic cloves, crushed

½ cup white wine
1 tsp sea salt

Directions

Combine olive oil with lemon juice, sugar, rosemary, oregano, crushed garlic, wine, and salt in a large bowl. Submerge fish in this mixture and marinate for one hour in the refrigerator. Remove from the refrigerator and drain but reserve the liquid for serving. Place fillets in a large vacuum-sealable bag and seal. Cook en Sous Vide for 40 minutes at 122 F. Drizzle the remaining marinade over fillets and serve.

Herb Butter Lemon Cod

Prep + Cook Time: 37 minutes | Servings: 6

Ingredients

8 tbsp butter

6 cod fillets

Salt and black pepper to taste

Zest of ½ lemon

1 tbsp minced fresh dill

½ tbsp minced fresh chives

½ tbsp minced fresh basil

½ tbsp minced fresh sage

Directions

Prepare a water bath and place the Sous Vide in it. Set to 134 F. Season the cod with salt and pepper. Place the cod and lemon zest in a vacuum-sealable bag. In a separate vacuum-sealable bag, place the butter, half of dill, chives, basil, and sage. Release air by the water displacement method, seal and submerge both bags in the bath.

Cook for 30 minutes. Once the timer has stopped, remove the cod and pat dry with kitchen towels. Discard the cooking juices. Remove the butter from the other bag and pour over the cod. Garnish with the remaining dill.

Tuna Flakes

Prep + Cook Time: 1 hour 45 minutes | Servings: 4

Ingredients

¼ lb tuna steak

1 tsp rosemary leaves

1 tsp thyme leaves

2 cups olive oil

1 clove garlic, minced

Directions

Make a water bath, place Sous Vide in it, and set to 135 F. Place the tuna steak, salt, rosemary, garlic, thyme, and two tablespoons of oil in the vacuum-sealable bag. Release air by the water displacement method, seal, and submerge the bag in the water bath. Set the timer for 1 hour 30 minutes.

Once the timer has stopped, remove the bag. Place the tuna in a bowl and set aside. Place a skillet over high heat, add the remaining olive oil. Once it has heated, pour over the tuna. Flake the tuna using two forks. Transfer and store in an airtight container with olive oil for up to a week. Serve in salads.

Salmon & Kale Salad with Avocado

Prep + Cook Time: 1 hour | Servings: 3

Ingredients

1 pound skinless salmon fillet

Salt and black pepper to taste

½ organic lemon, juiced

1 tbsp olive oil

1 cup kale leaves, shredded

½ cup roasted carrots, sliced

½ ripe avocado, cut into small cubes

1 tbsp fresh dill

1 tbsp fresh parsley leaves

Directions

Season the fillet with salt and pepper on both sides and place in a large vacuum-sealable bag. Seal the bag and cook en sous vide for 40 minutes at 122 F. Remove the salmon from a water bath and set aside.

Whisk together the lemon juice, a pinch of salt and black pepper in a mixing bowl and gradually add olive oil while whisking constantly. Add the shredded kale and toss to evenly coat with vinaigrette. Add in the roasted carrots, avocados, dill, and parsley. Toss to combine. Transfer to a serving bowl and serve with salmon on top.

Gingery Salmon

Prep + Cook Time: 45 minutes | Servings: 4

Ingredients

4 salmon fillets, with skin
2 tsp sesame oil

1 ½ olive oil
2 tbsp ginger, grated

2 tbsp sugar

Directions

Make a water bath, place Sous Vide in it, and set to 124F. Season salmon with salt and pepper. Place the remaining listed ingredient in a bowl and mix. Place salmon and sugar mixture into two vacuum-sealable bags, release air by the water displacement method, seal, and submerge the bag in the bath. Set the timer to 30 minutes.

Once the timer has stopped, remove and unseal the bag. Place a skillet over medium heat, place a piece of parchment paper at the bottom and preheat. Add the salmon, skin down, and sear for 1 minute each. Serve.

Chili Smelts

Prep + Cook Time: 1 hour 15 minutes | Servings: 5

Ingredients

1 pound fresh smelts
½ cup lemon juice
3 garlic cloves, crushed

1 tsp salt
1 cup extra virgin olive oil
2 tbsp fresh dill, finely chopped

1 tbsp chives, minced
1 tbsp chili pepper, ground

Directions

In a large bowl, combine olive oil with lemon juice, crushed garlic, sea salt, finely chopped dill, minced chives, and chili pepper. Place smelts into this mixture and cover. Refrigerate for 20 minutes.

Remove from the refrigerator and place in a large vacuum-sealable bag along with the marinade. Cook in sous vide for 40 minutes at 104 F. Remove from the water bath and drain but reserve the liquid.

Heat a large skillet over medium heat. Add smelts and briefly cook, for 3-4 minutes, turning them over. Remove from the heat and transfer to a serving plate. Drizzle with the marinade and serve immediately.

Marinated Catfish Fillets

Prep + Cook Time: 1 hour 20 minutes | Servings: 3

Ingredients

1 pound catfish fillet
½ cup lemon juice
½ cup parsley leaves, finely chopped
2 garlic cloves, crushed

1 cup onions, finely chopped
1 tbsp fresh dill, finely chopped
1 tbsp fresh rosemary, finely chopped
2 cups freshly squeezed apple juice

2 tbsp Dijon mustard
1 cup extra virgin olive oil

Directions

In a bowl, combine lemon juice, parsley, garlic, onions, dill, rosemary, apple juice, mustard, and olive oil. Whisk together until well incorporated. Submerge the fillets in the mixture and cover with a tight lid. Refrigerate for 30 minutes. Remove from the refrigerator and place in 2 vacuum-sealable bags. Seal and cook in sous vide for 40 minutes at 122 F. Remove and drain; reserve the liquid. Serve drizzled with its liquid.

Lemon Butter Sole

Prep + Cook Time: 45 minutes | Servings: 3

Ingredients

3 sole fillets
1 ½ tbsp unsalted butter

¼ cup lemon juice
½ tsp lemon zest

Lemon pepper to taste
1 tbsp parsley, chop

Directions

Make a water bath, place Sous Vide in it, and set to 132 F. Pat dry the sole and place in 3 separate vacuum-sealable bag. Release air by the water displacement method and seal the bags. Submerge in the water bath and set the timer for 30 minutes. Melt the butter in a pan over medium heat. Once it has melted, remove from the heat.

Add lemon juice and lemon zest and stir. Once the timer has stopped, remove and unseal the bag. Transfer the sole fillets to serving plates, drizzle butter sauce over and garnish with parsley. Serve with steamed vegetables.

Honey Salmon with Soba Noodles

Prep + Cook Time: 40 minutes | Servings: 4

Ingredients

Salmon

6 oz salmon fillets, skin-on	1 tsp sesame oil	1 tbsp fresh ginger, grated
Salt and black pepper to taste	1 cup olive oil	2 tbsp honey

Sesame Soba

4 oz dry soba noodles	1 tsp sesame oil	1 tsp toasted poppy seeds
1 tbsp grapeseed oil	2 tsp olive oil	Lime wedges for garnish
2 garlic cloves, chopped	¼ juiced lime	Sesame seeds for garnish
½ cauliflower head	1 sliced stalk green onion	2 tbsp cilantro, chopped
3 tbsp tahini	¼ cup cilantro, roughly chopped	

Directions

Prepare a water bath and place the Sous Vide in it. Set to 123 F. Season the salmon with salt and pepper. In a bowl, combine sesame oil, olive oil, ginger, and honey. Place the salmon and mixture in a vacuum-sealable bag. Release air by the water displacement method, seal, and submerge the bag in the bath. Cook for 20 minutes.

Meanwhile, prepare the soba noodles. Heat grapeseed oil in a skillet over high heat and stir-fry cauliflower and garlic for 6-8 minutes. In a bowl, combine well the tahini, olive oil, sesame oil, lime juice, cilantro, green onions and toasted sesame seeds. Drain the noodles and add to the cauliflower.

Heat a skillet over high heat. Cover with baking paper sheet. Once the timer has stopped, remove the salmon and transfer to the skillet. Sear for 1 minute. Serve the noodles in two bowls and add in salmon. Garnish with lime wedges, poppy seeds, and cilantro. Serve and enjoy!

Savory Creamy Cod with Parsley

Prep + Cook Time: 40 minutes | Servings: 6

Ingredients

For Cod

6 cod fillets	1 tbsp olive oil
Salt to taste	3 sprigs fresh parsley

For Sauce

1 cup white wine	1 finely chopped white onion	2 tsp black peppercorns
1 cup half-and-half cream	2 tbsp dill, chopped	

Directions

Prepare a water bath and place the Sous Vide in it. Set to 148 F.

Place seasoned with salt cod fillets in vacuum-sealable bags. Add olive oil and parsley. Release air by the water displacement method, seal, and submerge the bag in the water bath. Cook for 30 minutes.

Heat a saucepan over medium heat, add in wine, onion, black peppercorns and cook until reduced. Stir in half-and-half cream until thickened. Once the timer has stopped, plate the fish and drizzle with sauce.

Thai Salmon with Cauliflower & Egg Noodles

Prep + Cook Time: 55 minutes | Servings: 2

Ingredients

2 skin-on salmon fillets
Salt and black pepper to taste
1 tbsp olive oil
4 ½ tbsp soy sauce

2 tbsp minced fresh ginger
2 thinly sliced Thai Chilis
6 tbsp sesame oil
4 oz prepared egg noodles

6 oz cooked cauliflower florets
5 tsp sesame seeds

Directions

Prepare a water bath and place the Sous Vide in it. Set to 149 F. Prepare a baking tray lined with aluminium foil and put the salmon, season with salt and pepper and cover with another aluminium sheet. Bake in the oven for 30 minutes. Remove the baked salmon to a vacuum-sealable bag. Release air by the water displacement method, seal, and submerge the bag in the water bath. Cook for 8 minutes.

In a bowl, mix ginger, chilis, 4 tbsp of soy sauce, and 4 tbsp of sesame oil. Once the timer has stopped, remove the bag and transfer the salmon to a noodle bowl. Garnish with toasted seeds and salmon skin. Sprinkle with the ginger-chili sauce and serve.

Basil Cod Stew

Prep + Cook Time: 50 minutes | Servings: 4

Ingredients

1 pound cod fillet
1 cup fire-roasted tomatoes
1 tbsp basil, dried
1 cup fish stock

2 tbsp tomato paste
3 celery stalks, finely chopped
1 carrot, sliced
¼ cup olive oil

1 onion, finely chopped
½ cup button mushrooms

Directions

Heat olive oil in a large skillet, over medium heat. Add celery, onions, and carrot. Stir-fry for 10 minutes. Remove from the heat and transfer to a vacuum-sealable bag along with other ingredients. Cook in sous vide for 40 minutes at 122 F. Serve and enjoy!

Easy Tilapia

Prep + Cook Time: 1 hour 10 minutes | Servings: 3

Ingredients

3 (4 oz) tilapia fillets
3 tbsp butter

1 tbsp apple cider vinegar
Salt and black pepper to taste

Directions

Make a water bath, place Sous Vide in it, and set to 124 F. Season the tilapia with pepper and salt and place in a vacuum-sealable bag. Release air by the water displacement method and seal the bag.

Submerge it in the water bath and set the timer for 1 hour. Once the timer has stopped, remove and unseal the bag. Put a skillet over medium heat and add butter and vinegar. Simmer and stir continually to reduce vinegar by half. Add the tilapia and sear slightly. Season with salt and pepper as desired. Serve and enjoy!

Sesame-Crusted Cod Fillet

Prep + Cook Time: 45 minutes | Servings: 2

Ingredients

1 large cod fillet
2 tbsp sesame paste

1 ½ tbsp brown sugar
2 tbsp fish sauce

2 tbsp butter
Sesame seeds

Directions

Prepare a water bath and place the Sous Vide in it. Set to 131 F. Soak cod with the brown sugar, sesame paste and fish sauce mixture. Place in a vacuum-sealable bag. Release air by the water displacement method, seal, and submerge the bag in the water bath. Cook for 30 minutes. Melt butter in a skillet over medium heat.

Once the timer has stopped, remove the cod and transfer to the skillet and sear for 1 minute. Serve onto a platter. Pour cooking juices into the skillet and cook until reduced. Add 1 tbsp of butter and mix. Top cod with the sauce and garnish with sesame seeds. Serve with rice.

Salmon with Asparagus

Prep + Cook Time: 3 hours 15 minutes | Servings: 6

Ingredients

1 pound wild salmon fillet	12 medium asparagus spears	Salt and black pepper to taste
1 tbsp olive oil	4 white onion rings	
1 tbsp dried oregano	1 tbsp fresh parsley	

Directions

Season the fillet with oregano, salt, and pepper on both sides and lightly brush with olive oil. Place in a large vacuum-sealable along with other ingredients. Combine all spices in a mixing bowl. Rub the mixture evenly on both sides of the steak and place in a large vacuum-sealable bag. Seal the bag and cook in sous vide for 3 hours at 136 F. Serve and enjoy!

Creamy Salmon with Spinach & Mustard Sauce

Prep + Cook Time: 55 minutes | Servings: 2

Ingredients

4 skinless salmon fillets	1 cup heavy cream	Salt and black pepper to taste
1 large bunch of spinach	1 cup half-and-half cream	
½ cup Dijon mustard	1 tbsp lemon juice	

Directions

Prepare a water bath and place the Sous Vide in it. Set to 115 F. Place the salmon seasoned with salt in a vacuum-sealable bag. Seal and submerge the bag in the bath. Cook for 45 minutes.

Heat a pot over medium heat and cook spinach until softened. Lower the heat and pour in lemon juice, pepper and salt. Keep cooking. Heat a saucepan over medium heat and combine the half-and-half cream and Dijon mustard. Lower the heat and cook. Season with salt and pepper. Once the timer has stopped, remove the salmon and transfer to a plate. Drizzle with sauce. Serve with spinach.

Egg Bites with Salmon & Asparagus

Prep + Cook Time: 70 minutes | Servings: 6

Ingredients

6 whole eggs	4 spears asparagus	½ oz minced shallot
¼ cup crème fraiche	2 oz smoked salmon	2 tsp chopped, fresh dill
¼ cup goat cheese	2 oz chèvre cheese	Salt and black pepper to taste

Directions

Prepare a water bath and place the Sous Vide in it. Set to 172 F. Blend the eggs, crème fraiche, goat cheese and salt. Diced the asparagus and add to the mix with the shallots. Cut salmon and add to the bowl as well. Add the dill. Combine well. Add the egg and salmon mixture into 6 jars. Add 1/6 chevre into the jars, seal and submerge the jars in the water bath. Cook for 60 minutes. Once the timer has stopped, remove the jars and top with salt.

Salted Salmon in Hollandaise Sauce

Prep + Cook Time: 1 hour 50 minutes | Servings: 4

Ingredients

4 salmon fillets   Salt to taste

Hollandaise Sauce

4 tbsp butter   1 tsp lemon juice   ½ diced shallot
1 egg yolk   1 tsp water   A pinch of paprika

Directions

Season the salmon with salt. Allow chilling for 30 minutes. Prepare a water bath and place the Sous Vide in it. Set to 148 F. Place all the sauce ingredients in a vacuum-sealable bag. Release air by the water displacement method, seal, and submerge the bag in the water bath. Cook for 45 minutes.

Once the timer has stopped, remove the bag. Set aside. Lower the temperature of the Sous Vide to 120 F and place salmon in a vacuum-sealable bag. Release air by the water displacement method, seal, and submerge the bag in the water bath. Cook for 30 minutes. Transfer the sauce to a blender and mix until light yellow. Once the timer has stopped, remove the salmon and pat dry. Serve topped with the sauce.

Herby Lemon Salmon

Prep + Cook Time: 45 minutes | Servings: 2

Ingredients

2 skinless salmon fillets   1 shallot, sliced into thin rings   3 oz mixed greens
Salt and black pepper to taste   1 tbsp basil leaves, lightly chopped   1 lemon
¾ cup extra virgin olive oil   1 tsp allspice

Directions

Prepare a water bath and place the Sous Vide in it. Set to 128 F. Place the salmon and season with salt and pepper in a vacuum-sealable bag. Add in shallot rings, olive oil, allspice, and basil. Release air by the water displacement method, seal, and submerge the bag in the water bath. Cook for 25 minutes. Once the timer has stopped, remove the bag and transfer the salmon to a plate. Mix the cooking juices with some lemon juice and top salmon fillets. Serve.

Light Sea Bass with Dill

Prep + Cook Time: 35 minutes | Servings: 3

Ingredients

1 pound Chilean sea bass, skinless   Salt and black pepper to taste
1 tbsp olive oil   1 tbsp dill

Directions

Prepare a water bath and place the Sous Vide in it. Set to 134 F. Season the sea bass with salt and pepper and place in a vacuum-sealable bag. Add the dill and olive oil. Release air by the water displacement method, seal, and submerge the bag in the water bath. Cook for 30 minutes. Once the timer has stopped, remove the bag and transfer the sea bass to a plate. Serve and enjoy!

French Pot de Rillettes with Salmon

Prep + Cook Time: 2 hours 30 minutes | Servings: 2

Ingredients

½ pound salmon fillets, skin removed   6 tbsp butter   1 garlic clove, minced
1 tsp sea salt   1 onion, chopped   1 tbsp lime juice

Directions

Prepare a water bath and place the Sous Vide in it. Set to 130 F. Place the salmon, unsalted butter, sea salt, garlic cloves, onion and lemon juice in a vacuum-sealable bag. Release air by the water displacement method, seal, and submerge the bag in the water bath. Cook for 20 minutes.

Once the timer has stopped, remove the salmon and transfer into 8 small bowls. Season with cooking juices. Allow chilling in the fridge for 2 hours. Serve with toast bread slices.

Sage Salmon with Coconut Potato Mash

Prep + Cook Time: 1 hour 30 minutes | Servings: 2

Ingredients

2 salmon fillets, skin-on
2 tbsp olive oil
2 sprigs sage
4 garlic cloves

3 potatoes, peeled and chopped
¼ cup coconut milk
1 bunch rainbow chard
1 tbsp grated ginger

1 tbsp soy sauce
Sea salt to taste

Directions

Prepare a water bath and place the Sous Vide in it. Set to 122 F. Place salmon, sage, garlic, and olive oil in a vacuum-sealable bag. Release air by the water displacement method, seal, and submerge the bag in the water bath. Cook for 1 hour.

Heat an oven to 375 F. Brush the potatoes with oil and bake for 45 minutes. Transfer potatoes to a blender and add coconut milk. Season with salt and pepper. Blend for 3 minutes until smooth. Heat olive oil in a skillet over medium heat and sauté ginger, chard, and soy sauce. Once the timer has stopped, remove the salmon and transfer it to a hot pan. Sear for 2 minutes. Transfer to a plate, add the potato mash, and top with char to serve.

Amazing Lemon Salmon with Basil

Prep + Cook Time: 35 minutes | Servings: 4

Ingredients

2 pounds salmon
2 tbsp olive oil
1 tbsp chopped basil

Zest of 1 lemon
Juice of 1 lemon
¼ tsp garlic powder

Sea salt and black pepper to taste

Directions

Prepare a water bath and place the Sous Vide in it. Set to 115 F. Place the salmon in a vacuum-sealable bag. Release air by the water displacement method, seal, and submerge the bag in the water bath. Cook for 30 minutes.

Meanwhile, in a bowl combine well the pepper, salt, basil, lemon juice, and garlic powder until emulsified. Once the timer has stopped, remove the salmon and transfer it to a plate. Reserve the cooking juices. Heat olive oil in a pan over high heat and sauté the garlic slices. Set aside the garlic. Put the salmon in the pan and cook for 3 minutes until golden. Plate and top with the garlic slices.

Squid Rings

Prep + Cook Time: 1 hour 25 minutes | Servings: 3

Ingredients

2 cups squid rings

1 tbsp fresh rosemary

½ cup olive oil

Directions

Combine squid rings with rosemary, and olive oil in a large clean plastic bag. Seal the bag and shake a couple of times to coat well. Transfer to a large vacuum-sealable and seal the bag. Cook in sous vide for 1 hour and 10 minutes at 131 F. Remove from the water bath. Serve and enjoy!

Crabmeat Patties

Prep + Cook Time: 65 minutes | Servings: 4

Ingredients

1 pound lump crab meat
1 cup red onions, finely chopped
½ cup red bell peppers, finely chopped
2 tbsp chili pepper, finely chopped

1 tbsp celery leaves, finely chopped
1 tbsp parsley leaves, finely chopped
½ tsp tarragon, finely chopped
Salt and black pepper to taste

4 tbsp olive oil
2 tbsp almond flour
3 eggs, beaten

Directions

Heat 2 tablespoons of olive oil in a skillet and add onions. Stir-fry until translucent and add chopped red bell peppers and chili pepper. Cook for 5 minutes, stirring constantly. Transfer to a large bowl. Add crab meat, celery, parsley, tarragon, salt, pepper, almond flour, and eggs. Stir and mold the mixture into 2-inches diameter patties. Gently divide patties between 2 vacuum-sealable bags and seal them. Cook in sous vide for 40 minutes at 122 F.

Heat the remaining olive oil in a non-stick grill pan over high heat. Remove the patties from the water bath and transfer to a skillet. Briefly, brown on both sides for 3-4 minutes and serve.

Mussels in Fresh Lime Juice

Prep + Cook Time: 40 minutes | Servings: 2

Ingredients

1 pound fresh mussels, debearded
1 onion, peeled and finely chopped
Garlic cloves, crushed

½ cup freshly squeezed lime juice
¼ cup fresh parsley, finely chopped
1 tbsp rosemary, finely chopped

2 tbsp olive oil

Directions

Place mussels along with lime juice, garlic, onion, parsley, rosemary, and olive oil in a large vacuum-sealable bag. Cook en Sous Vide for 30 minutes at 122 F. Serve with green salad.

Parsley Prawns with Lemon

Prep + Cook Time: 35 minutes | Servings: 4

Ingredients

12 large prawns, peeled and deveined
1 tsp salt
1 tsp sugar

3 tsp olive oil
1 bay leaf
1 sprig parsley, chopped

2 tbsp lemon zest
1 tbsp lemon juice

Directions

Make a water bath, place Sous Vide in it, and set to 156 F. In a bowl, add prawns, salt, and sugar, mix and let it sit for 15 minutes. Place prawns, bay leaf, olive oil, and lemon zest in a vacuum-sealable bag. Release air by the water displacement method and seal. Submerge in the water bath and cook for 10 minutes. Once the timer has stopped, remove and unseal the bag. Dish prawns and drizzle with lemon juice.

Shrimp with Spicy Sauce

Prep + Cook Time: 40 minutes + Cooling Time | Servings: 5

Ingredients

2 pounds shrimp, deveined and peeled
1 cup tomato puree

2 tbsp horseradish sauce
1 tsp lemon juice

1 tsp Tabasco sauce
Salt and black pepper to taste

Directions

Prepare a water bath and place Sous Vide in it. Set to 137 F. Place shrimp in a vacuum-sealable bag. Release air by the water displacement method, seal and submerge bag in the bath. Cook for 30 minutes.

Once the timer has stopped, remove the bag and transfer into an ice water bath for 10 minutes. Allow to chill in the fridge for 1-6 hours. Combine well the tomato puree, horseradish sauce, soy sauce, lemon juice, Tabasco sauce, salt and pepper. Serve shrimp with the sauce.

Sweet Buttered Scallops with Pancetta

Prep + Cook Time: 45 minutes | Servings: 6

Ingredients

12 large scallops	Salt and black pepper to taste	2 tbsp honey
1 tbsp olive oil	4 pancetta slices, chopped	2 tbsp butter

Directions

Prepare a water bath and place the Sous Vide in it. Set to 126 F. Combine the scallops with olive oil, salt and pepper. Place in a vacuum-sealable bag. Release air by the water displacement method, seal, and submerge the bag in the water bath. Cook for 30 minutes. Once the timer has stopped, remove the scallops and pat them dry.

Cook the pancetta in a skillet over medium heat for 5 minutes. Stir in the butter, honey, and pepper for 2 minutes. Add the scallops and cook for 1 minute per side until golden brown. Plate the scallops and serve.

Cheesy Lemon Shrimp Pasta

Prep + Cook Time: 55 minutes | Servings: 4

Ingredients

2 cups Swiss chard, chopped	1 lemon, zested and juiced	1 ½ pounds shrimp, deveined, with
6 tbsp butter	1 tbsp fresh basil, chopped	tails
½ cup Parmesan cheese	Salt and black pepper to taste	8 oz pasta of choice
2 garlic cloves, minced	1 tsp red pepper flakes	

Directions

Prepare a water bath and place the Sous Vide in it. Set to 137 F.

Heat a pot over medium heat and combine the butter, Swiss chard, 1/4 cup of Pecorino Romano cheese, garlic, lemon zest and juice, basil, salt, pepper, and red pepper flakes. Cook for 5 minutes. Set aside.

Place the shrimp in a vacuum-sealable bag and pour in lemon mixture. Shake well. Release air by the water displacement method, seal, and submerge the bag in the water bath. Cook for 30 minutes.

Meanwhile, cook the pasta according to the package instructions. Drain and put in the pot. Once the timer has stopped, remove the shrimp and stir in the pasta for 3-4 minutes. Top with the remaining Pecorino and serve.

Creole Prawn Kabobs

Prep + Cook Time: 50 minutes | Servings: 4

Ingredients

Zest and juice of 1 lemon	Salt and white pepper to taste	1 tbsp chopped fresh dill
6 tbsp butter	1 tbsp Creole seasoning	Lemon wedges
2 garlic cloves, minced	1 ½ pounds prawns, deveined	

Directions

Prepare a water bath and place the Sous Vide in it. Set to 137 F. Melt butter in a saucepan over medium heat and add garlic, Creole seasoning, lemon zest and juice, salt, and pepper. Cook for 5 minutes. Allow to cool.

Place the prawns in a vacuum-sealable bag with the butter mix. Release air by the water displacement method, seal, and submerge the bag in the water bath. Cook for 30 minutes. Once the timer has stopped, remove the prawns and pat dry with kitchen towels. Discard the cooking juices. Thread the prawns onto kabobs and grill for 3 minutes on a preheated grill pan. Garnish with dill and squeeze lemon all over. Serve and enjoy!

Chili-Lemon Calamari Linguine

Prep + Cook Time: 2 hours 10 minutes | Servings: 4

Ingredients

4 calamari bodies, cleaned
Salt and black pepper to taste
10 ounces dried linguine
1 (16-ounce) can tomatoes

2 garlic cloves, minced
1 tsp red pepper flakes
1 tsp serrano pepper, chopped
Zest and juice of 1 lemon

2 tbsp chopped fresh parsley
3 tbsp chopped fresh dill

Directions

Prepare a water bath and place the Sous Vide in it. Set to 134 F. Season the calamari with salt and pepper. Place the calamari and 2 tbsp of olive oil in a vacuum-sealable bag. Release air by the water displacement method, seal, and submerge the bag in the water bath. Cook for 2 hours. After 1 hour and 45 minutes, cook the linguine according to the package instructions. Drain it.

Heat a saucepan over medium heat and add in the remaining olive oil, tomatoes, garlic, serrano pepper, lemon zest and juice, and parsley. Sauté for 3 minutes. Once the timer has stopped, remove the calamari and pat dry with kitchen towels. Cut into tiny slices and place in the saucepan. Add the pasta and stir. Serve and enjoy!

Crabmeat with Lime Butter Sauce

Prep + Cook Time: 70 minutes | Servings: 4

Ingredients

6 garlic cloves, minced
Zest and juice from ½ lime

1 pound crabmeat
4 tbsp butter

Directions

Prepare a water bath and place the Sous Vide in it. Set to 137 F. Combine well half of the garlic, lime zest, and half of the lime juice. Set aside. Place the crabmeat, butter, and lime mixture in a vacuum-sealable bag. Release air by the water displacement method, seal and submerge the bag in the water bath. Cook for 50 minutes. Once the timer has stopped, remove the bag. Discard the cooking juices.

Heat a saucepan over medium-low heat and pour in the remaining butter, remaining lime mixture, and remaining lime juice. Serve the crab in 4 ramekins, sprinkled with lime butter.

Paprika Scallops with Fresh Salad

Prep + Cook Time: 55 minutes | Servings: 4

Ingredients

1 pound scallops
1 tsp garlic powder

½ tsp onion powder
½ tsp paprika

¼ tsp cayenne pepper
Salt and black pepper to taste

Salad

3 cups corn kernels
½ pint halved cherry tomatoes

1 diced red bell pepper
2 tbsp chopped fresh parsley

Dressing

1 tbsp fresh basil

1 quartered lemon

Directions

Prepare a water bath and place the Sous Vide in it. Set to 122 F. Place the scallops in a vacuum-sealable bag. Season with salt and pepper. Combine garlic powder, paprika, onion powder, and cayenne pepper and pour in the bag. Release air by the water displacement method, seal, and submerge the bag in the bath. Cook for 30 minutes.

Meanwhile, preheat the oven to 400 F. In a baking tray, put the corn kernels and red pepper. Sprinkle olive oil and season with salt and pepper. Cook for 5-10 minutes. Transfer to a bowl and mix with parsley.

In a bowl, combined well the dressing ingredients and pour over corn kernels. Once the timer has stopped, remove the bag and transfer to a hot skillet. Sear for 2 minutes on each side. Serve on a platter, the scallops, and salad. Garnish with basil and lemon wedge. Serve and enjoy!

Divine Garlic-Lemon Crab Rolls

Prep + Cook Time: 60 minutes | Servings: 4

Ingredients

4 tbsp butter
1 pound cooked crabmeat
2 garlic cloves, minced

Zest and juice of ½ lemon
½ cup mayonnaise
1 fennel bulb, chopped

Salt and black pepper to taste
4 rolls, split, oiled, and toasted

Directions

Prepare a water bath and place Sous Vide in it. Set to 137 F. Combine garlic, lemon zest and 1/4 cup of lemon juice. Place the crabmeat in a vacuum-sealable bag with butter and lemon mix. Release air by the water displacement method, seal, and submerge the bag in the water bath. Cook for 50 minutes.

Once the timer has stopped, remove the bag and transfer it into a bowl. Discard the cooking juices. Combine the crabmeat with the remaining lemon juice, mayonnaise, fennel, dill, salt, and pepper. Fill the rolls with the crabmeat mixture before serving.

Spiced Charred Octopus with Lemon Sauce

Prep + Cook Time: 4 hours 15 minutes | Servings: 4

Ingredients

5 tbsp olive oil
1 pound octopus tentacles
Salt and black pepper to taste

2 tbsp lemon juice
1 tbsp lemon zest
1 tbsp minced fresh parsley

1 tsp thyme
1 tbsp paprika

Directions

Prepare a water bath and place the Sous Vide in it. Set to 179 F. Cut the tentacles into medium-size lengths. Season with salt and pepper. Place the lengths with olive oil in a vacuum-sealable bag. Release air by the water displacement method, seal, and submerge the bag in the water bath. Cook for 4 hours. Once the timer has stopped, remove the octopus and pat pat dry with kitchen towels. Discard the cooking juices. Drizzle with oil.

Heat a grill over medium heat and sear the tentacles for 10-15 seconds per side. Set aside. Combine well the lemon juice, lemon zest, paprika, thyme and parsley. Top the octopus with lemon dressing.

Octopus Grill

Prep + Cook Time: 5 hours 20 minutes | Servings: 3

Ingredients

½ lb medium octopus tentacles, blanched
Salt and black pepper to taste
3 tsp + 3 tbsp olive oil

2 tsp dried oregano
2 sprigs fresh parsley, chopped

Ice for an ice bath

Directions

Make a water bath, place Sous Vide in it, and set to 171 F.

Place the octopus, salt, 3 teaspoons of olive oil, and pepper in a vacuum-sealable bag. Release air by the water displacement method, seal and submerge the bag in the water bath. Set timer for 5 hours.

Once the timer has stopped, remove the bag and cover in an ice bath. Set aside. Preheat a grill. Once the grill is hot, transfer the octopus to a plate, add 3 tablespoons of olive oil and massage. Grill octopus to char nicely on each side. Dish octopus and garnish with parsley and oregano. Serve with a sweet, spicy dip.

Buttered Scallops

Prep + Cook Time: 55 minutes | Servings: 3

Ingredients

½ lb scallops   3 tsp butter   Salt and black pepper to taste

Directions

Make a water bath, place Sous Vide in it, and set to 140 F. Pat dry scallops using a paper towel. Place scallops, salt, 2 tablespoons of butter, and pepper in a vacuum-sealable bag. Release air by the water displacement method, seal, and submerge the bag in the water bath and set the timer for 40 minutes.

Once the timer has stopped, remove and unseal the bag. Pat dry the scallops using a paper towel and set aside. Set a skillet over medium heat and the remaining butter. Once it has melted, sear the scallops on both sides until golden brown. Serve with a side of buttered mixed vegetables.

Rosemary Squid

Prep + Cook Time: 1 hour and 15 minutes | Servings: 3

Ingredients

1 pound fresh squid, whole   1 tbsp of pink Himalayan salt   3 garlic cloves, crushed
½ cup extra virgin olive oil   1 tbsp of dried rosemary   3 cherry tomatoes, halved

Directions

Thoroughly rinse each squid under the running water. Using a sharp paring knife, remove the heads and clean each squid. In a large bowl, combine olive oil with salt, dried rosemary, cherry tomatoes, and crushed garlic. Submerge squid in this mixture and refrigerate for 1 hour. Then remove and drain. Place squid and cherry tomatoes in a large vacuum-sealable bag. Cook en sous vide for one hour at 136 F.

Fried Lemon Shrimps

Prep + Cook Time: 50 minutes | Servings: 3

Ingredients

1 pound shrimps, peeled and deveined   ½ cup freshly squeezed lemon juice   1 tsp fresh rosemary, crushed
3 tbsp olive oil   1 garlic clove, crushed   1 tsp sea salt

Directions

Combine olive oil with lemon juice, crushed garlic, rosemary, and salt. Using a kitchen brush, spread the mixture over each shrimp and place in a large vacuum-sealable bag. Cook in sous vide for 40 minutes at 104 F.

Buttery Cockles with Peppercorns

Prep + Cook Time: 1 hour 30 minutes | Servings: 2

Ingredients

4 oz canned cockles   1 bay leaf   2 garlic cloves, minced
¼ cup dry white wine   1 tbsp black peppercorns   Salt to taste
1 diced celery stalk   1 tbsp olive oil   1 tsp freshly cracked black pepper
1 diced parsnip   8 tbsp butter, room temperature   ¼ cup panko breadcrumbs
1 quartered shallot   1 tbsp minced fresh parsley   1 baguette, sliced

Directions

Prepare a water bath and place the Sous Vide in it. Set to 154 F. Place the cockles, shallots, celery, parsnip, wine, peppercorns, olive oil and bay leaf in a vacuum-sealable bag. Release air by the water displacement method, seal, and submerge the bag in the water bath. Cook for 60 minutes.

In a blender, pour the butter, parsley, salt, garlic and ground pepper. Mix at medium speed until combined. Put the mixture into a plastic bag and roll it. Move into the fridge and allow chilling. Once the timer has stopped, remove the snail and veggies. Discard the cooking juices. Heat a skillet over high heat. Top the cockles with butter, sprinkle some breadcrumbs over and cook for 3 minutes until melted. Serve with warm baguette slices.

Chili Shrimp & Avocado Salad

Prep + Cook Time: 45 minutes | Servings: 4

Ingredients

1 chopped red onion
Juice of 2 limes
1 tsp olive oil
¼ tsp sea salt

⅛ tsp white pepper
1 pound raw shrimp, peeled and deveined
1 diced tomato

1 diced avocado
1 green chili pepper, seeded and diced
1 tbsp chopped cilantro

Directions

Prepare a water bath and place the Sous Vide in it. Set to 148 F. Place the lime juice, red onion, sea salt, white pepper, olive oil, and shrimp in a vacuum-sealable bag. Release air by the water displacement method, seal, and submerge the bag in the water bath. Cook for 24 minutes. Once the timer has stopped, transfer the shrimp to an ice-water bath for 10 minutes. In a bowl, combine tomato, avocado, chili pepper, and cilantro. Top with shrimp.

Saucy Scallops with Mango

Prep + Cook Time: 50 minutes | Servings: 4

Ingredients

1 pound large scallops

1 tbsp butter

Sauce

1 tbsp lemon juice

2 tbsp olive oil

Garnish

1 tbsp lime zest
1 tbsp orange zest

1 cup diced mango
1 thinly sliced Serrano pepper

2 tbsp chopped mint leaves

Directions

Place the scallops in a vacuum-sealable bag. Season with salt and pepper. Allow chilling in the fridge all night. Prepare a water bath and place the Sous Vide in it. Set to 122 F. Release air by the water displacement method, seal, and submerge the bag in the water bath. Cook for 15-35 minutes.

Heat a skillet over medium heat. In a bowl, combine well the sauce ingredients. Once the timer has stopped, remove the scallops and transfer to the skillet and sear until browned. Serve in a plate. Sprinkle the sauce and add the garnish ingredients.

Savory Buttery Lobster Tails

Prep + Cook Time: 1 hour 10 minutes | Servings: 2

Ingredients

8 tbsp butter
2 lobster tails, shells removed

2 sprigs fresh tarragon
2 tbsp sage

Salt to taste
Lemon wedges

Directions

Prepare a water bath and place the Sous Vide in it. Set to 134 F. Place the lobster tails, butter, salt, sage and tarragon in a vacuum-sealable bag. Release air by the water displacement method, seal, and submerge the bag in the water bath. Cook for 60 minutes. Once the timer has stopped, remove the bag and transfer the lobster to a plate. Sprinkle butter on top. Garnish with lemon wedges.

Leek & Shrimp with Mustard Vinaigrette

Prep + Cook Time: 1 hour 20 minutes | Servings: 4

Ingredients

6 leeks
5 tbsp olive oil
Salt and black pepper to taste

1 shallot, minced
1 tbsp rice vinegar
1 tsp Dijon mustard

1/3 pound cooked bay shrimp
Chopped fresh parsley

Directions

Prepare a water bath and place the Sous Vide in it. Set to 183 F. Cut the top of the leeks and remove the bottom parts. Wash them in cold water and sprinkle with some olive oil. Season with salt and pepper. Place in a vacuum-sealable bag. Release air by the water displacement method, seal, and submerge in the bath. Cook for 1 hour.

In a bowl, combine the shallot, Dijon mustard, vinegar, and 1/4 cup of olive oil. Season with salt and pepper. Once the timer has stopped, remove the bag and transfer to an ice-water bath. Allow cooling. Put the leeks in 4 plates and season with salt. Add the shrimp and drizzle with vinaigrette. Garnish with parsley.

Coconut Shrimp Soup

Prep + Cook Time: 55 minutes | Servings: 6

Ingredients

6 raw shrimp, peeled and deveined

1 tbsp butter

Salt and black pepper to taste

For Soup

1 pound zucchini
4 tbsp lime juice
2 yellow onions, chopped
1-2 small red chilis, finely chopped
1 stem of lemongrass, white part only,

chopped
1 tsp shrimp paste
1 tsp sugar
1 ½ cups coconut milk
1 tsp tamarind paste

1 cup water
½ cup coconut cream
1 tbsp fish sauce
2 tbsp fresh basil, chopped

Directions

Prepare a water bath and place the Sous Vide in it. Set to 142 F. Place the shrimp and butter in a vacuum-sealable bag. Season with salt and pepper. Release air by the water displacement method, seal, and submerge the bag in the water bath. Cook for 15-35 minutes.

Meanwhile, peel the zucchini and discard the seeds. Chop in cubes. In a food processor, add the onion, lemongrass, chili, shrimp paste, sugar, and 1/2 cup of coconut milk. Blend until purée.

Heat a casserole over lower heat and combine the onion mixture, remaining coconut milk, tamarind paste and water. Add in zucchini and cook for 10 minutes. Once the timer has stopped, remove the shrimp and transfer to the soup. Whisk the coconut cream, lime juice and basil. Serve in soup bowls.

Dill Baby Octopus Bowl

Prep + Cook Time: 60 minutes | Servings: 4

Ingredients

1 pound baby octopus
1 tbsp olive oil

1 tbsp freshly squeezed lemon juice
Salt and black pepper to taste

1 tbsp dill

Directions

Prepare a water bath and place the Sous Vide in it. Set to 134 F. Place the octopus in a vacuum-sealable bag. Release air by the water displacement method, seal, and submerge the bag in the water bath. Cook for 50 minutes. Once the timer has stopped, remove the octopus and pat dry. Mix the octopus with some olive oil and lemon juice. Season with salt, pepper and dill.

Gourmet Lobster with Mayonnaise

Prep + Cook Time: 40 minutes | Servings: 2

Ingredients

2 lobster tails
1 tbsp butter

2 sweet onions, chopped
3 tbsp mayonnaise

Salt and black pepper to taste
2 tsp lemon juice

Directions

Prepare a water bath and place the Sous Vide in it. Set to 138 F. Heat water in a casserole over high heat until boiling. Open the lobster tail shells and immerse them into the water. Cook for 90 seconds. Transfer to an ice-water bath. Allow cooling for 5 minutes. Crack the shells and remove the tails.

Place the tails with butter in a vacuum-sealable bag. Release air by the water displacement method, seal, and submerge the bag in the water bath. Cook for 25 minutes. Once the timer has stopped, remove the tails and pat dry. Seat aside. Allow chilling for 30 minutes. In a bowl, combine the mayonnaise, sweet onions, pepper, and lemon juice. Chop the tails, add to the mayonnaise mixture, and stir well. Serve with toasted bread.

Party Shrimp Cocktail

Prep + Cook Time: 40 minutes | Servings: 2

Ingredients

1 pound shrimp, peeled and deveined
Salt and black pepper to taste
4 tbsp fresh dill, chopped
1 tbsp butter

4 tbsp mayonnaise
2 tbsp green onions, minced
2 tsp freshly squeezed lemon juice
2 tsp tomato puree

1 tbsp tabasco sauce
4 oblong dinner rolls
8 leaves of lettuce
½ lemon, sliced into wedges

Directions

Prepare a water bath and place the Sous Vide in it. Set to 149 F. For the seasoning, combine well the mayonnaise, green onions, lemon juice, tomato puree, and Tabasco sauce. Season with salt and pepper.

Place the shrimp and seasoning in a vacuum-sealable bag. Add 1 tbsp of dill and 1/2 tbsp of butter in each pack. Release air by the water displacement method, seal, and submerge the bag in the water bath. Cook for 15 minutes.

Preheat oven over to 400 F. and cook the dinner rolls for 15 minutes. Once the timer has stopped, remove the bag and drain. Put the shrimp in a bowl with the dressing and mix well. Serve on top of the lettuce rolls with lemon.

Garlicky Mustard Shrimp

Prep + Cook Time: 2 hours 45 minutes | Servings: 2

Ingredients

½ tsp yellow mustard seeds
¼ tsp celery seeds
½ tsp red pepper flakes
½ tsp coriander seeds
½ tsp fennel seeds

¾ cup olive oil
½ cup freshly squeezed lemon juice
4 tbsp rice vinegar
Salt and black pepper to taste
1 bay leaves

1 tbsp Old Bay Seasoning
2 garlic cloves, very thinly sliced
1 pound deveined shrimp
½ yellow onion, cut into thin slices

Directions

Prepare a water bath and place the Sous Vide in it. Set to 149 F.

Heat a saucepan over medium heat and toast the mustard seeds, red pepper flakes, celery, fennel and coriander seeds. Cook until pop. Set aside and allow cooling.

In a canning jar pour the olive oil, lemon juice, toasted spices, black pepper, rice vinegar, bay leaves, garlic cloves and seasoning. Seal and submerge the jars in the water bath. Cook for 30 minutes. Once the timer has stopped, remove the jars and allow cooling for 5 minutes. Transfer to an ice-water bath for cooling. Put in the fridge for 2 hours before serving.

Sweet Chili Shrimp Stir-Fry

Prep + Cook Time: 40 minutes | Servings: 6

Ingredients

1 ½ pound shrimp	6 garlic cloves, smashed	2 tsp sugar
3 dried red chilis	2 tbsp champagne wine	½ tsp cornstarch
1 tbsp grated ginger	1 tbsp soy sauce	3 green onions, chopped

Directions

Prepare a water bath and place the Sous Vide in it. Set to 135 F. Combine the ginger, garlic cloves, chilis, champagne wine, sugar, soy sauce, and cornstarch. Place the peeled shrimp with the mixture in a vacuum-sealable bag. Release air by the water displacement method, seal and submerge in the water bath.

Cook for 30 minutes. Place green onions in a skillet over medium heat. Add in oil and cook for 20 seconds. Once the timer has stopped, remove the cooked shrimp and transfer to a bowl. Garnish with onion. Serve with rice.

Fruity Thai Shrimp

Prep + Cook Time: 25 minutes | Servings: 4

Ingredients

2 pounds shrimp, peeled and deveined	2 shallots, sliced	2 tbsp basil, chopped
4 pieces peeled and chopped papaya	¾ cup cherry tomatoes, halved	¼ cup toasted peanuts

Thai Dressing

¼ cup lime juice	5 tbsp fish sauce	4 small red chili
6 tbsp sugar	4 garlic cloves	

Directions

Prepare a water bath and place the Sous Vide in it. Set to 135 F. Place the shrimp in a vacuum-sealable bag. Release air by the water displacement method, seal, and submerge the bag in the water bath.

Cook for 15 minutes. Combine well in a bowl the lime juice, fish sauce and sugar. Mash the garlic and chilis. Add to the dressing mixture. Once the timer has stopped, remove the shrimp from the bag and transfer to a bowl. Add the papaya, basil, shallots, cherry tomatoes, and peanuts. Glaze with the dressing.

Dublin-Style Lemon Shrimp Dish

Prep + Cook Time: 1 hour 15 minutes | Servings: 4

Ingredients

4 tbsp butter	1 tsp fresh lime zest	½ cup of panko bread crumbs
2 tbsp lime juice	Salt and black pepper to taste	1 tbsp fresh parsley, minced
2 cloves fresh garlic, minced	1 pound jumbo shrimp, deveined	

Directions

Prepare a water bath and place the Sous Vide in it. Set to 135 F.

Heat 3 tbsp of butter in a skillet over medium heat and add in lime juice, salt, pepper, garlic, and zest. Allow cooling for 5 minutes. Place the shrimp and mixture in a vacuum-sealable bag. Release air by the water displacement method, seal, and submerge the bag in the water bath. Cook for 30 minutes.

Meanwhile, heat the butter in a pan over medium and toast the panko breadcrumbs. Once the timer has stopped, remove the shrimp, transfer to a pot over high heat, and cook with the cooking juices. Serve in 4 soup bowls and top with the breadcrumbs.

Juicy Scallops with Chili Garlic Sauce

Prep + Cook Time: 75 minutes | Servings: 2

Ingredients

2 tbsp yellow curry powder
1 tbsp tomato paste
½ cup coconut cream

1 tsp chili garlic sauce
1 tbsp lemon juice
6 scallops

Cooked brown rice, for serving
Fresh cilantro, chopped

Directions

Prepare a water bath and place the Sous Vide in it. Set to 134 F. Combine the coconut cream, tomato paste, curry powder, lime juice, and chili-garlic sauce. Place the mixture with the scallops in a vacuum-sealable bag. Release air by the water displacement method, seal, and submerge the bag in the water bath. Cook for 60 minutes.

Once the timer has stopped, remove the bag and transfer to a plate. Serve the brown rice and top with the scallops. Garnish with cilantro.

Curry Shrimp with Noodles

Prep + Cook Time: 25 minutes | Servings: 2

Ingredients

1 pound shrimp, tail-on
8 oz vermicelli noodles, cooked
1 tsp rice wine

1 tsp curry powder
1 tbsp soy sauce
1 green onion, sliced

2 tbsp vegetable oil

Directions

Prepare a water bath and place the Sous Vide in it. Set to 149 F. Place the shrimp in a vacuum-sealable bag. Release air by the water displacement method, seal, and submerge the bag in the water bath. Cook for 15 minutes.

Heat oil in a pan over medium heat and add in rice wine, curry powder, and soy sauce. Mix well and add the noodles. Once the timer has stopped, remove the shrimp, and transfer to the noodle mix. Top with green onion.

Yummy Cheesy Lobster Risotto

Prep + Cook Time: 55 minutes | Servings: 4

Ingredients

1 tall lobster, shell removed
Salt and black pepper to taste
6 tbsp butter

2½ cups chicken stock
¾ cup Arborio rice
2 tbsp red wine

¼ cup grated Grana Padano cheese
2 minced chives

Directions

Prepare a water bath and place the Sous Vide in it. Set to 138 F. Season the lobster with salt and pepper and place in a vacuum-sealable bag with 3 tbsp of butter. Release air by the water displacement method, seal, and submerge the bag in the water bath. Cook for 25 minutes.

Heat 3 tbsp of butter in a skillet over medium heat and cook the rice. Stir in 1/4 cup of chicken stock. Keep cooking until the stock evaporated. Add 1/4 cup of chicken stock. Repeat the process until the rice is creamy.

Once the timer has stopped, remove the lobster and chop in bites. Add the lobster to the rice. Stir the remaining chicken stock and red wine. Cook until liquid is absorbed. Top with Grana Padano cheese and season with salt and pepper. Garnish with chives and more cheese.

EGGS

Ground Beef Omelet

Prep + Cook Time: 35 minutes | Servings: 3

Ingredients

1 cup lean ground beef
¼ cup finely chopped onions

¼ tsp dried thyme, ground
½ tsp dried oregano, ground

Salt and black pepper to taste
1 tbsp olive oil

Directions :

Preheat the oil in a skillet over medium heat. Add onions and stir-fry for about 3-4 minutes, or until translucent. Add ground beef and cook for 5 minutes, stirring occasionally. Sprinkle with some salt, pepper, thyme, and oregano. Stir well and cook for a minute more. Remove from the heat and set aside.

Prepare a water bath and place the Sous Vide in it. Set to 170 F. Whisk the eggs in a medium bowl and pour in a vacuum-resealable bag. Add beef mixture. Release air by the water displacement method and seal the bag.

Immerse the bag in the water bath and set the timer for 15 minutes. Using a glove, massage the bag every 5 minutes to ensure even cooking. Once the timer stopped, remove the bag from the water bath and transfer the omelet to a serving plate.

Light Vegetarian Frittata

Prep + Cook Time: 1 hour 40 minutes | Servings: 5

Ingredients

1 tbsp olive oil
1 medium onion, chopped
Salt to taste
4 cloves minced garlic
1 daikon, peeled and diced

2 carrots, peeled and diced
1 parsnip, peeled and diced
1 cup butternut squash, peeled and diced
6 oz oyster mushrooms, chopped

¼ cup parsley leaves, freshly minced
A pinch of red pepper flakes
5 large eggs
¼ cup whole milk

Directions

Prepare a water bath and place the Sous Vide in it. Set to 175 F. Grease a few jars with oil. Set aside.

Heat a skillet over high heat with oil. Add the onion sweat for 5 minutes. Add garlic and cook for 30 seconds. Season with salt. Combine carrots, daikon, squash and parsnips. Season with salt and cook 10 minutes more. Add the mushrooms and season with pepper flakes and parsley. Cook for 5 minutes.

In a bowl, whisk the eggs and milk Season with salt. Separate the mixture amongst the jars with the vegetables. Seal and submerge the jars in the bath. Cook for 60 minutes. Once ready, remove the jars. Let cool and serve.

Avocado & Egg Sandwich

Prep + Cook Time: 70 minutes | Servings: 4

Ingredients

8 slices of Bread
4 eggs
1 avocado

1 tsp paprika
4 tsp Hollandaise sauce
1 tbsp chopped parsley

Salt and black pepper to taste

Directions

Prepare a water bath and place the Sous Vide in it. Set to 145 F. Scoop out the avocado flesh and mash it. Stir in sauce and spices. Place the eggs in a vacuum-sealable bag. Release air by the water displacement method, seal, and submerge the bag in the water bath. Set the timer for 1 hour. Once done, immediately place in an ice bath to cool. Peel and slice the eggs. Spread half of the egg slices with the avocado mash and top with egg slices. Top with the remaining bread slices.

Devilled Eggs

Prep + Cook Time: 75 minutes | Servings: 6

Ingredients

6 eggs
Juice from 1 lemon
2 tbsp chopped parsley

1 tomato, minced
2 tbsp minced black olives
1 tbsp yogurt

1 tbsp olive oil
1 tsp mustard
1 tsp chili powder

Directions

Prepare a water bath and place the Sous Vide in it. Set to 170 F. Place the eggs in a vacuum-sealable bag. Release air by the water displacement method, seal, and submerge the bag in the water bath. Set the timer for 1 hour.

Once ready, remove the bag and into an ice bath to cool and peel. Cut in half and scoop out the yolks. Add the remaining ingredients to the yolks and stir to combine. Fill the eggs with the mixture.

Hard-Boiled Eggs

Prep + Cook Time: 1 hour 10 minutes | Servings: 3

Ingredients

3 large eggs

Ice bath

Directions

Make a water bath, place Sous Vide in it, and set to 165 F. Place the eggs in the water bath and set the timer for 1 hour. Once the timer has stopped, transfer the eggs to an ice bath. Peel eggs. Serve as a snack or in salads.

Pickled Eggs

Prep + Cook Time: 2 hours 10 minutes | Servings: 6

Ingredients

6 eggs
1 tbsp peppercorns
Juice from a can of beets

1 cup vinegar
½ tbsp salt
2 garlic cloves

1 bay leaf
¼ cup sugar

Directions

Prepare a water bath and place Sous Vide in it. Set to 170 F.

Carefully lower the eggs into the water and cook for 1 hour. Using a slotted spoon, transfer them to a large bowl with ice cold water and let them cool for a couple of minutes. Peel and place in a 1 quart canister jar with a hinged lid. In a small bowl combine the remaining ingredients. Pour over the eggs, seal and immerse in the bath. Cook for 1 hour. Remove the jar from the water bath and cool to room temperature.

Dill & Turmeric Egg Scramble

Prep + Cook Time: 35 minutes | Servings: 8

Ingredients

8 eggs
1 tbsp turmeric powder

¼ cup dill
1 tsp salt

Pinch of paprika

Directions

Prepare a water bath and place the Sous Vide in it. Set to 165 F.

Beat the eggs in a bowl along with the remaining ingredients. Transfer to a vacuum-sealable bag. Release air by the water displacement method, seal, and submerge the bag in the water bath. Set the timer for 15 minutes. Once the timer has stopped, remove the bag and massage carefully to combine. Cook for another 15 minutes. Remove the bag from the water carefully. Serve warm.

Soft and Chili Eggs

Prep + Cook Time: 60 minutes | Servings: 5

Ingredients

1 tbsp chili powder   5 eggs   Salt and black pepper to taste

Directions

Prepare a water bath and place Sous Vide in it. Set to 147 F. Place eggs in a vacuum-sealable bag. Release air by the water displacement method, seal and submerge in the bath. Cook for 50 minutes. Once the timer has stopped, remove the bag and place them in an ice bath to cool and peel. Sprinkle the eggs with the spices and serve.

Eggs Benedict

Prep + Cook Time: 70 minutes | Servings: 4

Ingredients

4 eggs   5 tbsp Hollandaise sauce   Salt and black pepper to taste
3 ounces bacon, sliced   4 biscuit muffins

Directions

Prepare a water bath and place the Sous Vide in it. Set to 150 F. Place the eggs in a vacuum-sealable bag. Release air by the water displacement method, seal, and submerge the bag in the water bath. Set the timer for 1 hour.

Once the timer has stopped, remove the bag and separate. Peel the eggs and place them on top of the muffins. Drizzle with sauce and sprinkle with salt and pepper. Top with bacon.

Poached Eggs

Prep + Cook Time: 65 minutes | Servings: 4

Ingredients

4 cups water   1 tbsp mayonnaise
4 eggs paprika   Salt and black pepper to taste

Directions

Prepare a water bath and place Sous Vide in it. Set to 145 F. Place eggs in a vacuum-sealable bag. Release air by the water displacement method, seal and submerge bath. Set the timer for 55 minutes.

Once the timer has stopped, remove the bag and transfer to an ice bath to cool and peel. Meanwhile, bring the water to a boil in a saucepan. Lace the peeled eggs inside and cook for a minute. While the eggs are cooking, whisk together the remaining ingredients. Drizzle over the eggs.

Eggs in Bacon

Prep + Cook Time: 7 hours 15 minutes | Servings: 4

Ingredients

4 boiled eggs   7 ounces bacon, sliced   4 ounces mozzarella cheese, sliced
1 tsp butter   1 tbsp Dijon mustard   Salt and black pepper to taste

Directions

Prepare a water bath and place the Sous Vide in it. Set to 140 F. Rub bacon with butter and pepper. Place a slice of mozzarella cheese on top of each egg and wrap the eggs along with the cheese in bacon.

Brush with mustard and place them in a vacuum-sealable bag. Release air by the water displacement method, seal, and submerge the bag in the water bath. Set the timer for 7 hours. Once the timer has stopped, remove the bag and transfer to a plate. Serve warm.

Cherry Tomato Eggs

Prep + Cook Time: 40 minutes | Servings: 6

Ingredients

10 eggs
1 cup cherry tomatoes, halved
2 tbsp sour cream

1 tbsp chives
½ cup milk
½ tsp nutmeg

1 tsp butter
1 tsp salt

Directions

Prepare a water bath and place the Sous Vide in it. Set to 170 F.

Place cherry tomatoes in a large vacuum-sealable bag. Whisk the eggs with the remaining ingredients and pour over the tomatoes. Release air by the water displacement method, seal, and submerge the bag in the water bath. Set the timer for 30 minutes. Once done, remove the bag and transfer to a plate.

Pastrami Scramble

Prep + Cook Time: 25 minutes | Servings: 3

Ingredients

6 eggs
½ cup pastrami

2 tbsp heavy cream
Salt and black pepper to taste

2 tbsp butter, melted
3 slices of toast

Directions

Prepare a water bath and place the Sous Vide in it. Set to 167 F. Whisk together the butter, eggs, cream and spices in a vacuum-sealable bag. Release air by the water displacement method, seal, and submerge the bag in the water bath. Set the timer for 15 minutes. Once the timer has stopped, remove the bag and transfer eggs to a plate. Serve on top of the toast.

Tomato Shakshuka

Prep + Cook Time: 2 hours 10 minutes | Servings: 3

Ingredients

28 ounces canned crushed tomatoes
6 eggs
1 tbsp paprika

2 garlic cloves, minced
Salt and black pepper to taste
2 tsp cumin

¼ cup minced cilantro

Directions

Prepare a water bath and place the Sous Vide in it. Set to 148 F. Place the eggs in a vacuum-sealable bag. Release air by the water displacement method, seal, and submerge the bag in the water bath. Combine the remaining ingredients in another vacuum-sealable bag. Set the timer for 2 hours. Divide the tomato sauce between three bowls. Once the timer has stopped, remove the bag. Peel the eggs and place 2 in each bowl.

Arugula & Prosciutto Omelet

Prep + Cook Time: 25 minutes | Servings: 2

Ingredients

4 thin slices prosciutto
5 large eggs

¼ cup fresh arugula, finely chopped
¼ cup sliced avocado

Salt and black pepper to taste

Directions

Prepare a water bath, place Sous Vide in it, and set to 167 F. Whisk the eggs with arugula, salt, and pepper. Transfer to a vacuum-sealable bag. Press to remove the air and then seal the lid. Cook for 15 minutes. Once the timer has stopped, transfer the omelet to a serving plate and top with avocado slices and prosciutto.

Spinach Omelet

Prep + Cook Time: 20 minutes | Servings: 2

Ingredients

4 large eggs, beaten
¼ cup Greek yogurt

¾ cup fresh spinach, finely chopped
1 tbsp butter

¼ cup cheddar cheese, grated
¼ tsp salt

Directions

Prepare a water bath, place Sous Vide in it, and set to 165 F. Beat the eggs in a medium bowl. Stir in the yogurt, salt, and cheese. Place the mixture into a vacuum resealable bag and seal. Submerge the bag in the water bath. Cook for 10 minutes. Melt butter in a pan over medium heat. Add spinach and cook for 5 minutes. Set aside. Once the timer has stopped, transfer the eggs to a serving plate. Top with spinach and fold the omelet.

Ginger Spring Onion Omelet

Prep + Cook Time: 20 minutes | Servings: 2

Ingredients

8 free-range eggs, beaten
½ cup spring onions

1 tsp ginger, freshly grated
1 tbsp extra-virgin olive oil

Salt and black pepper to taste

Directions

Prepare a water bath, place Sous Vide in it, and set to 165 F. In a bowl, whisk the eggs, ginger, salt, and pepper. Transfer the mixture to a vacuum resealable bag and seal. Submerge the bag in the water bath. Cook for 10 minutes. Heat oil in a saucepan over medium heat. Cook spring onions for 2 minutes. Once the timer has stopped, remove the omelet to a serving plate. Slice thinly, top with onions and fold the omelet to serve.

Leek & Garlic Eggs

Prep + Cook Time: 35 minutes | Servings: 2

Ingredients

2 cups fresh leek, chopped into bite-sized pieces
5 garlic cloves, whole

1 tbsp butter
2 tbsp extra virgin olive oil
4 large eggs

1 tsp salt

Directions

Whisk together eggs, butter, and salt. Transfer to a vacuum-sealable bag and cook in Sous Vide for ten minutes at 165 F. Gently transfer to a plate. Heat the oil in a large skillet over medium heat. Add garlic and chopped leek. Stir-fry for ten minutes. Remove from the heat and use to top eggs.

Spinach & Mushroom Egg Quiche

Prep + Cook Time: 20 minutes | Servings: 2

Ingredients

1 cup Cremini mushrooms, sliced
1 cup fresh spinach, chopped
2 large eggs, beaten

2 tbsp whole milk
1 garlic clove, minced
¼ cup Parmesan cheese, grated

1 tbsp butter
½ tsp salt

Directions

In a large vacuum-sealable bag, place mushrooms, spinach, milk, garlic, and salt. Seal the bag and cook in sous vide for 10 minutes at 180 F. Melt the butter in a saucepan over medium heat. Remove the vegetable mixture from the bag and add to a saucepan. Cook for 1 minute, and then add beaten eggs. Stir well until incorporated and cook until eggs are set. Sprinkle with grated cheese and remove from heat to serve.

APPETIZERS AND SNACKS

Italian Chicken Fingers

Prep + Cook Time: 2 hours 20 minutes | Servings: 3

Ingredients

1 pound chicken breasts
1 cup almond flour
1 tsp minced garlic

1 tsp salt
½ tsp cayenne pepper
2 tsps mixed Italian herbs

¼ tsp black pepper
2 eggs, beaten
¼ cup olive oil

Directions

Rinse the meat under cold running water and pat dry with kitchen paper. Season with mixed Italian herbs and place in a large vacuum-sealable. Seal the bag and cook the chicken in sous vide for 2 hours at 167 F. Remove from the water bath and set aside. Now combine together flour, salt, cayenne, Italian herbs, and pepper in a bowl and set aside. In a separate bowl, beat the eggs and set aside.

Heat olive oil in a large skillet, over medium heat. Dip the chicken into the beaten egg and coat with the flour mixture. Fry for 5 minutes on each side, or until golden brown.

Cherry Chicken Bites

Prep + Cook Time: 1 hour and 40 minutes | Servings: 3

Ingredients

1 pound chicken breast, boneless and skinless, cut into bite-sized pieces
1 red bell pepper, chopped into chunks
1 green bell pepper, chopped into chunks

1 cup cherry tomatoes, whole
1 cup olive oil
1 tsp Italian seasoning mix
1 tsp cayenne pepper

½ tsp dried oregano
Salt and black pepper to taste

Directions

Rinse the meat under cold running water and pat dry with kitchen paper. Cut into bite-sized pieces and set aside. Wash the bell peppers and cut them into chunks. Wash the cherry tomatoes and remove the green stems. Set aside. In a bowl, combine olive oil with Italian seasoning, cayenne, salt, and pepper.

Stir until well incorporated. Add the meat and coat well with the marinade. Set aside for 30 minutes to allow flavors to meld and penetrate into the meat. Place the meat along with vegetables in a large vacuum-sealable bag. Add three tablespoons of the marinade and seal the bag. Cook in sous vide for 1 hour at 149 F.

Herby Italian Sausage Pannini

Prep + Cook Time: 3 hours 15 minutes | Servings: 4

Ingredients

1 pound Italian sausage
1 red bell pepper, sliced
1 yellow bell pepper, sliced
1 onion, sliced

1 garlic clove, minced
1 cup tomato juice
1 tsp dried oregano
1 tsp dried basil

1 tsp olive oil
Salt and black pepper to taste
4 bread slices

Directions

Prepare a water bath and place the Sous Vide in it. Set to 138 F. Place the sausages in a vacuum-sealable bag. Add the garlic, basil, onion, pepper, tomato juice, and oregano in each bag. Release air by the water displacement method, seal and submerge the bags in the water bath. Cook for 3 hours.

Once the timer has stopped, remove the sausages and transfer to a hot skillet. Fry them for 1 minute per side. Set aside. Add the remaining ingredients in the skillet, season with salt and pepper. Cook until water has evaporated. Serve the sausages and the remaining ingredients in between the bread.

Cinnamon Persimmon Toast

Prep + Cook Time: 4 hours 10 minutes | Servings: 6

Ingredients

4 Bread Slices, toasted
4 Persimmons, chopped

3 tbsp Sugar
½ tsp Cinnamon

2 tbsp Orange Juice
½ tsp Vanilla Extract

Directions

Prepare a water bath and place the Sous Vide in it. Set to 155 F.

Place persimmons in a vacuum-sealable bag. Add in orange juice, vanilla extract, sugar, and cinnamon. Close the bag and shake well to coat the persimmon pieces. Release air by the water displacement method, seal, and submerge the bag in the water bath. Set the timer for 4 hours. Once the timer has stopped, remove the bag and transfer the persimmons to a food processor. Blend until smooth. Spread the persimmon mixture over bread.

Chicken Wings with Ginger

Prep + Cook Time: 2 hours 25 minutes | Servings: 4

Ingredients

2 pounds chicken wings
¼ cup extra virgin olive oil
4 garlic cloves
1 tbsp rosemary leaves, finely chopped

1 tsp white pepper
1 tsp cayenne pepper
1 tbsp fresh thyme, finely chopped
1 tbsp fresh ginger, grated

¼ cup lime juice
½ cup apple cider vinegar

Directions

In a large bowl, combine olive oil with garlic, rosemary, white pepper, cayenne pepper, thyme, ginger, lime juice, and apple cider vinegar. Submerge wings in this mixture and cover. Refrigerate for one hour. Transfer the wings along with the marinade in a large vacuum-sealable bag. Seal the bag and cook in sous vide for 1 hour and 15 minutes at 149 F. Remove from the vacuum-sealable bag and brown before serving. Serve and enjoy!

Beef Patties

Prep + Cook Time: 1 hour 55 minutes | Servings: 4

Ingredients

1 pound lean ground beef
1 egg
2 tbsp almonds, finely chopped

2 tbsp almond flour
1 cup onions, finely chopped
2 garlic cloves, crushed

¼ cup olive oil
Salt and black pepper to taste
¼ cup parsley leaves, finely chopped

Directions

In a bowl, combine ground beef with finely chopped onions, garlic, oil, salt, pepper, parsley, and almonds. Mix well with a fork and gradually add some almond flour. Whisk in one egg and refrigerate for 40 minutes. Remove the meat from the refrigerator and gently form into one-inch-thick patties, about 4-inches in diameter. Place in a two separate vacuum-sealable bags and cook in sous vide for one hour at 129 F.

Carrots & Nuts Stuffed Peppers

Prep + Cook Time: 2 hours 35 minutes | Servings: 5

Ingredients

4 shallots, chopped
4 carrots, chopped
4 garlic cloves, minced
1 cup raw cashews, soaked and drained
1 cup pecans, soaked and drained

1 tbsp balsamic vinegar
1 tbsp soy sauce
1 tbsp ground cumin
2 tsp paprika
1 tsp garlic powder

1 pinch cayenne pepper
4 fresh thyme sprigs
Zest of 1 lemon
4 bell peppers, tops cut off and seeded

Directions

Prepare a water bath and place the Sous Vide in it. Set to 186 F. In a blender, pulse the carrots, garlic, shallots, cashews, pecans, balsamic vinegar, soy sauce, cumin, paprika, garlic powder, cayenne, thyme, and lemon zest.

Pour the mixture into the bell peppers shells and place in a vacuum-sealable bag. Release air by the water displacement method, seal, and submerge the bag in the water bath. Cook for 1 hour and 15 minutes. Once the timer has stopped, remove the peppers and transfer to a plate.

Easy Spiced Hummus

Prep + Cook Time: 3 hours 35 minutes | Servings: 6

Ingredients

1 ½ cups dried chickpeas, soaked overnight
2 quarts water
¼ cup lemon juice

¼ cup tahini paste
2 garlic cloves, minced
2 tbsp olive oil
½ tsp caraway seeds

½ tsp salt
1 tsp cayenne pepper

Directions

Prepare a water bath and place the Sous Vide in it. Set to 196 F.

Strain the chickpeas and place in a vacuum-sealable bag with 1 quart of water. Release air by the water displacement method, seal, and submerge the bag in the water bath. Cook for 3 hours. Once the timer has stopped, remove the bag and transfer into an ice water bath and allow to chill.

In a blender, mix the lemon juice and tahini paste for 90 seconds. Add in garlic, olive oil, caraway seeds, and salt, mix for 30 seconds until smooth. Remove the chickpeas and drain it.

For a smoother hummus, peel the chickpeas. In a food processor, combine the half of chickpeas with the tahini mix and blend for 90 seconds. Add the remaining chickpeas and blend until smooth. Put the mixture in a plate and garnish with cayenne pepper and the reserved chickpeas.

Green Pea Dip

Prep + Cook Time: 45 minutes | Servings: 8

Ingredients

2 cups green peas
3 tbsp heavy cream

1 tbsp tarragon
1 tsp olive oil

Salt and black pepper to taste
¼ cup diced apple

Directions

Prepare a water bath and place the Sous Vide in it. Set to 185 F. Place all the ingredients in a vacuum-sealable bag. Release air by the water displacement method, seal, and submerge the bag in the water bath. Set the timer for 32 minutes. Once the timer has stopped, remove the bag and blend with a hand blender until smooth.

Mustard Drumsticks

Prep + Cook Time: 1 hour | Servings: 5

Ingredients

2 pounds chicken drumsticks
¼ cup Dijon mustard

2 garlic cloves, crushed
2 tbsp coconut aminos

1 tsp pink Himalayan salt
½ tsp black pepper

Directions

In a small bowl, combine Dijon with crushed garlic, coconut aminos, salt, and pepper. Spread the mixture over the meat with a kitchen brush and place in a large vacuum-sealable bag. Seal the bag and cook in sous vide for 45 minutes at 167 F. Serve and enjoy!

French Fries

Prep + Cook Time: 45 | Servings: 6

Ingredients

3 pounds potatoes, sliced
5 cups water

Salt and black pepper to taste
¼ tsp baking soda

Directions

Prepare a water bath and place the Sous Vide in it. Set to 195 F. Place the potato slices, water, salt, and baking soda in a vacuum-sealable bag. Release air by the water displacement method, seal, and submerge the bag in the water bath. Set the timer for 25 minutes.

Meanwhile, heat the oil in a saucepan over medium heat. Once the timer has stopped, remove the potato slices from the brine and pat dry them. Cook in the oil for a few minutes, until golden.

Stuffed Collard Greens

Prep + Cook Time: 65 minutes | Servings: 3

Ingredients

1 pound collard greens, steamed
1 pound lean ground beef

1 small onion, finely chopped
1 tbsp olive oil

Salt and black pepper to taste
1 tsp fresh mint, finely chopped

Directions

Boil a large pot of water and add in greens. Briefly cook, for 2-3 minutes. Drain and gently squeeze the greens and set aside. In a large bowl, combine ground beef, onion, oil, salt, pepper, and mint. Stir well until incorporated.

Place leaves on your work surface, vein side up. Use one tablespoon of the meat mixture and place it in the bottom center of each leaf. Fold the sides over and roll up tightly. Tuck in the sides and gently transfer to a large vacuum-sealable bag. Seal the bag and cook in sous vide for 45 minutes at 167 F.

Lemon & Garlick Artichokes

Prep + Cook Time: 2 hours 15 minutes | Servings: 4

Ingredients

1 lb Artichoke hearts
Juice from 3 Lemons

1 tbsp Mustard
5 Garlic Cloves, minced

1 tbsp minced Green Onion
4 tbsp Olive Oil

Directions

Prepare a water bath and place the Sous Vide in it. Set to 195 F. Place the artichokes in a plastic bowl. Add the remaining ingredients and shake to coat. Place all the mixture in a plastic bag. Seal and submerge the bag in the bath. Set the timer for 2 hours. Once the timer has stopped, cook the artichoke on the grill for a minute per side.

Ginger Balls

Prep + Cook Time: 1 hour 30 minutes | Servings: 3

Ingredients

1 pound ground beef
1 cup onions, finely chopped
3 tbsp olive oil

¼ cup fresh cilantro, finely chopped
¼ cup fresh mint, finely chopped
2 tsp ginger paste

1 tsp cayenne pepper
Salt to taste

Directions

In a large bowl, combine ground beef, onions, olive oil, cilantro, mint, cilantro, ginger paste, cayenne pepper, and salt. Mold patties and refrigerate for 15 minutes. Remove from the refrigerator and transfer to separate vacuum-sealable bags. Cook in Sous Vide for 1 hour at 154 F. Serve and enjoy!

Sweet Tofu Kebabs with Veggies

Prep + Cook Time: 65 minutes | Servings: 6

Ingredients

1 zucchini, sliced
1 eggplant, sliced
1 yellow bell pepper, chopped

1 red bell pepper, chopped
1 green bell pepper, chopped
16 ounces tofu cheese

¼ cup olive oil
1 tsp honey
Salt and black pepper to taste

Directions

Prepare a water bath and place the Sous Vide in it. Set to 186 F.

Place the zucchini and eggplant in a vacuum-sealable bag. Place the bell pepper chunks in a vacuum-sealable bag. Release air by the water displacement method, seal and submerge the bags in the water bath. Cook for 45 minutes. After 10 minutes, heat a skillet over medium heat.

Strain the tofu and pat dry. Chop into cubes. Brush with olive oil and transfer to the skillet and sear until golden brown on each side. Transfer into a bowl, pour in honey and cover. Allow to chill. Once the timer has stopped, remove the bags and transfer all the contents into a bowl. Season with salt and pepper. Discard cooking juices. Place the veggies and tofu, alternating, into the kebabs.

Onion & Bacon Muffins

Prep + Cook Time: 3 hours 45 minutes | Servings: 5

Ingredients

1 onion, chopped
6 ounces bacon, chopped
1 cup flour

4 tbsp butter, melted
1 egg
1 tsp baking soda

1 tbsp vinegar
¼ tsp salt

Directions

Prepare a water bath and place the Sous Vide in it. Set to 196 F.

Meanwhile, in a skillet over medium heat, cook the bacon until crispy. Transfer to a bowl and add the onion to the bacon grease and cook for 3 minutes until soft.

Transfer to a bowl and stir in the remaining ingredients. Divide the muffin batter into 5 small jars. Make sure not to fill more than halfway. Place the jars into a water bath and set the timer for 3 hours and 30 minutes. Once the timer stopped, remove the jars and serve.

Tarragon Asparagus Mix

Prep + Cook Time: 25 minutes | Servings: 3

Ingredients

1 ½ lb medium asparagus
5 tbsp butter
2 tbsp lemon juice

½ tsp lemon zest
1 tbsp chives, sliced
1 tbsp parsley, chopped

1 tbsp + 1 tbsp fresh dill, chopped
1 tbsp + 1 tbsp tarragon, chopped

Directions

Make a water bath, place the Sous Vide in it, and set to 183 F. Cut off and discard the tight bottoms of the asparagus. Place the asparagus in a vacuum-sealable bag. Release air by the water displacement method, seal and submerge in the water bath and set the timer for 10 minutes.

Once the timer has stopped, remove the bag and unseal. Place a skillet over low heat, add in butter and steamed asparagus. Season with salt and pepper and toss continually. Add lemon juice and zest and cook for 2 minutes. Turn heat off and add parsley, 1 tablespoon of dill, and 1 tablespoon of tarragon. Toss evenly. Garnish with remaining dill and tarragon. Serve warm as a side dish.

Cod Bite Balls

Prep + Cook Time: 105 minutes | Servings: 5

Ingredients

12 ounces minced cod
2 ounces bread
1 tbsp butter

¼ cup flour
1 tbsp semolina
2 tbsp water

1 tbsp minced garlic
Salt and black pepper to taste
¼ tsp paprika

Directions

Prepare a water bath and place the Sous Vide in it. Set to 125 F. Combine the bread and water and mash the mixture. Add in the remaining ingredients and mix well to combine. Make balls out of the mixture.

Spray a skillet with cooking spray and cook the bite balls over medium heat for about 15 seconds per side until lightly toasted. Place the cod bites in a vacuum-sealable bag. Release air by the water displacement method, seal, and submerge the bag in the water bath. Set the timer for 1 hour and 30 minutes. Once the timer has stopped, remove the bag and plate the cod bites. Serve.

Panko Yolk Croquettes

Prep + Cook Time: 60 minutes | Servings: 5

Ingredients

2 eggs plus 5 yolks
1 cup panko breadcrumbs
3 tbsp olive oil

5 tbsp flour
¼ tsp Italian seasoning
½ tsp salt

¼ tsp paprika

Directions

Prepare a water bath and place the Sous Vide in it. Set to 150 F. Place the yolk inside the water (without a bag or glass) and cook for 45 minutes, turning over halfway through. Let cool slightly. Beat the eggs along with the other ingredients, except the oil. Dip the yolks in the egg and panko mixture. Heat the oil in a skillet. Fry the yolks for a few minutes per side, until golden.

Chili Hummus

Prep + Cook Time: 4 hours 15 minutes | Servings: 9

Ingredients

16 ounces chickpeas, soaked overnight
2 garlic cloves, minced
1 tsp sriracha

¼ tsp chili powder
½ tsp chili flakes
½ cup olive oil

1 tbsp salt
6 cups water

Directions

Prepare a water bath and place the Sous Vide in it. Set to 195 F. Place the chickpeas and water in a plastic bag. Release air by the water displacement method, seal, and submerge the bag in the water bath. Set the timer for 4 hours. Once the timer has stopped, remove the bag, drain the water and transfer the chickpeas to a food processor. Add in the remaining ingredients. Blend until smooth.

Turkey Salad with Cucumber

Prep + Cook Time: 2 hours 20 minutes | Servings: 3

Ingredients

1 pound turkey breasts, sliced
½ cup chicken broth
2 garlic cloves, minced
2 tbsp olive oil

1 tsp salt
¼ tsp Cayenne pepper
2 bay leaves
1 medium-sized tomato, chopped

1 large red bell pepper, chopped
1 medium-sized cucumber
½ tsp Italian seasoning

Directions

Season turkey with salt and cayenne pepper. Place in a vacuum-sealable along with chicken broth, garlic, and bay leaves. Seal the bag and cook in Sous Vide for 2 hours at 167 F. Remove and set aside. Place the vegetables in a large bowl and add turkey. Mix with Italian seasoning and olive oil. Toss well to combine and serve immediately.

Eggplant Rounds with Pistachios

Prep + Cook Time: 8 hours 10 minutes | Servings: 8

Ingredients

3 eggplants, sliced
¼ cup crushed pistachios
1 tbsp miso

1 tbsp mirin
2 tsp olive oil
1 tsp chives

Salt and black pepper to taste

Directions

Prepare a water bath and place the Sous Vide in it. Set to 185 F.

Whisk together the oil, mirin, chives, miso, and pepper. Brush the eggplant slices with the mixture. Arrange some eggplant slices on in a single layer in a vacuum-sealable bag and top with pistachios. Repeat the process until you use all of the ingredients. Release air by the water displacement method, seal, and submerge the bag in the water bath. Set the timer for 8 hours. Once the timer has stopped, remove the bag and plate.

Creamy Artichoke Dip

Prep + Cook Time: 1 hour 45 minutes | Servings: 6

Ingredients

2 tbsp butter
2 onions, quartered
3 cloves garlic, minced

15 oz artichoke hearts, chopped
18 oz frozen spinach, thawed
5 oz green chilies

3 tbsp mayonnaise
3 tbsp whipped cream cheese

Directions

Make a water bath, place Sous Vide in it, and to 181 F. Divide onions, garlic, artichoke hearts, spinach, and green chilies into 2 vacuum-sealable bags. Release air by the water displacement method, seal and submerge the bags in the water bath. Set the timer for 30 minutes to cook.

Once the timer has stopped, remove and unseal the bags. Puree the ingredients using a blender. Place a pan over medium heat and add in butter. Put in vegetable puree, lemon juice, mayonnaise, and cream cheese. Season with salt and pepper. Stir and cook for 3 minutes. Serve warm with vegetable strips.

"Eat-me" Fruity Chorizo

Prep + Cook Time: 75 minutes | Servings: 4

Ingredients

2½ cups seedless white grapes, stems removed
1 tbsp fresh rosemary, chopped
2 tbsp butter

4 chorizo sausages
2 tbsp balsamic vinegar

Salt and black pepper to taste

Directions

Prepare a water bath and place the Sous Vide in it. Set to 165 F. Place the butter, white grapes, rosemary and chorizo in a vacuum-sealable bag. Shake well. Release air by the water displacement method, seal, and submerge the bag in the water bath. Cook for 60 minutes.

Once the timer has stopped, transfer the chorizo mix to a plate. In a preheated saucepan, pour the cooking liquids along with grapes and balsamic vinegar. Stir for 3 minutes. Top chorizo with grape sauce.

Radish Cheese Dip

Prep + Cook Time: 1 hour 15 minutes | Servings: 4

Ingredients

30 radishes, green leaves removed
1 tbsp Chardonnay vinegar

Sugar to taste
1 cup water for steaming

1 tbsp grapeseed oil
12 oz cream cheese

Directions

Make a water bath, place Sous Vide in it, and set to 183 F. Put the radishes, salt, pepper, water, sugar, and vinegar in a vacuum-sealable bag. Release air from the bag, seal and submerge in the water bath. Cook for 1 hour. Once the timer has stopped, remove the bag, unseal and transfer the radishes with a little steaming water into a blender. Add cream cheese and puree to get a smooth paste. Serve.

Celery Dip

Prep + Cook Time: 50 minutes | Servings: 3

Ingredients

½ lb celery root, sliced
1 cup heavy cream

3 tbsp butter
1 tbsp lemon juice

Salt to taste

Directions

Make a water bath, place Sous Vide in it, and set to 183 F. Place celery, heavy cream, lemon juice, butter, and salt in a vacuum-sealable bag. Release air from the bag, seal and submerge in the bath. Cook for 40 minutes. Once the timer has stopped, remove and unseal the bag. Puree the ingredients using a blender. Serve.

Chicken & Mushrooms in Marsala Sauce

Prep + Cook Time: 2 hours 25 minutes | Servings: 2

Ingredients

2 chicken breasts
1 cup Marsala wine
1 cup chicken broth

14 ounces mushrooms, sliced
½ tbsp flour
1 tbsp butter

Salt and black pepper to taste
2 garlic cloves, minced
1 shallot, minced

Directions

Prepare a water bath and place the Sous Vide in it. Set to 140 F. Season the chicken with salt and pepper and place in a vacuum-sealable bag along with the mushrooms. Release air by the water displacement method, seal and submerge in the water bath. Cook for 2 hours.

Once the timer has stopped, remove the bag. Melt the butter in a pan over medium heat, whisk in the flour and the remaining ingredients. Cook until the sauce thickens. Add chicken and cook for 1 minute.

White Wine Mussels

Prep + Cook Time: 1 hour 20 minutes | Servings: 3

Ingredients

1 pound fresh mussels
3 tbsp extra virgin olive oil
1 cup onions, finely chopped

¼ cup fresh parsley, finely chopped
3 tbsp fresh thyme, chopped
1 tbsp lemon zest

1 cup dry white wine

Directions

Heat the oil in a medium-sized skillet over medium heat. Add onions and stir-fry until translucent, 3 minutes. Add lemon zest, parsley, and thyme. Give it a good stir and transfer to a vacuum-sealable bag. Add mussels and one cup of dry white wine. Seal the bag and cook in Sous Vide for 40 minutes at 104 F. Serve and enjoy!

Scallops with Bacon

Prep + Cook Time: 50 minutes | Servings: 6

Ingredients

10 ounces scallops
3 ounces bacon, sliced

½ onion, grated
½ tsp white pepper

1 tbsp olive oil

Directions

Prepare a water bath and place the Sous Vide in it. Set to 140 F.

Top the scallops with the grated onion and wrap with bacon slices. Sprinkle with white pepper and drizzle with oil. Place in a plastic bag. Release air by the water displacement method, seal, and submerge the bag in the water bath. Set the timer for 35 minutes. Once the timer has stopped, remove the bag. Serve.

Chicken Liver Spread

Prep + Cook Time: 5 hours 15 minutes | Servings: 8

Ingredients

1 pound chicken liver
6 eggs
8 ounces bacon, minced

2 tbsp soy sauce
3 ounces shallot, chopped
3 tbsp vinegar

Salt and black pepper to taste
4 tbsp butter
½ tsp paprika

Directions

Prepare a water bath and place the Sous Vide in it. Set to 156 F.

Cook the bacon in a skillet over medium heat, add shallots and cook for 3 minutes. Stir in the soy sauce and vinegar. Transfer to a blender along with the remaining ingredients. Blend until smooth. Place all the ingredients in a mason jar and seal. Cook for 5 hours. Once the timer has stopped, remove the jar and serve.

Sweet & Spicy Duck

Prep + Cook Time: 70 minutes | Servings: 4

Ingredients

1 pound duck breast
1 tsp thyme
1 tsp oregano

2 tbsp honey
½ tsp chili powder
½ tsp paprika

1 tsp garlic salt
1 tbsp sesame oil

Directions

Prepare a water bath and place the Sous Vide in it. Set to 158 F.

Whisk together the honey, oil, spices and herbs. Brush the duck with the mixture and place in a vacuum-sealable bag. Release air by the water displacement method, seal, and submerge the bag in the water bath. Set the timer for 60 minutes. Once the timer has stopped, remove the bag and slice the duck breast. Serve warm.

Glazed Baby Carrots

Prep + Cook Time: 3 hours 10 minutes | Servings: 4

Ingredients

1 cup baby carrots
4 tbsp brown sugar

1 cup chopped shallot
1 tbsp butter

Salt and black pepper to taste
1 tbsp dill

Directions

Prepare a water bath and place Sous Vide in it. Set to 165 F. Place all the ingredients in a vacuum-sealable bag. Shake to coat. Release air by the water displacement method, seal and submerge in the water bath. Set the timer for 3 hours. Once the timer has stopped, remove the bag. Serve warm.

Tamari Corn on The Cob

Prep + Cook Time: 3 hours 15 minutes | Servings: 8

Ingredients

1 pound corn on cob
1 tbsp butter

¼ cup tamari sauce
2 tbsp miso paste

1 tsp salt

Directions

Prepare a water bath and place the Sous Vide in it. Set to 185 F.

Whisk together the tamari, butter, miso, and salt. Place the corn in a plastic bag and pour the mixture over. Shake to coat. Release air by the water displacement method, seal, and submerge the bag in the water bath. Set the timer for 3 hours. Once the timer has stopped, remove the bag. Serve warm.

Shrimp Appetizer

Prep + Cook Time: 75 minutes | Servings: 8

Ingredients

1 pound shrimps
3 tbsp sesame oil

3 tbsp lemon juice
½ cup parsley

Salt and white pepper to taste

Directions

Prepare a water bath and place the Sous Vide in it. Set to 140 F.

Place all ingredients in a vacuum-sealable bag. Shake to coat the shrimp well. Release air by the water displacement method, seal, and submerge the bag in the water bath. Set the timer for 1 hour. Once the timer has stopped, remove the bag. Serve warm.

Gingery Squash Veggies

Prep + Cook Time: 70 minutes | Servings: 8

Ingredients

14 ounces butternut squash
1 tbsp grated ginger

1 tsp butter, melted
1 tsp lemon juice

Salt and black pepper to taste
¼ tsp turmeric

Directions

Prepare a water bath and place the Sous Vide in it. Set to 185 F.

Peel and slice the squash into wedges. Place all the ingredients in a vacuum-sealable bag. Shake to coat well. Release air by the water displacement method, seal, and submerge the bag in the water bath. Set the timer for 55 minutes. Once the timer has stopped, remove the bag. Serve warm.

Lobster Tails

Prep + Cook Time: 50 minutes | Servings: 6

Ingredients

1 pound lobster tails, peeled
½ lemon

½ tsp garlic powder
¼ tsp onion powder

1 tbsp rosemary
1 tsp olive oil

Directions

Prepare a water bath and place the Sous Vide in it. Set to 140 F.

Season lobster with garlic and onion powder. Place in a vacuum-sealable bag. Add the rest of the ingredients and shake to coat. Release air by the water displacement method, seal, and submerge the bag in the water bath. Set the timer for 40 minutes. Once the timer has stopped, remove the bag. Serve warm.

BBQ Tofu

Prep + Cook Time: 2 hours 15 minutes | Servings: 8

Ingredients

15 ounces tofu
3 tbsp barbecue sauce

2 tbsp tamari sauce
1 tsp onion powder

1 tsp salt

Directions

Prepare a water bath and place the Sous Vide in it. Set to 180 F.

Cut the tofu into cubes. Place it in a plastic bag. Release air by the water displacement method, seal, and submerge the bag in the water bath. Set the timer for 2 hours. Once the timer has stopped, remove the bag and transfer to a bowl. Add the remaining ingredients and toss to combine.

Tasty French Toast

Prep + Cook Time: 100 minutes | Servings: 2

Ingredients

2 eggs
4 bread slices

½ cup milk
½ tsp cinnamon

1 tbsp butter, melted

Directions

Prepare a water bath and place the Sous Vide in it. Set to 150 F.

Whisk together the eggs, milk, butter and cinnamon. Place the bread slices in a vacuum-sealable bag and pour the egg mixture over. Shake to coat well. Release air by the water displacement method, seal, and submerge the bag in the water bath. Set the timer to 1 hour and 25 minutes. Once the timer has stopped, remove the bag. Serve.

Milky Mashed Potatoes with Rosemary

Prep + Cook Time: 1 hour 45 minutes | Servings: 4

Ingredients

2 pounds red potatoes
5 garlic cloves

8 oz butter
1 cup whole milk

3 sprigs rosemary
Salt and white pepper to taste

Directions

Prepare a water bath and place the Sous Vide in it. Set to 193 F. Wash the potatoes and peel them and slice. Take the garlic, peel and mash them. Combine the potatoes, garlic, butter, salt, and rosemary. Place in a vacuum-sealable bag. Release air by the water displacement method, seal, and submerge the bag in the water bath.

Cook for 1 hour and 30 minutes. Once the timer has stopped, remove the bag and transfer into a bowl and mash them. Stir the blended butter and milk. Season with salt and pepper. Top with rosemary and serve.

Sous Vide Pickled Rhubarb

Prep + Cook Time: 40 minutes | Servings: 8

Ingredients

2 pounds rhubarb, sliced
7 tbsp apple cider vinegar

1 tbsp brown sugar
¼ celery stalk, minced

¼ tsp salt

Directions

Prepare a water bath and place the Sous Vide in it. Set to 180 F. Place all the ingredients in a vacuum-sealable bag. Shake to coat well. Release air by the water displacement method, seal, and submerge the bag in the water bath.Cook for 25 minutes. Once the timer has stopped, remove the bag. Serve warm.

Hot Chicken Wings

Prep + Cook Time: 4 hours 15 minutes | Servings: 4

Ingredients

2 pound chicken wings
½ butter stick, melted

¼ cup hot red sauce
½ tsp salt

Directions

Prepare a water bath and place Sous Vide in it. Set to 170 F. Season chicken with salt and place in 2 vacuum-sealable bags. Release air by the water displacement method, seal and submerge in bath. Cook for 4 hours. Once done, remove the bags. Whisk the sauce and butter. Toss the wings with the mixture.

Sweet Thighs with Sun-Dried Tomatoes

Prep + Cook Time: 75 minutes | Servings: 7

Ingredients

2 pounds chicken thighs
3 ounces sun-dried tomatoes, chopped
1 yellow onion, chopped

1 tsp rosemary
1 tbsp sugar
2 tbsp olive oil

1 egg, beaten

Directions

Prepare a water bath and place the Sous Vide in it. Set to 149 F. Combine all the ingredients in a vacuum-sealable bag and shake to coat well. Release air by the water displacement method, seal, and submerge the bag in the water bath. Set the timer for 63 minutes. Once the timer has stopped, remove the bag and serve as desired.

Dijon Chicken Filets

Prep + Cook Time: 65 minutes | Servings: 4

Ingredients

1 pound chicken filets
3 tbsp Dijon mustard
2 onions, grated
2 tbsp cornstarch

½ cup milk
1 tbsp lemon zest
1 tsp thyme
1 tsp oregano

Garlic salt and black pepper to taste
1 tbsp olive oil

Directions

Prepare a water bath and place the Sous Vide in it. Set to 146 F. Whisk together all the ingredients and place in a vacuum-sealable bag. Release air by the water displacement method, seal, and submerge the bag in the water bath. Set the timer for 45 minutes. Once the timer has stopped, remove the bag and transfer to a saucepan and cook over medium heat for 10 minutes.

Adobo Chicken

Prep + Cook Time: 4 hours 25 minutes | Servings: 6

Ingredients

2 pounds chicken thighs
3 tbsp peppercorns

1 cup chicken stock
½ cup soy sauce

2 tbsp vinegar
1 tbsp garlic powder

Directions

Prepare a water bath and place the Sous Vide in it. Set to 155 F.

Place the chicken, soy sauce and garlic powder in a vacuum-sealable bag. Release air by the water displacement method, seal, and submerge the bag in the water bath. Set the timer for 4 hours. Once the timer has stopped, remove the bag and place in a saucepan. Add the remaining ingredients. Cook for 15 more minutes.

Bacon-Wrapped Turkey Leg

Prep + Cook Time: 6 hours 15 minutes | Servings: 5

Ingredients

14 ounces turkey leg
5 ounces bacon, sliced
½ tsp chili flakes

2 tsp olive oil
1 tbsp sour cream
½ tsp oregano

½ tsp paprika
¼ lemon, sliced

Directions

Prepare a water bath and place the Sous Vide in it. Set to 160 F. Combine in a bowl the herbs and spices with the sour cream and brush over the turkey. Wrap in bacon and drizzle with olive oil. Place in a vacuum-sealable bag along with lemon. Release air by the water displacement method, seal, and submerge the bag in the water bath. Set timer for 6 hours. Once the timer has stopped, remove the bag and slice. Serve warm.

Mexican Butter Corn

Prep + Cook Time: 40 minutes | Servings: 2

Ingredients

2 ears of corn, shucked
2 tbsp cold butter
Salt and black pepper to taste

¼ cup mayonnaise
½ tbsp Mexican style chili powder
½ tsp grated lime zest

¼ cup crumbled feta cheese
¼ cup chopped, fresh cilantro
Lime wedges for serving

Directions

Prepare a water bath and place the Sous Vide in it. Set to 183 F. Place the corn ears and butter in a vacuum-sealable bag. Season with salt and pepper. Release air by the water displacement method, seal, and submerge the bag in the water bath. Cook for 30 minutes. Once the timer has stopped, remove the corn. In a bowl, mix the mayo, lime zest, feta, and chili powder. Top the corn ears with mayonnaise mix and serve.

Vanilla Apricots with Whiskey

Prep + Cook Time: 45 minutes | Servings: 4

Ingredients

2 apricots, pitted and quartered
½ cup rye whiskey

½ cup ultrafine sugar
1 tsp vanilla extract

Salt to taste

Directions

Prepare a water bath and place Sous Vide in it. Set to 182 F. Place all ingredients in a vacuum-sealable bag. Release air by the water displacement method, seal and submerge in the water bath. Cook for 30 minutes. Once the timer has stopped, remove the bag and transfer into an ice bath.

Kaffir Lime Drumsticks

Prep + Cook Time: 80 minutes | Servings: 7

Ingredients

16 ounces chicken drumsticks
2 tbsp cilantro leaves
1 tsp dried mint

1 tsp thyme
Salt and white pepper to taste
1 tbsp olive oil

1 tbsp chopped Kaffir lime leaves

Directions

Prepare a water bath and place the Sous Vide in it. Set to 153 F. Place all the ingredients in a vacuum-sealable bag. Massage to coat the chicken well. Release air by the water displacement method, seal, and submerge the bag in the water bath. Set the timer for 70 minutes. Once done, remove the bag. Serve warm.

Orange Duck with Paprika & Thyme

Prep + Cook Time: 15 hours 10 minutes | Servings: 4

Ingredients

16 ounces duck legs	1 tsp salt	2 tsp sesame oil
1 tsp orange zest	1 tsp sugar	½ tsp paprika
2 tbsp Kaffir leaves	1 tbsp orange juice	½ tsp thyme

Directions

Prepare a water bath and place the Sous Vide in it. Set to 160 F. Dump all the ingredients in a vacuum-sealable bag. Massage to combine well. Release air by the water displacement method, seal, and submerge the bag in the water bath. Set the timer for 15 hours. Once the timer has stopped, remove the bag. Serve warm.

Spicy Cauliflower Steaks

Prep + Cook Time: 35 minutes | Servings: 5

Ingredients

1 pound cauliflower, sliced	½ tsp garlic powder	1 tbsp heavy
1 tbsp turmeric	1 tsp sriracha	2 tbsp butter
1 tsp chili powder	1 tbsp chipotle	

Directions

Prepare a water bath and place the Sous Vide in it. Set to 185 F. Whisk together all of the ingredients, except cauliflower. Brush the cauliflower steaks with the mixture. Place them in a vacuum-sealable bag. Release air by the water displacement method, seal, and submerge the bag in the water bath. Set the timer for 18 minutes. Once the timer has stopped, remove the bag and preheat your grill and cook the steaks for a minute per side.

Cayenne Potato Strips with Mayo Dressing

Prep + Cook Time: 1 hour 50 minutes | Servings: 6

Ingredients

2 large gold potatoes, cut into strips	1 tsp paprika	¾ cup vegetable oil
Salt and black pepper to taste	½ tsp cayenne pepper	Salt and black pepper to taste
1 ½ tbsp olive oil	1 egg yolk	
1 tsp thyme	2 tbsp cider vinegar	

Directions

Prepare a water bath and place the Sous Vide in it. Set to 186 F. Place the potatoes with a pinch of salt in a vacuum-sealable bag. Release air by the water displacement method, seal and submerge in the water bath.

Cook for 1 hour and 30 minutes. Once the timer has stopped, remove the potatoes and pat dry with kitchen towels. Discard cooking juices. Heat oil in a pan over medium heat. Add in fries and sprinkle with paprika, cayenne, thyme, black pepper, and salt. Stir for 7 minutes until the potatoes turn golden brown on all sides.

To make the mayo: mix well the egg yolk and half of the vinegar. Slowly, pour in vegetable oil while stirring until smooth. Add the remaining vinegar. Season with salt and pepper and mix well. Serve with fries.

Cheesy Pears with Walnuts

Prep + Cook Time: 55 minutes | Servings: 2

Ingredients

1 pear, sliced	4 tbsp shaved Grana Padano cheese	2 tbsp lemon juice
1 pound honey	2 cups rocket leaves	2 tbsp olive oil
½ cup walnuts	Salt and black pepper to taste	

Directions

Prepare a water bath and place the Sous Vide in it. Set to 158 F. Combine the honey and pears. Place in a vacuum-sealable bag. Release air by the water displacement method, seal, and submerge the bag in the water bath. Cook for 45 minutes. Once the timer has stopped, remove the bag and transfer into a bowl. Top with the dressing.

Nutty Baked Sweet Potatoes

Prep + Cook Time: 3 hours 45 minutes | Servings: 2

Ingredients

1 pound sweet potatoes, sliced
Salt to taste

¼ cup walnuts
1 tbsp coconut oil

Directions

Prepare a water bath and place the Sous Vide in it. Set to 146 F.

Place the potatoes and salt in a vacuum-sealable bag. Release air by the water displacement method, seal, and submerge the bag in the water bath. Cook for 3 hours. Heat a skillet over medium heat and toast the walnuts. Chop them.

Preheat the over to 375 F and lined a baking tray with parchment foil. Once the timer has stopped, remove the potatoes and transfer to the baking tray. Sprinkle with coconut oil and bake for 20-30 minutes. Toss once. Serve topped with toasted walnuts.

Tasty Parsnips with Honey Glaze

Prep + Cook Time: 1 hour 8 minutes | Servings: 4

Ingredients

1 pound parsnips, peeled and trimmed
3 tbsp butter

2 tbsp honey
1 tsp olive oil

Salt and black pepper to taste
1 tbsp chopped fresh parsley

Directions

Prepare a water bath and place the Sous Vide in it. Set to 186 F.

Place the parsnips, butter, honey, olive oil, salt, and pepper in a vacuum-sealable bag. Release air by the water displacement method, seal, and submerge the bag in the water bath. Cook for 1 hour.

Heat a skillet over medium heat. Once the timer has stopped, remove the bag and transfer the contents into the skillet and cook for 2 minutes until the liquid turns a glaze. Add the parsley and mix quickly. Serve.

Buttery & Sweet Duck

Prep + Cook Time: 7 hours 10 minutes | Servings: 7

Ingredients

2 pounds duck wings
2 tbsp sugar
3 tbsp butter

1 tbsp maple syrup
1 tsp black pepper
1 tsp salt

1 tbsp tomato paste

Directions

Prepare a water bath and place the Sous Vide in it. Set to 175 F. Whisk together the ingredients in a bowl and brush the wings with the mixture. Place the wings in a vacuum-sealable bag and pour over the remaining mixture.

Release air by the water displacement method, seal, and submerge the bag in the water bath. Set the timer for 7 hours. Once the timer has stopped, remove the bag and slice. Serve warm.

Paprika & Rosemary Potatoes

Prep + Cook Time: 55 minutes | Servings: 4

Ingredients

8 oz fingerling potatoes
Salt and black pepper to taste

1 tbsp butter
1 sprig rosemary

1 tsp paprika

Directions

Prepare a water bath and place the Sous Vide in it. Set to 178 F.

Combine the potatoes with salt, paprika and pepper. Place them in a vacuum-sealable bag. Release air by the water displacement method, seal, and submerge the bag in the water bath. Cook for 45 minutes.

Once the timer has stopped, remove the potatoes and cut them by half. Heat the butter in a skillet over medium heat and stir in rosemary and potatoes. Cook for 3 minutes. Sprinkle with salt. Serve on a plate.

Buttery Yams

Prep + Cook Time: 1 hour 10 minutes | Servings: 4

Ingredients

1 pound yams, sliced
8 tbsp butter

½ cup heavy cream
Salt to taste

Directions

Prepare a water bath and place the Sous Vide in it. Set to 186 F. Combine the heavy cream, yams, kosher salt, and butter. Place in a vacuum-sealable bag. Release air by the water displacement method, seal, and submerge the bag in the water bath. Cook for 60 minutes. Once the timer has stopped, remove the bag and pour the contents into a a food processor; blend until smooth and serve.

Broccoli & Blue Cheese Mash

Prep + Cook Time: 1 hour 40 minutes | Servings: 6

Ingredients

1 head broccoli, cut into florets
3 tbsp butter

Salt and black pepper to taste
1 tbsp parsley

5 oz blue cheese, crumbled

Directions

Prepare a water bath and place the Sous Vide in it. Set to 186 F. Place broccoli, butter, salt, parsley, and black pepper in a vacuum-sealable bag. Release air by the water displacement method, seal, and submerge the bag in the water bath. Cook for 1 hour and 30 minutes. Once the timer has stopped, remove the bag and transfer into a blender. Put the cheese inside and mix at high speed for 3-4 minutes until smooth. Serve.

Turkey Meatballs

Prep + Cook Time: 2 hours 10 minutes | Servings: 4

Ingredients

12 ounces ground turkey
2 tsp tomato sauce
1 egg

1 tsp cilantro
1 tbsp butter
Salt and black pepper to taste

1 tbsp breadcrumbs
½ tsp thyme

Directions

Prepare a water bath and place the Sous Vide in it. Set to 142 F. Combine all the ingredients in a bowl. Shape the mixture into meatballs. Place in a vacuum-sealable bag. Release air by the water displacement method, seal, and submerge the bag in the water bath. Set the timer for 2 hours. Serve warm and enjoy!

Curried Zucchinis

Prep + Cook Time: 40 minutes | Servings: 3

Ingredients

3 small zucchinis, diced
2 tsp curry powder

1 tbsp olive oil
Salt and black pepper to taste

¼ cup cilantro

Directions

Make a water bath, place Sous Vide in it, and set to 185 F. Place zucchinis in a vacuum-sealable bag. Release air by the water displacement method, seal, and submerge the bag in the water bath. Cook for 20 minutes. Once the timer has stopped, remove and unseal the bag. Place a skillet over medium, add olive oil. Once it has heated, add the zucchinis and the remaining listed ingredients. Season with salt and stir-fry for 5 minutes. Serve and enjoy!

Spicy Pickled Beets

Prep + Cook Time: 50 minutes | Servings: 4

Ingredients

12 oz beets, sliced
½ jalapeno pepper

1 diced garlic clove
2/3 cup white vinegar

2/3 cup water
2 tbsp pickling spice

Directions

Prepare a water bath and place the Sous Vide in it. Set to 192 F. In 5 mason jars, combine jalapeño pepper, beets and garlic cloves. Heat a saucepan and boil the pickling spice, water and white vinegar. Drain and pour over the beets mixture inside the jars. Seal and submerge the jars in the water bath. Cook for 40 minutes. Once the timer has stopped, remove the jars and allow cooling. Serve.

Spicy Butter Corn

Prep + Cook Time: 35 minutes | Servings: 5

Ingredients

5 tbsp butter
5 ears yellow corn, husked

1 tablespoon fresh parsley
½ tsp Cayenne pepper

Salt to taste

Directions

Prepare a water bath and place the Sous Vide in it. Set to 186 F. Place 3 ears of corn in each vacuum-sealable bag. Release air by the water displacement method, seal and submerge the bags in the water bath. Cook for 30 minutes. Once the timer has stopped, remove the corn from the bags and transfer into a plate. Garnish with cayenne pepper and parsley.

Jarred Pumpkin Bread

Prep + Cook Time: 3 hours 40 minutes | Servings: 4

Ingredients

1 egg, beaten
6 tbsp canned pumpkin puree
6 ounces flour

1 tsp baking powder
1 tsp cinnamon
¼ tsp nutmeg

1 tbsp sugar
¼ tsp salt

Directions

Prepare a water bath and place the Sous Vide in it. Set to 195 F. Sift the flour along with the baking powder, salt, cinnamon, and nutmeg in a bowl. Stir in beaten egg, sugar and pumpkin puree. Mix to form a dough.

Divide the dough between two mason jars and seal. Place in the water bath and cook for 3 hours and 30 minutes. Once the time passed, remove the jars and let it cool before serving.

SAUCES, STOCKS AND BROTHS

Spicy BBQ Sauce

Prep + Cook Time: 1 hour 15 minutes | Servings: 10

Ingredients

1 ½ lb small tomatoes
¼ cup apple cider vinegar
¼ tsp sugar
1 tbsp Worcestershire sauce

½ tbsp liquid hickory smoke
2 tsp smoked paprika
2 tsp garlic powder
1 tsp onion powder

Salt to taste
½ tsp chili powder
½ tsp cayenne pepper
4 tbsp water

Directions

Make a water bath, place Sous Vide in it, and set to 185 F. Place the tomatoes into two vacuum-sealable bags. Release air by the water displacement method, seal and submerge the bags in the bath. Set the timer to 40 minutes.

Once the timer has stopped, remove and unseal the bags. Transfer the tomatoes to a blender and puree until smooth and thick. Do not add water. Put a pot over medium heat, add in tomato puree and the remaining ingredients. Bring to a boil, stirring continuously for 20 minutes. A thick consistency should be achieved.

Peri Peri Sauce

Prep + Cook Time: 40 minutes | Servings: 15

Ingredients

2 lb red chili peppers
4 cloves garlic, crushed
2 tsp smoked paprika

1 cup cilantro leaves, chopped
½ cup basil leaves, chopped
1 cup olive oil

2 lemons' juice

Directions

Make a water bath, place Sous Vide in it, and set to 185 F. Place the peppers in a vacuum-sealable bag. Release air by the water displacement method, seal, and submerge the bag in the water bath. Set the timer for 30 minutes.

Once the timer has stopped, remove and unseal the bag. Transfer the pepper and the remaining listed ingredients to a blender and puree to smooth. Store in an airtight container, refrigerate, and use for up to 7 days.

Onion Pomodoro Sauce

Prep + Cook Time: 30 minutes | Servings: 4

Ingredients

4 cups tomatoes, halved and cored
½ onion, chopped
½ tsp sugar

¼ cup fresh oregano
2 garlic cloves, minced
Salt and black pepper to taste

5 tbsp olive oil

Directions

Prepare a water bath and place the Sous Vide in it. Set to 175 F. Place the tomatoes, oregano, garlic, onion and sugar in a vacuum-sealable bag. Release air by the water displacement method, seal, and submerge the bag in the water bath. Cook for 15 minutes. Once the timer has stopped, remove the bag and transfer the content into a blender and mix for 1 minute until smooth. Top with black pepper.

Ginger Syrup

Prep + Cook Time: 1 hour 10 minutes | Servings: 10

Ingredients

1 cup ginger, sliced thinly
1 large white onion, peeled

2 ½ cups water
¼ cup sugar

Directions

Make a water bath, place Sous Vide in it, and set to 185 F. Place onion in a vacuum-sealable bag. Release air by the water displacement method, seal and submerge in the water bath. Cook for 40 minutes.

Once the timer has stopped, remove and unseal the bag. Transfer the onion with 4 tablespoons of water to a blender and puree to smooth. Place a pot over medium heat, add the onion puree and the remaining listed ingredients. Bring to a boil for 15 minutes. Turn off heat, cool, and strain through a fine sieve. Store in a jar, refrigerate, and use for up to 14 days. Use it as a spice in other foods.

Chicken Stock

Prep + Cook Time: 12 hours 25 minutes | Servings: 4

Ingredients

2 lb chicken, any parts – thighs, breasts   2 celery sticks, chopped   2 white onions, chopped

Directions

Make a water bath, place Sous Vide in it, and set to 194 F. Separate all the ingredients in 2 vacuum bags, fold the top of the bags 2–3 times. Place in the water bath. Set the timer for 12 hours.

Once the timer has stopped, remove the bags and transfer the ingredients to a pot. Boil the ingredients over high heat for 10 minutes. Turn off heat and strain. Use the stock as a soup base.

Jalapeno Seasoning

Prep + Cook Time: 70 minutes | Servings: 6

Ingredients

2 jalapeno peppers   1 onion, peeled only   2 tsp rosemary powder
2 green chili peppers   3 tsp oregano powder   10 tsp aniseed powder
2 cloves garlic, crushed   3 tsp black pepper powder

Directions

Make a water bath, place Sous Vide in it, and set to 185 F. Place the peppers and onion in a vacuum-sealable bag. Release air by the water displacement method, seal, and submerge the bag in the water bath. Set the timer for 40 minutes. Once the timer has stopped, remove and unseal the bag. Transfer the pepper and onion with 2 tablespoons of water to a blender and puree to smooth.

Place a pot over low heat, add in pepper puree and the remaining ingredients. Simmer for 15 minutes. Turn off heat and cool. Store in a spice jar, refrigerate, and use for up to 7 days. Use it as a spice.

Honey & Onion Balsamic Dressing

Prep + Cook Time: 1 hour 55 minutes | Servings: 1

Ingredients

3 sweet onions, chopped   Salt and black pepper to taste   1 tbsp honey
1 tbsp butter   2 tbsp balsamic vinegar   2 tsp of fresh thyme leaves

Directions

Prepare a water bath and place the Sous Vide in it. Set to 186 F. Heat a skillet over medium heat with butter. Add onions, season with salt and pepper and cook for 10 minutes. Add in balsamic vinegar and cook for 1 minute. Remove from the heat and pour in honey.

Place the mix in a vacuum-sealable bag. Release air by the water displacement method, seal, and submerge the bag in the water bath. Cook for 90 minutes. Once the timer has stopped, remove the bag and transfer to a platter. Garnish with fresh thyme. Serve with pizza or sandwich.

Seafood Stock

Prep + Cook Time: 10 hours 10 minutes | Servings: 6

Ingredients

1 lb shrimp shells, with heads and tails
3 cups water
1 tbsp olive oil

2 tsp salt
2 sprigs rosemary
½ head garlic, crushed

½ cup celery leaves, chopped

Directions

Make a water bath, place Sous Vide in it, and set to 180 F. Toss the shrimp with the olive oil. Place the shrimp with the remaining listed ingredients in a vacuum-sealable bag. Release air, seal and submerge the bag into the water bath, and set the timer for 10 hours.

Fish Broth

Prep + Cook Time: 10 hours 15 minutes | Servings: 4

Ingredients

5 cups water
½ lb fish fillets, skin

1 lb fish head
5 medium green onions

3 sweet onion
¼ lb black seaweed (Kombu)

Directions

Make a water bath, place Sous Vide in it, and set to 194 F. Separate all the listed ingredients equally into 2 vacuum bags, fold the top of the bags 2 times. Place them in the water bath and clip it to the Sous Vide container.

Set the timer for 10 hours. Once the timer has stopped, remove the bags and transfer the ingredients to a pot. Boil the ingredients over high heat for 5 minutes Turn off heat and strain. Refrigerate and use for up to 14 days.

Garlic Basil Rub

Prep + Cook Time: 55 minutes | Servings: 15

Ingredients

2 heads garlic, crushed
2 tsp olive oil
A pinch salt

1 head fennel bulb, chopped
2 lemons, zested and juiced
¼ sugar

25 basil leaves

Directions

Make a water bath, place Sous Vide in it, and set to 185 F. Place the fennel and sugar in a vacuum-sealable bag. Release air by the water displacement method, seal, and submerge the bag in the water bath. Set the timer for 40 minutes. Once the timer has stopped, remove and unseal the bag. Transfer the fennel, sugar, and remaining listed ingredients to a blender and puree to smooth. Store in a spice container and use up to a week with refrigeration.

Tomato Sauce

Prep + Cook Time: 55 minutes | Servings: 4

Ingredients

1 (16-oz) can tomatoes, crushed
1 small white onion, diced
1 cup fresh basil leaves

1 tbsp olive oil
1 clove garlic, crushed
Salt to taste

1 bay leaf
1 red chili

Directions

Make a water bath, place Sous Vide in it, and set to 185 F. Place all the listed ingredients in a vacuum-sealable bag. Release air by the water displacement method, seal, and submerge the bag in the water bath. Set the timer for 40 minutes. Once the timer has stopped, remove and unseal the bag. Discard the bay leaf and transfer the remaining ingredients to a blender and puree smooth. Serve as a side sauce.

Mustard Asparagus Dressing

Prep + Cook Time: 30 minutes | Servings: 2

Ingredients

1 lb large asparagus, trimmed
Salt and black pepper to taste
¼ cup olive oil

1 tsp Dijon mustard
1 tsp dill
1 tsp red wine vinegar

1 hard-boiled egg, chopped
Fresh parsley, chopped

Directions

Prepare a water bath and place the Sous Vide in it. Set to 186 F. Peel the bottom of the stalk and place in a vacuum-sealable bag. Release air by the water displacement method, seal, and submerge the bag in the bath.

Cook for 15 minutes. Once the timer has stopped, remove the bag and transfer to an ice bath. Separate the cooking juices. In a bowl, for the vinaigrette, combine olive oil, vinegar and mustard; stir well. Season with salt and move it to a mason jar. Seal and shake until well combined. Top with parsley, egg, and the vinaigrette.

Vegetable Stock

Prep + Cook Time: 12 hours 35 minutes | Servings: 10

Ingredients

1 ½ cups celery root, diced
1 ½ cups leeks, diced
½ cup fennel bulb, diced
4 cloves garlic, crushed

1 tbsp olive oil
6 cups water
1 ½ cups mushrooms
½ cup parsley, chopped

1 tbsp black peppercorns
1 bay leaf

Directions

Make a water bath, place Sous Vide in it, and set to 180 F. Preheat an oven to 450 F. Place the leeks, celery, fennel, garlic, and olive oil in a bowl. Toss them. Transfer to a roasting pan and tuck them in the oven.

Roast for 20 minutes. Place the roasted vegetables with its juices, water, parsley, peppercorns, mushrooms, and bay leaf in a vacuum-sealable bag. Release air, seal and submerge the bag into the water bath and set the timer for 12 hours. Cover the water bath container with plastic wrap to reduce evaporation. Once the timer has stopped, remove and unseal the bag. Strain the ingredients. Cool and use frozen for up to 1 month.

Beef Broth

Prep + Cook Time: 13 hours 25 minutes | Servings: 6

Ingredients

3 lb beef feet
1 ½ lb beef bones
½ lb grounded beef
5 cups tomato paste

6 sweet onions
3 heads garlic
6 tbsp black pepper
5 sprigs thyme

4 bay leaves
10 cups water

Directions

Preheat an oven to 425 F. Place beef bones and beef feet in a roasting pan and rub them with the tomato paste. Add garlic and onion. Set aside. Place and crumble ground beef in another roasting pan. Place the roasting pans in the oven and roast until dark brown.

Once done, drain fat from the roasting pans. Make a water bath in a large container, place Sous Vide in it, and set to 195 F. Separate the ground beef, roasted vegetables, black pepper, thyme, and bay leaves in 3 vacuum bags. Deglaze the roasting pans with water and add it to the bags. Fold the top of the bags 2 to 3 times.

Place the bags in the water bath and clip it to the Sous Vide container. Set the timer for 13 hours. Once the timer has stopped, remove the bags and transfer the ingredients to a pot. Bring the ingredients to a boil over high heat. Cook for 15 minutes. Turn off heat and strain. Use the stock as a soup base.

VEGETARIAN & VEGAN

Cream of Tomatoes with Cheese Sandwich

Prep + Cook Time: 55 minutes | Servings: 8

Ingredients

½ cup cream cheese
2 pounds tomatoes, cut into wedges
Salt and black pepper to taste
2 tbsp olive oil

2 garlic cloves, minced
½ tsp chopped fresh sage
⅛ tsp red pepper flakes
½ tsp white wine vinegar

2 tbsp butter
4 slices bread
2 slices halloumi cheese

Directions

Prepare a water bath and place the Sous Vide in it. Set to 186 F. Put the tomatoes in a colander over a bowl and season with salt. Stir well. Allow to chill for 30 minutes. Discard the juices. Combine the olive oil, garlic, sage, black pepper, salt, and pepper flakes.

Place in a vacuum-sealable bag. Release air by the water displacement method, seal, and submerge the bag in the water bath. Cook for 40 minutes. Once the timer has stopped, remove the bag and transfer into a blender. Add in vinegar and cream cheese. Mix until smooth. Transfer to a plate and season with salt and pepper if needed.

To make the cheese bars: heat a skillet over medium heat. Grease the bread slices with butter and put into the skillet. Lay cheese slices over the bread and place over another buttery bread. Toast for 1-2 minutes. Repeat with the remaining bread. Cut into cubes. Serve over the warm soup.

Garlic Tabasco Edamame Cheese

Prep + Cook Time: 1 hour 6 minutes | Servings: 4

Ingredients

1 tbsp olive oil
4 cups fresh edamame in pods

1 tsp salt
1 garlic clove, minced

1 tbsp red pepper flakes
1 tbsp Tabasco sauce

Directions

Prepare a water bath and place the Sous Vide in it. Set to 186 F.

Heat a pot with water over high heat and blanch the edamame pots for 60 seconds. Strain them and transfer into an ice water bath. Combine the garlic, red pepper flakes, Tabasco sauce, and olive oil. Place the edamame in a vacuum-sealable bag. Pour the Tabasco sauce. Release air by the water displacement method, seal, and submerge the bag in the water bath. Cook for 1 hour. Serve and enjoy!

Citrus Corn with Tomato Sauce

Prep + Cook Time: 55 minutes | Servings: 8

Ingredients

⅓ cup olive oil
4 ears yellow corn, husked
Salt and black pepper to taste

1 large tomato, chopped
3 tbsp lemon juice
2 garlic cloves, minced

1 serrano pepper, seeded
4 scallions, green parts only, chopped
½ bunch fresh cilantro leaves, chopped

Directions

Prepare a water bath and place the Sous Vide in it. Set to 186 F. Whisk the corns with olive oil and season with salt and pepper. Place them in a vacuum-sealable bag. Release air by the water displacement method, seal, and submerge the bag in the water bath. Cook for 45 minutes.

Meantime, combine well the tomato, lemon juice, garlic, serrano pepper, scallions, cilantro, and the remaining olive oil in a bowl. Preheat a grill over high heat. Once the timer has stopped, remove the corns and transfer to the grill and cook for 2-3 minutes. Allow to cool. Cut the kernels from the cob and pour in tomato sauce. Serve.

Sage Roasted Potato Mash

Prep + Cook Time: 1 hour 35 minutes | Servings: 6

Ingredients

¼ cup butter
12 sweet potatoes, unpeeled
10 garlic cloves, chopped

4 tsp salt
6 tbsp olive oil
5 fresh sage sprigs

1 tbsp paprika

Directions

Prepare a water bath and place the Sous Vide in it. Set to 192 F. Combine the potatoes, garlic, salt, olive oil and 2 or 3 thyme springs and place in a vacuum-sealable bag. Release air by the water displacement method, seal, and submerge the bag in the water bath. Cook for 1 hour and 15 minutes.

Preheat the oven to 450 F. Once the timer has stopped, remove the potatoes and transfer into a bowl. Separate the cooking juices. Combine well the potatoes with butter and the remaining sage springs. Transfer into a baking tray, previously lined with aluminium foil. Make a hole in the center of the potatoes and pour the cooking juices in. Bake the potatoes for 10 minutes, turning 5 minutes later. Discard the sage. Serve sprinkled with paprika.

Maple Beet Salad with Cashews & Queso Fresco

Prep + Cook Time: 1 hour 35 minutes | Servings: 8

Ingredients

6 large beets, cut into chunks
Salt and black pepper to taste
3 tbsp maple syrup
2 tbsp butter

Zest of 1 large orange
1 tbsp olive oil
½ tsp cayenne pepper
1 ½ cups cashews

6 cup arugula
3 tangerines, peeled and segmented
1 cup queso fresco, crumbled

Directions

Prepare a water bath and place the Sous Vide in it. Set to 186 F. Place the beet chunks in a vacuum-sealable bag. Season with salt and pepper. Add 2 tbsp of maple syrup, butter, and orange zest. Release air by the water displacement method, seal, and submerge the bag in the water bath. Cook for 1 hour and 15 minutes.

Preheat the oven to 350 F. Mix the remaining maple syrup, olive oil, salt, and cayenne. Add in cashews and stir well. Transfer the cashew mixture into a baking tray, previously lined with wax pepper and bake for 10 minutes.

Allow to cool. Once the timer has stopped, remove the beets and discard the cooking juices. Put the arugula on a serving plate, beets, and tangerine wedges all over. Scatter with queso fresco and cashew mix to serve.

Celery & Leek Potato Soup

Prep + Cook Time: 2 hours 15 minutes | Servings: 8

Ingredients

8 tbsp butter
4 red potatoes, sliced
1 yellow onion, cut into ¼-inch pieces
1 celery stalk, cut into ½-inch pieces

4 cups chopped leeks, white parts only
1 cup vegetable stock
1 carrot, chopped
4 garlic cloves, minced

2 bay leaves
Salt and black pepper to taste
2 cups heavy cream
¼ cup chopped fresh chives

Directions

Prepare a water bath and place the Sous Vide in it. Set to 186 F. Place the potatoes, carrots, onion, celery, leeks, vegetable stock, butter, garlic, and bay leaves in a vacuum-sealable bag. Release air by the water displacement method, seal, and submerge the bag in the water bath. Cook for 2 hours.

Once the timer has stopped, remove the bag and transfer into a blender. Discard the bay leaves. Mix the contents and season with salt and pepper. Pour the cream slowly and blend 2-3 minutes until smooth. Drain the contents and garnish with chives to serve.

Cheesy Bell Peppers with Cauliflower

Prep + Cook Time: 52 minutes | Servings: 5

Ingredients

½ cup shaved Provolone cheese
1 head cauliflower, cut florets
2 garlic cloves, minced

Salt and black pepper to taste
2 tbsp butter
1 tbsp olive oil

½ large red bell pepper, cut strips
½ yellow bell pepper, cut into strips
½ orange bell pepper, cut into strips

Directions

Prepare a water bath and place the Sous Vide in it. Set to 186 F. Combine well the cauliflower florets, 1 clove of garlic, salt, pepper, half of butter, and half of olive oil. In another bowl, mix the bell peppers, remaining garlic, remaining salt, pepper, remaining butter, and remaining olive oil.

Place the cauliflower in a vacuum-sealable bag. Place the bell peppers in another vacuum-sealable bag. Release air by the water displacement method, seal and submerge the bags in the water bath. Cook for 40 minutes.

Once the timer has stopped, remove the bags and transfer the contents into a serving bowl. Discard the cooking juices. Combine the vegetables and top with Provolone cheese.

Herby Mashed Snow Peas

Prep + Cook Time: 55 minutes | Servings: 6

Ingredients

½ cup vegetable broth
1 pound fresh snow peas
Zest of 1 lemon

2 tbsp chopped fresh basil
1 tbsp olive oil
Salt and black pepper to taste

2 tbsp chopped fresh chives
2 tbsp chopped fresh parsley
¾ tsp garlic powder

Directions

Prepare a water bath and place the Sous Vide in it. Set to 186 F. Combine the peas, lemon zest, basil, olive oil, black pepper, chives, parsley, salt, and garlic powder and place them in a vacuum-sealable bag. Release air by the water displacement method, seal, and submerge the bag in the water bath. Cook for 45 minutes. Once the timer has stopped, remove the bag and transfer into a blender and mix well.

Buttered Asparagus with Thyme & Cheese

Prep + Cook Time: 21 minutes | Servings: 6

Ingredients

¼ cup shaved Pecorino Romano cheese
16 oz fresh asparagus, trimmed

4 tbsp butter, cubed
Salt to taste

1 garlic clove, minced
1 tbsp thyme

Directions

Prepare a water bath and place the Sous Vide in it. Set to 186 F.

Place the asparagus in a vacuum-sealable bag. Add the butter cubes, garlic, salt, and thyme. Release air by the water displacement method, seal, and submerge the bag in the water bath. Cook for 14 minutes. Once the timer has stopped, transfer the asparagus to a plate. Top with cooking juices. Garnish with Pecorino Romano cheese.

Fall Squash Cream Soup

Prep + Cook Time: 2 hours 20 minutes | Servings: 6

Ingredients

¾ cup heavy cream
1 winter squash, chopped
1 large pear

½ yellow onion, diced
3 fresh thyme sprigs
1 garlic clove, chopped

1 tsp ground cumin
Salt and black pepper to taste
4 tbsp crème fraîche

Directions

Prepare a water bath and place the Sous Vide in it. Set to 186 F. Combine the squash, pear, onion, thyme, garlic, cumin, and salt. Place in a vacuum-sealable bag. Release air by the water displacement method, seal and submerge in the water bath. Cook for 2 hours.

Once the timer has stopped, remove the bag and transfer all the contents into a blender. Puree until smooth. Add in cream and stir well. Season with salt and pepper. Transfer the mix into serving bowls and top with some créme fraiche. Garnish with pear chunks.

Lemon Collard Greens Salad with Cranberries

Prep + Cook Time: 15 minutes | Servings: 6

Ingredients

6 cups fresh collard greens, stemmed	2 garlic cloves, crushed	½ tsp salt
6 tbsp olive oil	4 tbsp lemon juice	¾ cup dried cranberries

Directions

Prepare a water bath and place the Sous Vide in it. Set to 196 F. Combine the collard greens with 2 tbsp of olive oil. Place it in a vacuum-sealable bag. Release air by the water displacement method, seal, and submerge the bag in the water bath. Cook for 8 minutes.

Stir the remaining olive oil, garlic, lemon juice and salt. Once the timer has stopped, remove the collard greens and transfer onto a serving plate. Sprinkle with the dressing. Garnish with cranberries.

Ginger Tamari Brussels Sprouts with Sesame

Prep + Cook Time: 43 minutes | Servings: 6

Ingredients

1 ½ pounds Brussels sprouts, halved	1 tbsp tamari sauce	¼ tsp toasted sesame oil
2 garlic cloves, minced	1 tsp grated ginger	1 tbsp sesame seeds
2 tbsp vegetable oil	¼ tsp red pepper flakes	

Directions

Prepare a water bath and place Sous Vide in it. Set to 186 F. Heat a pot over medium heat and combine the garlic, vegetable oil, tamari sauce, ginger, and red pepper flakes. Cook for 4-5 minutes. Set aside.

Place the brussels sprouts in a vacuum-sealable bag and pour in tamari mixture. Release air by the water displacement method, seal, and submerge the bag in the water bath. Cook for 30 minutes.

Once the timer has stopped, remove the bag and pat dry with kitchen towels. Reserve the cooking juices. Transfer the sprouts to a bowl and combine with the sesame oil. Plate the sprouts and sprinkle with cooking juices. Garnish with sesame seeds.

Buttered Peas with Mint

Prep + Cook Time: 25 minutes | Servings: 2

Ingredients

1 tbsp butter	1 tbsp mint leaves, chopped	Sugar to taste
½ cup snow peas	A pinch salt	

Directions

Make a water bath, place Sous Vide in it, and set to 183 F. Place all the ingredients in a vacuum-sealable bag. Release air by the water displacement method, seal and submerge in the bath. Cook for 15 minutes. Once the timer has stopped, remove and unseal the bag. Transfer the ingredients to a serving plate. Serve as a condiment.

Beet Spinach Salad

Prep + Cook Time: 2 hours 25 minutes | Servings: 3

Ingredients

1 ¼ cup beets, trimmed and cut into bite-sized pieces
1 cup fresh spinach, chopped

2 tbsp olive oil
1 tbsp lemon juice, freshly juiced
1 tsp balsamic vinegar

2 garlic cloves, crushed
1 tbsp butter
Salt and black pepper to taste

Directions

Rinse well and clean beets. Chop into bite-sized pieces and place in a vacuum-sealable bag along with butter and crushed garlic. Cook in Sous Vide for 2 hours at 185 F. Set aside to cool.

Place the spinach in a vacuum-sealable bag and cook in Sous Vide for 10 minutes at 180 F. Remove from the water bath and cool completely. Place in a large bowl and add cooked beets. Season with salt, pepper, vinegar, olive oil, and lemon juice. Serve immediately.

Garlic Greens with Mint

Prep + Cook Time: 30 minutes | Servings: 2

Ingredients

½ cup fresh chicory, torn
½ cup wild asparagus, finely chopped
½ cup Swiss chard, torn

¼ cup fresh mint, chopped
¼ cup arugula, torn
2 garlic cloves, minced

½ tsp salt
4 tbsp lemon juice, freshly squeezed
2 tbsp olive oil

Directions

Fill a large pot with salted water and add greens. Cook for 3 minutes. Remove and drain. Gently squeeze with your hands and then chop the greens. Transfer to a large vacuum-sealable bag and cook in Sous Vide for 10 minutes at 162 F. Remove from the water bath and set aside.

Heat olive oil over medium heat in a large skillet. Add garlic and stir-fry for 1 minute. Stir in greens and season with salt. Sprinkle with fresh lemon juice and serve.

Brussel Sprouts in White Wine

Prep + Cook Time: 35 minutes | Servings: 4

Ingredients

1 pound Brussels sprouts, trimmed
½ cup extra virgin olive oil

½ cup white wine
Salt and black pepper to taste

2 tbsp fresh parsley, finely chopped
2 garlic cloves, crushed

Directions

Place Brussels sprouts in a large vacuum-sealable bag with three tablespoons of olive oil. Cook in Sous Vide for 15 minutes at 180 F. Remove from the bag.

In a large, non-stick grill pan, heat the remaining olive oil. Add Brussels sprouts, crushed garlic, salt, and pepper. Briefly grill, shaking the pan a couple of times until lightly charred on all sides. Add wine and bring it to a boil. Stir well and remove from the heat. Top with finely chopped parsley and serve.

Cauliflower Broccoli Soup

Prep + Cook Time: 70 minutes | Servings: 2

Ingredients

1 head cauliflower, cut into florets
½ lb broccoli, cut into small florets
1 green bell pepper, chopped

1 onion, diced
1 tsp olive oil
1 clove garlic, crushed

½ cup vegetable stock
½ cup skimmed milk

Directions

Make a water bath, place the Sous Vide in it, and set it to 185 F. Place the cauliflower, broccoli, bell pepper, and white onion in a vacuum-sealable bag and pour olive oil into it. Release air by the water displacement method and seal the bag. Submerge the bag in the water bath. Set the timer for 50 minutes and cook.

Once the timer has stopped, remove the bag and unseal. Transfer the vegetables to a blender, add garlic and milk, and puree to smooth. Place a pan over medium heat, add the vegetable puree and vegetable stock and simmer for 3 minutes. Season with salt and pepper. Serve warm as a side dish.

Bell Pepper Puree

Prep + Cook Time: 40 minutes | Servings: 4

Ingredients

8 red bell peppers, cored	2 tbsp lemon juice	2 tsp sweet paprika
⅓ cup olive oil	3 cloves garlic, crushed	

Directions

Make a water bath and place Sous Vide in it and set to 183 F. Put the bell peppers, garlic, and olive oil in a vacuum-sealable bag. Release air by the water displacement method, seal and submerge the bags in the water bath. Set the timer for 20 minutes and cook. Once the timer has stopped, remove the bag and unseal.

Transfer the bell pepper and garlic to a blender and puree to smooth. Place a pan over medium heat; add bell pepper puree and the remaining ingredients. Cook for 3 minutes. Serve warm or cold as a dip.

Radish with Herb Cheese

Prep + Cook Time: 1 hour 15 minutes | Servings: 3

Ingredients

10 oz goat cheese	3 tbsp pesto	2 clove garlic
4 oz cream cheese	3 tsp lemon juice	9 large radishes, sliced.
¼ cup red bell pepper, minced	2 tbsp parsley	

Directions

Make a water bath, place Sous Vide in it, and set to 181 F.Place the radish slices in a vacuum-sealable bag, release air and seal it. Submerge the bag in the water bath and set the timer for 1 hour.

In a bowl, mix the remaining listed ingredients and pour the mixture into a piping bag. Set aside. Once the timer has stopped, remove the bag and unseal. Arrange the radish slices on a serving platter and pipe the cheese mixture on each slice. Serve as a snack.

Smoked Paprika Veggie Wontons

Prep + Cook Time: 5 hours 15 minutes | Servings: 9

Ingredients

10 ounces wonton wraps	1 tsp olive oil	½ tsp garlic powder
10 ounces veggies by choice, grated	½ tsp chili powder	Salt and black pepper to taste
2 eggs	½ tsp smoked paprika	

Directions

Prepare a water bath and place the Sous Vide in it. Set to 165 F. Beat the eggs along with the spices. Stir in the veggies and oil. Pour the mixture into a vacuum-sealable bag-Release air by the water displacement method, seal, and submerge the bag in the water bath. Set the timer for 5 hours.

Once the timer has stopped, remove the bag and transfer to a bowl. Divide the mixture between the ravioli, wrap and pinch the edges to seal. Cook in boiling water for 4 minutes over medium heat.

Tomato Soup

Prep + Cook Time: 60 minutes | Servings: 3

Ingredients

2 lb tomatoes, halved
1 onion, diced
1 celery stick, chopped

3 tbsp olive oil
1 tbsp tomato puree
A pinch sugar

1 bay leaf

Directions

Make a water bath, place Sous Vide in it, and set to 185 F. Place all the listed ingredients except salt in bowl and toss. Put them in a vacuum-sealable bag. Release air by the water displacement method, seal and submerge the bag into the water bath. Set the timer for 40 minutes.

Once the timer has stopped, remove the bag and unseal. Puree the ingredients using a blender. Pour the blended tomato into a pot and set it over medium heat. Season with salt and cook for 10 minutes. Dish soup into bowls and cool. Serve warm.

Brussels Sprouts in Sweet Syrup

Prep + Cook Time: 75 minutes | Servings: 3

Ingredients

4 lb Brussels sprouts, halved
3 tbsp olive oil
¾ cup fish sauce

3 tbsp water
2 tbsp sugar
1 ½ tbsp rice vinegar

2 tsp lime juice
3 red chilies, sliced thinly
2 cloves garlic, minced

Directions

Make a water bath, place Sous Vide in it, and set to 183 F. Pour Brussels sprouts, salt, and oil in a vacuum-sealable bag, release air by the water displacement method, seal, and submerge the bag in the water bath. Set the timer for 50 minutes.

Once the timer has stopped, remove the bag and transfer the Brussels sprouts to a foiled baking sheet. Preheat a broiler to high, place the baking sheet in it, and broil for 6 minutes. Pour the Brussels sprouts into a bowl.

Make the sauce: in a bowl, add the remaining listed cooking ingredients and stir. Add the sauce to the Brussels sprouts and toss evenly. Serve as a side dish.

Beetroot & Goat Cheese Salad

Prep + Cook Time: 2 hours 20 minutes | Servings: 3

Ingredients

1 lb beetroot, cut into wedges
½ cup almonds, blanched
2 tbsp hazelnuts, skinned
2 tsp olive oil

1 clove garlic, finely minced
1 tsp cumin powder
1 tsp lemon zest
Salt to taste

½ cup goat cheese, crumbled
Fresh mint leaves to garnish

Dressing:

2 tbsp olive oil

1 tbsp apple cider vinegar

Directions

Make a water bath, place the Sous Vide in it, and set to 183 F. Place the beetroots in a vacuum-sealable bag. Release air by the water displacement method, seal, and submerge the bag in the water bath and set the timer for 2 hours. Once the timer has stopped, remove and unseal the bag. Place the beetroot aside.

Put a pan over medium heat, add almonds and hazelnuts, and toast for 3 minutes. Transfer to a cutting board and chop. Add oil to the same pan, place garlic and cumin. Cook for 30 seconds. Turn heat off. In a bowl, mix the goat cheese, almond mixture, lemon zest, and garlic mixture. Drizzle with olive oil and vinegar and serve.

Eggplant Lasagna

Prep + Cook Time: 3 hours | Servings: 3

Ingredients

1 lb eggplants, peeled and thinly sliced
1 tsp salt
1 cup tomato sauce, divided into 3

2 oz fresh mozzarella, thinly sliced
1 oz Parmesan cheese, grated
2 oz Italian blend cheese, grated

3 tbsp fresh basil, chopped

Topping:

½ tbsp macadamia nuts, toasted and chopped
1 oz Parmesan cheese, grated

1 oz Italian blend cheese, grated

Directions

Make a water bath, place Sous Vide in it, and set to 183 F. Season eggplants with salt. Lay a vacuum-sealable bag on its side, make a layer of half the eggplant, spread one portion of tomato sauce, layer mozzarella, then parmesan, then cheese blend, then basil. Top with the second portion of tomato sauce.

Seal the bag carefully by the water displacement method, keeping it flat as possible. Submerge the bag flat in the water bath. Set the timer for 2 hours and cook. Release air 2 to 3 times within the first 30 minutes as eggplant releases gas as it cooks.

Once the timer has stopped, remove the bag gently and poke one corner of the bag using a pin to release liquid from the bag. Lay the bag flat on a serving plate, cut open the top of it and gently slide the lasagna onto the plate. Top with remaining tomato sauce, macadamia nuts, cheese blend, and Parmesan cheese. Melt and brown the cheese using a torch.

Mushroom Soup

Prep + Cook Time: 50 minutes | Servings: 3

Ingredients

1 lb mixed mushrooms
2 onions, diced
3 cloves garlic

2 sprigs parsley leaves, chopped
2 tbsp thyme powder
2 tbsp olive oil

2 cups cream
2 cups vegetable stock

Directions

Make a water bath, place Sous Vide in it, and set to 185 F. Place the mushrooms, onion, and celery in a vacuum-sealable bag. Release air by the water displacement method, seal, and submerge the bag in the water bath. Set the timer for 30 minutes. Once the timer has stopped, remove and unseal the bag.

Blend the ingredients from the bag in a blender. Put a pan over medium heat, add olive oil. Once it starts to heat, add in pureed mushrooms and the remaining ingredients, except for the cream. Cook for 10 minutes. Turn off heat and add cream. Stir well and serve.

Poached Tomatoes

Prep + Cook Time: 45 minutes | Servings: 3

Ingredients

4 cups cherry tomatoes
5 tbsp olive oil

½ tbsp fresh rosemary leaves, minced
½ tbsp fresh thyme leaves, minced

Salt and black pepper to taste

Directions

Make a water bath, place Sous Vide in it, and set to 131 F. Divide the listed ingredients into 2 vacuum-sealable bags, season with salt and pepper. Release air by the water displacement method and seal the bags. Submerge them in the water bath and set the timer to cook for 30 minutes. Once the timer has stopped, remove the bags and unseal. Transfer the tomatoes with the juices into a bowl. Serve as a side dish.

Ratatouille

Prep + Cook Time: 2 hours 10 minutes | Servings: 3

Ingredients

2 zucchinis, sliced

2 tomatoes, chopped

2 red capsicum, seeded and cut into 2-inch dices

1 small eggplant, sliced

1 onion, cut into 1-inch dices

Salt to taste

½ red pepper flakes

8 cloves garlic, crushed

2 ½ tbsp olive oil

5 sprigs + 2 sprigs Basil Leaves

Directions

Make a water bath, place Sous Vide in it, and set to 185 F. Place the tomatoes, zucchini, onion, bell pepper and eggplant each in 5 separate vacuum-sealable bags. Put garlic, basil leaves, and 1 tablespoon of olive oil in each bag. Release air by the water displacement method, seal and submerge the bags in the water bath and set the timer for 20 minutes.

Once the timer has stopped, remove the bag with the tomatoes. Set aside. Reset the timer for 30 minutes. Once the timer has stopped, remove the bags with the zucchinis and red bell peppers. Set aside. Reset the timer for 1 hour. Once the timer has stopped, remove the remaining bags and discard garlic and basil leaves. In a bowl, add tomatoes and use a spoon to mash them lightly. Chop the remaining vegetables and add to the tomatoes. Season with salt, red pepper flakes, remaining olive oil, and basil. Serve as a side dish.

Green Soup

Prep + Cook Time: 55 minutes | Servings: 3

Ingredients

4 cups vegetable stock

1 tbsp olive oil

1 clove garlic, crushed

1-inch ginger, sliced

1 tsp coriander powder

1 large zucchini, diced

3 cups kale

2 cups broccoli, cut into florets

1 lime, juiced and zested

Directions

Make a water bath, place Sous Vide in it, and set to 185 F. Place the broccoli, zucchini, kale, and parsley in a vacuum-sealable bag. Release air by the water displacement method, seal, and submerge the bag in the water bath. Set the timer for 30 minutes.

Once the timer has stopped, remove and unseal the bag. Add the steamed ingredients to a blender with garlic and ginger. Puree to smooth. Pour the green puree into a pot and add the remaining listed ingredients. Put the pot over medium heat and simmer for 10 minutes. Serve as a light dish.

Mixed Vegetable Soup

Prep + Cook Time: 55 minutes | Servings: 3

Ingredients

1 sweet onion, sliced

1 tsp garlic powder

2 cups zucchini, cut in small dices

3 oz Parmesan rind

2 cups baby spinach

2 tbsp olive oil

1 tsp red pepper flakes

2 cups vegetable stock

1 sprig rosemary

Salt to taste

Directions

Make a water bath, place Sous Vide in it, and set to 185 F. Toss all the ingredients with olive oil except the garlic and salt, and place them in a vacuum-sealable bag. Release air by water displacement method, seal, and submerge the bag in the water bath. Set the timer for 30 minutes.

Once the timer has stopped, remove and unseal the bag. Discard the rosemary. Pour the remaining ingredients into a pot and add salt and garlic powder. Put the pot over medium heat and simmer for 10 minutes. Serve.

Radish & Basil Salad

Prep + Cook Time: 50 minutes | Servings: 2

Ingredients

20 small radishes, trimmed
1 tbsp white wine vinegar
¼ cup chopped basil

½ cup feta cheese
1 tsp sugar
1 tbsp water

¼ tsp salt

Directions

Prepare a water bath and place the Sous Vide in it. Set to 200 F. Place the radishes in a large vacuum-sealable bag and add vinegar, sugar, salt, and water. Shake to combine. Release air by the water displacement method, seal and submerge in the water bath. Cook for 30 minutes. Once the timer has stopped, remove the bag and let it cool in an ice bath. Serve warm. Serve tossed with the basil and feta.

Bell Pepper Mix

Prep + Cook Time: 35 minutes | Servings: 2

Ingredients

1 red bell pepper, chopped
1 yellow bell pepper, chopped

1 green bell pepper, chopped
1 large orange bell pepper, chopped

Salt to taste

Directions

Make a water bath, place Sous Vide in it, and set to 183 F. Place all the bell peppers with salt in a vacuum-sealable bag. Release air by the water displacement method, seal and submerge in the water bath. Set the timer for 15 minutes. Once the timer has stopped, remove and unseal the bag. Serve bell peppers with their juices.

Cilantro Turmeric Quinoa

Prep + Cook Time: 105 minutes | Servings: 6

Ingredients

3 cups quinoa
2 cups heavy cream
½ cup water

3 tbsp cilantro leaves
2 tsp turmeric powder
1 tbsp butter

½ tbsp salt

Directions

Prepare a water bath and place the Sous Vide in it. Set to 180 F. Place all the ingredients in a vacuum-sealable bag. Stir to combine well. Release air by the water displacement method, seal, and submerge the bag in the water bath. Set the timer for 90 minutes. Once the timer has stopped, remove the bag. Serve warm.

Vegetarian Parmesan Risotto

Prep + Cook Time: 65 minutes | Servings: 5

Ingredients

2 cups Arborio rice
½ cup plain white rice
1 cup veggie stock

1 cup water
6-8 ounces Parmesan cheese, grated
1 onion, chopped

1 tbsp butter
Salt and black pepper to taste

Directions

Prepare a water bath and place Sous Vide in it. Set to 185 F. Melt the butter in a saucepan over medium heat. Add onions, rice, and spices and cook for a few minutes. Transfer to a vacuum-sealable bag. Release air by the water displacement method, seal, and submerge the bag in the water bath. Set the timer for 50 minutes. Once the timer has stopped, remove the bag and stir in the Parmesan cheese.

Potato & Date Salad

Prep + Cook Time: 3 hours 15 minutes | Servings: 6

Ingredients

2 pounds potatoes, cubed
5 ounces dates, chopped
½ cup crumbled goat cheese
1 tsp oregano

1 tbsp olive oil
1 tbsp lemon juice
3 tbsp butter
1 tsp cilantro

1 tsp salt
1 tbsp chopped parsley
¼ tsp garlic powder

Directions

Prepare a water bath and place the Sous Vide in it. Set to 190 F.

Place the potatoes, butter, dates, oregano, cilantro, and salt in a vacuum-sealable bag. Release air by the water displacement method, seal, and submerge the bag in the water bath. Set the timer for 3 hours.

Once the timer has stopped, remove the bag and transfer to a bowl. Whisk together the olive oil, lemon juice, parsley, and garlic powder and drizzle over the salad. If using cheese, sprinkle it over.

Quinoa & Celeriac Miso Dish

Prep + Cook Time: 2 hours 25 minutes | Servings: 6

Ingredients

1 celeriac, chopped
1 tbsp miso paste
6 cloves garlic
5 sprigs thyme

1 tsp onion powder
3 tbsp ricotta cheese
1 tbsp mustard seeds
Juice of ¼ a large lemon

5 cherry tomatoes roughly cut
Chopped parsley
8 ounces vegan butter
8 ounce cooked quinoa

Directions

Prepare a water bath and place the Sous Vide in it. Set to 186 F.

Melt the butter in a skillet over medium heat and add the garlic, thyme, mustard seeds. Cook for about 2 minutes. Stir in onion powder and set aside. Place the celeriac in a vacuum-sealable bag. Release air by the water displacement method, seal, and submerge the bag in the water bath. Cook for 2 hours.

Once the timer has stopped, remove the bag and transfer to a skillet and stir until golden brown. Season with miso. Set aside. Heat a pan over medium heat, add tomatoes, mustard and quinoa. Combine with lemon juice and parsley. Serve by mixing the celeriac and tomato mix.

Curry Ginger & Nectarine Chutney

Prep + Cook Time: 60 minutes | Servings: 3

Ingredients

½ cup granulated sugar
½ cup water
¼ cup white wine vinegar
1 garlic clove, minced
¼ cup white onion, finely chopped

Juice of 1 lime
2 tsp grated fresh ginger
2 tsp curry powder
A pinch of red pepper flakes
Salt and black pepper to taste

Pepper flakes to taste
4 large pieces nectarine, sliced into wedges
¼ cup chopped up fresh basil

Directions

Prepare a water bath and place the Sous Vide in it. Set to 168 F. Heat a saucepan over medium heat and combine the water, sugar, white wine vinegar, and garlic. Moving until the sugar softens. Add lime juice, onion, curry powder, ginger, and red pepper flakes. Season with salt and black pepper. Stir well. Place the mixture in a vacuum-sealable bag. Release air by the water displacement method, seal, and submerge the bag in the bath.

Cook for 40 minutes. Once the timer has stopped, remove the bag and place in an ice bath. Transfer the food to a serving plate. Garnish with basil.

Minty Chickpea and Mushroom Bowl

Prep + Cook Time: 4 hours 15 minutes | Servings: 8

Ingredients

9 ounces mushrooms
3 cups veggie broth
1 pound chickpeas, soaked overnight
1 tsp butter

1 tsp paprika
1 tbsp mustard
2 tbsp tomato juice
1 tsp salt

¼ cup chopped mint
1 tbsp olive oil

Directions

Prepare a water bath and place the Sous Vide in it. Set to 195 F. Place broth and chickpeas in a vacuum-sealable bag. Release air by the water displacement method, seal, and submerge the bag in the water bath.

Set the timer for 4 hours. Once the timer has stopped, remove the bag. Heat oil in a pan over medium heat. Add in mushrooms, tomato juice, paprika, salt, and mustard. Cook for 4 minutes. Drain the chickpeas and add them to the pan. Cook for another 4 minutes. Stir in butter and mint.

Braised Beetroot

Prep + Cook Time: 1 hour 15 minutes | Servings: 3

Ingredients

2 beets, peeled and sliced
⅓ cup balsamic vinegar

½ tsp olive oil
⅓ cup toasted walnuts

⅓ cup Grana Padano cheese, grated
Salt and black pepper to taste

Directions

Make a water bath, place Sous Vide in it, and set to 183 F. Place the beets, vinegar, and salt in a vacuum-sealable bag. Release air by the water displacement method, seal, and submerge the bag in the water bath. Set the timer for 1 hour. Once the timer has stopped, remove and unseal the bag. Transfer the beets to a bowl, add olive oil and toss. Sprinkle walnuts and cheese over it. Serve as a side dish.

Paprika Grits

Prep + Cook Time: 3 hours 10 minutes | Servings: 4

Ingredients

10 ounces grits
4 tbsp butter

1 ½ tsp paprika
10 ounces water

½ tsp garlic salt

Directions

Prepare a water bath and place the Sous Vide in it. Set to 180 F. Place all the ingredients in a vacuum-sealable bag. Stir with a spoon to combine well. Release air by the water displacement method, seal, and submerge the bag in the water bath. Set the timer for 3 hours. Once the timer has stopped, remove the bag. Serve and enjoy!

Oregano White Beans

Prep + Cook Time: 5 hours 15 minutes | Servings: 8

Ingredients

12 ounces white beans
1 cup tomato paste
8 ounces veggie stock

1 tbsp sugar
3 tbsp butter
1 cup chopped onions

1 bell pepper, chopped
1 tbsp oregano
2 tsp paprika

Directions

Prepare a water bath and place the Sous Vide in it. Set to 185 F. Combine all the ingredients in a vacuum-sealable bag. Stir to combine. Release air by the water displacement method, seal, and submerge the bag in the water bath. Set the timer for 5 hours. Once the timer has stopped, remove the bag. Serve warm.

Cabbage & Pepper in Tomato Sauce

Prep + Cook Time: 4 hours 45 minutes | Servings: 6

Ingredients

2 pounds cabbage, sliced
1 cup sliced bell pepper
1 cup tomato paste

2 onions, sliced
1 tbsp sugar
Salt and black pepper to taste

1 tbsp cilantro
1 tbsp olive oil

Directions

Prepare a water bath and place the Sous Vide in it. Set to 184 F.

Place the cabbage and onion in a vacuum-sealable bag and season with the spices. Add in tomato paste and stir to combine well. Release air by the water displacement method, seal, and submerge the bag in the water bath. Set the timer for 4 hours and 30 minutes. Once the timer has stopped, remove the bag.

Balsamic Braised Cabbage

Prep + Cook Time: 1 hour 45 minutes | Servings: 3

Ingredients

1 lb red cabbage, quartered and core removed
1 shallot, thinly sliced
2 cloves garlic, thinly sliced

½ tbsp balsamic vinegar
½ tbsp unsalted butter

Salt to taste

Directions

Make a water bath, place Sous Vide in it, and set to 185 F. Divide cabbage and remaining ingredients into 2 vacuum-sealable bags. Release air by the water displacement method and seal the bags. Submerge them in the water bath and set the timer to cook for 1 hour 30 minutes.

Once the timer has stopped, remove and unseal the bags. Transfer the cabbage with juices into serving plates. Season with salt and vinegar to taste. Serve as a side dish.

Grape Vegetable Mix

Prep + Cook Time 105 minutes | Servings: 9

Ingredients

8 sweet potatoes, sliced
2 red onions, sliced

4 ounces tomato, pureed
1 tsp minced garlic

Salt and black pepper to taste
1 tsp grape juice

Directions

Prepare a water bath and place Sous Vide in it. Set to 183 F. Place all the ingredients with ¼ cup water in a vacuum-sealable bag.Release air by the water displacement method, seal, and submerge the bag in the water bath. Set the timer for 90 minutes. Once the timer has stopped, remove the bag. Serve warm.

Vegetable Caponata

Prep + Cook Time: 2 hours 15 minutes | Servings: 4

Ingredients

4 canned plum tomatoes, crushed
2 bell peppers, sliced
2 zucchinis, sliced

½ onion, sliced
2 eggplants, sliced
6 garlic cloves, minced

2 tbsp olive oil
6 basil leaves
Salt and black pepper to taste

Directions

Prepare a water bath and place the Sous Vide in it. Set to 185 F. Combine all of the ingredients in a vacuum-sealable bag. Release air by the water displacement method, seal, and submerge the bag in the water bath. Set the timer for 2 hours. Once the timer has stopped, transfer to a serving platter.

Braised Swiss Chard with Lime

Prep + Cook Time: 25 minutes | Servings: 2

2 pounds Swiss chard
4 tbsp of extra virgin olive oil

2 garlic cloves, crushed
1 whole lime, juiced

2 tsps sea salt

Directions

Thoroughly rinse Swiss chard and drain in a colander. Using a sharp paring knife roughly chop and transfer to a large bowl. Stir in 4 tablespoons of olive oil, crushed garlic, lime juice, and sea salt. Transfer to a large vacuum-sealable bag and seal. Cook en sous vide for 10 minutes at 180 F.

Root Veggie Mash

Prep + Cook Time: 3 hours 15 minutes | Servings: 4

Ingredients

2 parsnips, peeled and chopped
1 turnip, peeled and chopped
1 large sweet potatoes, peeled and

chopped
1 tbsp butter
Salt and black pepper to taste

Pinch of nutmeg
¼ tsp thyme

Directions

Prepare a water bath and place Sous Vide in it. Set to 185 F. Place the veggies in a vacuum-sealable bag. Release air by the water displacement method, seal and submerge in the water bath. Cook for 3 hours. Once done, remove the bag and mash the veggies with a potato masher. Stir in the remaining ingredients.

Mustardy Lentil & Tomato Dish

Prep + Cook Time: 105 minutes | Servings: 8

Ingredients

2 cups lentils
1 can chopped tomatoes, undrained
1 cup green peas
3 cups veggie stock

3 cups water
1 onion, chopped
1 carrot, sliced
1 tbsp butter

2 tbsp mustard
1 tsp red pepper flakes
2 tbsp lime juice
Salt and black pepper to taste

Directions

Prepare a water bath and place Sous Vide in it. Set to 192 F. Place all the ingredients in a large vacuum-sealable bag. Release air by water displacement method, seal and submerge in bath. Cook for 90 minutes. Once the timer has stopped, remove the bag and transfer to a large bowl and stir before serving.

Buttery Summer Squash

Prep + Cook Time: 1 hour 35 minutes | Servings: 4

Ingredients

2 tbsp butter
¾ cup onion, chopped
1 ½ pounds summer squash, sliced

Salt and black pepper to taste
½ cup whole milk
2 large whole eggs

½ cup crumbled plain potato chips

Directions

Prepare a water bath and place the Sous Vide in it. Set to 175 F. Grease a few jars. Heat a large skillet over medium heat and melt the butter. Add in onions and sauté for 7 minutes. Add the squash, season with salt and pepper and sauté for 10 minutes. Divide the mix in the jars. Allow it cool and set aside.

Whisk the milk, salt and eggs in a bowl. Season with pepper. Pour the mixture over the jars, seal and submerge the jars in the water bath. Cook for 60 minutes. Once the timer has stopped, remove the jars and allow cooling for 5 minutes. Serve over potato chips.

Bell Pepper Rice Pilaf with Raisins

Prep + Cook Time: 3 hours 10 minutes | Servings: 6

Ingredients

2 cups white rice
2 cups veggie stock
⅔ cup water

3 tbsp raisins, chopped
2 tbsp sour cream
½ cup chopped red onion

1 bell pepper, chopped
Salt and black pepper to taste
1 tsp thyme

Directions

Prepare a water bath and place the Sous Vide in it. Set to 180 F. Place all the ingredients in a vacuum-sealable bag. Stir to combine well. Release air by the water displacement method, seal, and submerge the bag in the water bath. Set the timer for 3 hours. Once the timer has stopped, remove the bag. Serve warm.

Yogurt Caraway Soup

Prep + Cook Time: 2 hours 20 minutes | Servings: 4

Ingredients

1 tbsp olive oil
1 ½ tsp caraway seeds
1 medium onion, diced
1 leek, halved and thinly sliced

Salt to taste
2 pounds carrots, chopped
1 bay leaf
3 cups vegetable broth

½ cup whole milk yogurt
Apple cider vinegar
Fresh dill fronds

Directions

Prepare a water bath and place the Sous Vide in it. Set to 186 F. Heat olive oil in a large skillet over medium heat and add caraway seeds. Toast them for 1 minute. Add in onion, salt, and leek. Sauté for 5-7 minutes or until tender. Combine the onion, bay leaf, carrots and 1/2 tbsp of salt into a large bowl.

Distribute the mixture in a vacuum-sealable bag. Release air by the water displacement method, seal, and submerge the bag in the water bath. Cook for 2 hours. Once the timer has stopped, remove the bag and pour into a bowl. Mix in broth. Stir in yogurt. Season the soup with some salt and vinegar and serve garnished dill fronds.

Rosemary Russet Potatoes Confit

Prep + Cook Time: 1 hour 15 minutes | Servings: 4

Ingredients

1 pound russet potatoes, chopped
Salt to taste

¼ tsp ground white pepper
1 tsp chopped fresh rosemary

2 tbsp whole butter
1 tbsp corn oil

Directions

Prepare a water bath and place Sous Vide in it. Set to 192 F. Season potatoes with rosemary, salt and pepper. Combine the potatoes with butter and oil. Place in a vacuum-sealable bag. Release air by the water displacement method, seal, and submerge the bag in the water bath. Cook for 60 minutes. Once the timer has stopped, remove the bag and transfer into a large bowl. Garnish with butter and serve.

Honey Apple & Arugula Salad

Prep + Cook Time: 3 hours 50 minutes | Servings: 4

Ingredients

2 tbsp honey
2 apples, cored, halved and sliced
Dressing

½ cup walnuts, toasted and chopped
½ cup shaved Grana Padano cheese

4 cups arugula
Sea salt to taste

¼ cup olive oil
1 tbsp white wine vinegar

1 tsp Dijon mustard
1 garlic clove, minced

Salt to taste

Directions

Prepare a water bath and place the Sous Vide in it. Set to 158 F. Place the honey in a glass bowl and heat for 30 seconds, add the apples and mix well. Place it in a vacuum-sealable bag. Release air by the water displacement method, seal, and submerge the bag in the water bath. Cook for 30 minutes.

Once the timer has stopped, remove the bag and transfer into an ice-water bath for 5 minutes. Refrigerate for 3 hours. Combine all the dressing ingredients in a jar and shake well. Allow cooling in the fridge for a moment.

In a bowl, mix the arugula, walnuts, and Grana Padano cheese. Add the peach slices. Top with the dressing. Season with salt and pepper and serve.

Rice & Leek Pilaf with Walnuts

Prep + Cook Time: 3 hours 15 minutes | Servings: 4

Ingredients

1 tbsp olive oil
1 leek, thinly sliced
1 minced garlic clove

Salt to taste
1 cup rinsed wild rice
¼ cup currants

2 cups vegetable broth
¼ cup walnuts, toasted and chopped

Directions

Prepare a water bath and place the Sous Vide in it. Set to 182 F.

Heat a saucepan over medium heat with oil. Stir in garlic, leek and 1/2 tbsp of salt. Cook until the leek is fragrant. Remove from the heat. Add in rice and currants. Mix well. Place the mixture in a vacuum-sealable bag.

Release air by the water displacement method, seal, and submerge the bag in the water bath. Cook for 3 hours. Once the timer has stopped, remove the bag and transfer to a bowl. Top with walnuts.

Delicious Chutney of Dates & Mangoes

Prep + Cook Time: 1 hour 45 minutes | Servings: 4

Ingredients

2 pounds mangoes, chopped
1 small onion, diced
½ cup light brown sugar
¼ cup dates

2 tbsp apple cider vinegar
2 tbsp freshly squeezed lemon juice
1 ½ tsp yellow mustard seeds
1 ½ tsp coriander seeds

Salt to taste
¼ tsp curry powder
¼ tsp dried turmeric
⅛ tsp cayenne

Directions

Prepare a water bath and place the Sous Vide in it. Set to 183 F. Combine all the ingredients. Place in a vacuum-sealable bag. Release air by the water displacement method, seal, and submerge the bag in the water bath. Cook for 90 minutes. Once the timer has stopped, remove the bag and pour into a pot.

Mandarin & Green Bean Salad with Walnuts

Prep + Cook Time: 1 hour 10 minutes | Servings: 8

Ingredients

2 pounds green beans, trimmed
2 mandarins

2 tbsp butter
Salt to taste

2 oz walnuts

Directions

Prepare a water bath and place the Sous Vide in it. Set to 186 F. Combine the green beans, salt and butter. Place in a vacuum-sealable bag. Add in mandarin zest and juice. Release air by the water displacement method, seal, and submerge the bag in the water bath. Cook for 1 hour. Once the timer has stopped, remove the bag and transfer to a serving platter. Top with mandarin zest and walnuts.

Tangerine & Green Bean Platter with Hazelnuts

Prep + Cook Time: 1 hour 20 minutes | Servings: 9

Ingredients

1 pound green beans, trimmed
2 small tangerines

2 tbsp butter
Salt to taste

2 oz hazelnuts

Directions

Prepare a water bath and place the Sous Vide in it. Set to 186 F.

Combine the green beans, butter and salt. Place in a vacuum-sealable bag. Zest one of the tangerines inside. Release air by the water displacement method, seal, and submerge the bag in the water bath. Cook for 60 minutes.

Once the timer has stopped, remove the bag. Preheat the oven yo 400 F. and toast the hazelnuts for 7 minutes. Peel and chop, and top the beans with hazelnuts and tangerine zest.

Curry Pears & Coconut Cream

Prep + Cook Time: 1 hour 10 minutes | Servings: 4

Ingredients

2 pears, cored, peeled and sliced

1 tbsp curry powder

2 tbsp coconut cream

Directions

Prepare a water bath and place the Sous Vide in it. Set to 186 F. Combine all the ingredients and place in a vacuum-sealable bag. Release air by the water displacement method, seal, and submerge the bag in the water bath. Cook for 60 minutes. Once the timer has stopped, remove the bag and transfer to a large bowl. Divide in serving plates and serve.

Soft Broccoli Purée

Prep + Cook Time: 2 hours 15 minutes | Servings: 4

Ingredients

1 head broccoli, cut into florets
½ tsp garlic powder

Salt to taste
1 tbsp butter

1 tbsp heavy whipping cream

Directions

Prepare a water bath and place the Sous Vide in it. Set to 183 F. Combine the broccoli, salt, garlic powder, and heavy cream. Place in a vacuum-sealable bag. Release air by the water displacement method, seal, and submerge the bag in the water bath. Cook for 2 hours. Once the timer has stopped, remove the bag and transfer into a blender to pulse. Season and serve.

Green Pea Cream with Nutmeg

Prep + Cook Time: 1 hour 10 minutes | Servings: 8

Ingredients

1 pound fresh green peas
1 cup whipping cream
¼ cup butter

1 tbsp cornstarch
¼ tsp ground nutmeg
4 cloves

2 bay leaves
Black pepper to taste

Directions

Prepare a water bath and place the Sous Vide in it. Set to 184 F. Combine the cornstarch, nutmeg and cream into a bowl. Whisk until the cornstarch soften. Place the mixture in a vacuum-sealable bag. Release air by the water displacement method, seal, and submerge the bag in the water bath. Cook for 1 hour. Once the timer has stopped, extract the bag and remove the bay leaf. Serve.

Chili Cabbage Goulash

Prep + Cook Time: 1 hour 15 minutes | Servings: 2

Ingredients

2 pounds white cabbage, chopped
2 tbsp olive oil
Salt to taste
¼ cup fish sauce

2 tbsp water
1 ½ tbsp granulated sugar
1 tbsp rice vinegar
1 ½ tsp lime juice

12 pieces thinly sliced chilis
1 small minced garlic clove
Chopped fresh mint
Chopped fresh cilantro

Directions

Prepare a water bath and place the Sous Vide in it. Set to 183 F.

Combine the cabbage, olive oil and salt. Place in a vacuum-sealable bag. Release air by the water displacement method, seal, and submerge the bag in the water bath. Cook for 50 minutes. For the vinaigrette, in a bowl, mix the fish sauce, sugar, water, rice vinegar, lime juice, garlic, and chilis.

Once the timer has stopped, remove the bag and transfer to an aluminum foil and heat up. Sear the cabbage for 5 minutes. Serve in a bowl with the vinaigrette. Top with mint and cilantro.

Broiled Onions with Sunflower Pesto

Prep + Cook Time: 2 hours 25 minutes | Servings: 4

Ingredients

4 spring onions, trimmed and halved
½ cup + 2 tbsp olive oil
Salt and black pepper to taste

2 tbsp sunflower seeds
2 cloves garlic, peeled
3 cups loosely packed fresh basil leaves

3 tbsp grated Grana Padano cheese
1 tbsp freshly squeezed lemon juice

Directions

Prepare a water bath and place the Sous Vide in it. Set to 183 F. Place the onions in a vacuum-sealable bag. Season with salt, pepper and 2 tbsp of olive oil. Release air by the water displacement method, seal, and submerge the bag in the water bath. Cook for 2 hours.

Meanwhile, for the pesto sauce, combine in a processor food the sunflower seeds, garlic, and basil, and blend until finely chopped. Carefully add the remaining oil. Add in lemon juice and stop. Season with salt and pepper. Set aside. Once the timer has stopped, remove the bag and transfer the onions to a skillet and cook for 10 minutes. Serve and top with the pesto sauce.

Red Chili Broccoli Soup

Prep + Cook Time: 1 hour 25 minutes | Servings: 8

Ingredients

2 tbsp olive oil
1 large onion, diced
2 garlic cloves, sliced

Salt to taste
⅛ tsp crushed red chili flakes
1 broccoli head, cut into florets

1 apple, peeled and diced
6 cups vegetable broth

Directions

Prepare a water bath and place the Sous Vide in it. Set to 183 F.

Heat a skillet over medium heat with the oil, until shimmer. Sauté the onion, 1/4 tbsp of salt and garlic for 7 minutes. Add in chili flakes and mix well. Remove from the heat. Allow cooling.

Place the apple, broccoli, onion mix and 1/4 tbsp of salt in a vacuum-sealable bag. Release air by the water displacement method, seal, and submerge the bag in the water bath. Cook for 1 hour.

Once the timer has stopped, remove the bag and transfer to a pot. Pour in vegetable broth and blend. Season with salt. Serve and enjoy!

Easy Broccoli Puree

Prep + Cook Time: 60 minutes | Servings: 4

Ingredients

1 head broccoli
1 cup vegetable stock

3 tbsp butter
Salt to taste

Directions

Prepare a water bath and place the Sous Vide in it. Set to 186 F.

Combine the broccoli, butter and vegetable stock. Place in a vacuum-sealable bag. Release air by the water displacement method, seal, and submerge the bag in the water bath. Cook for 45 minutes.

Once the timer has stopped, remove the bag and drain. Reserve the cooking juices. Put the broccoli into a blender and puree until smooth. Pour some cooking juices. Season with salt and pepper to serve.

Allspice Miso Corn with Sesame & Honey

Prep + Cook Time: 45 minutes | Servings: 4

Ingredients

4 ears of corn
6 tbsp butter
3 tbsp red miso paste

1 tsp honey
1 tsp allspice
1 tbsp canola oil

1 scallion, thinly sliced
1 tsp toasted sesame seeds

Directions

Prepare a water bath and place the Sous Vide in it. Set to 183 F. Clean the corn and cut the ears. Cover each corn with 2 tbsp of butter. Place in a vacuum-sealable bag. Release air by the water displacement method, seal, and submerge the bag in the water bath. Cook for 30 minutes.

Meanwhile, combine 4 tbsp of butter, 2 tbsp of miso paste, honey, canola oil, and allspice in a bowl. Stir well. Set aside. Once the timer has stopped, remove the bag and sear the corn. Spread the miso mixture on top. Garnish with sesame oil and scallions.

Creamy Gnocchi with Peas

Prep + Cook Time: 1 hour 50 minutes | Servings: 2

Ingredients

1 pack gnocchi
1 tbsp butter
½ thinly sliced sweet onion

Salt and black pepper to taste
½ cup frozen peas
¼ cup heavy cream

½ cup grated Pecorino Romano cheese

Directions

Prepare a water bath and place the Sous Vide in it. Set to 183 F. Place the gnocchi in a vacuum-sealable bag. Release air by the water displacement method, seal, and submerge the bag in the water bath.

Cook for 1 hour and 30 minutes. Once the timer has stopped, remove the bag and set aside. Heat a skillet over medium heat with butter and sauté the onion for 3 minutes. Add the frozen peas and cream and cook. Combine the gnocchi with the cream sauce, season with pepper and salt and serve in a plate.

Light Broccoli Sauté

Prep + Cook Time: 45 minutes | Servings: 4

Ingredients

1 pound fresh broccoli
¼ cup butter, melted

Salt and black pepper to taste

Directions

Prepare a water bath and place the Sous Vide in it. Set to 183 F. Chunk the broccoli in quarters. Place them in a vacuum-sealable bag. Season with salt and pepper. Add in butter. Release air by the water displacement method, seal, and submerge the bag in the water bath. Cook for 30 minutes. Once the timer has stopped, remove the bag.

Nutmeg Sweet Pea Cream

Prep + Cook Time: 1 hour 10 minutes | Servings: 8

Ingredients

1 pound frozen fresh sweet peas	1 tbsp cornstarch	2 bay leaves
1 cup half-and-half cream	¼ tsp ground nutmeg	Black pepper to taste
¼ cup butter	4 cloves	

Directions

Prepare a water bath and place the Sous Vide in it. Set to 183 F. In a bowl, combine the cream, nutmeg and cornstarch. Mix until the cornstarch dissolved. Place the mix and remaining ingredients in a vacuum-sealable bag. Release air by the water displacement method, seal, and submerge the bag in the water bath. Cook for 1 hour. Once the timer has stopped, remove the bag. Top with black pepper. Serve and enjoy!

Sesame Zucchini Miso

Prep + Cook Time: 3 hours 15 minutes | Servings: 2

Ingredients

1 zucchini, sliced	2 tbsp sake	Salt to taste
¼ cup white miso	1 tbsp sugar	2 tbsp sesame seeds, toasted
2 tbsp Italian seasoning	1 tsp sesame oil	2 tbsp scallions, thinly sliced

Directions

Prepare a water bath and place the Sous Vide in it. Set to 186 F.

Place the zucchini in a vacuum-sealable bag. Release air by the water displacement method, seal, and submerge the bag in the water bath. Cook for 3 hours.

Once the timer has stopped, remove the bag and transfer to a baking sheet. Discard the cooking juice. For the miso sauce, combine the miso, sake, sugar, Italian seasoning, and sesame oil in a small bowl. Whisk until smooth. Brush the zucchini with the sauce and caramelize for 3-5 minutes. Serve on a platter and top with sesame seeds.

Chili Garbanzo Bean Stew

Prep + Cook Time: 3 hours 10 minutes | Servings: 4

Ingredients

1 cup garbanzo beans, soaked overnight	½ tsp ground cumin	1/8 tsp cayenne pepper
3 cups water	½ tsp ground coriander	Chopped fresh cilantro
1 tbsp olive oil	¼ tsp ground cinnamon	Harissa sauce, to taste
Salt to taste	1/8 tsp ground cloves	

Directions

Prepare a water bath and place the Sous Vide in it. Set to 192 F.

Place beans in a vacuum-sealable bag with cumin, salt, olive oil, cloves, cinnamon, cilantro, and cayenne. Release air by water displacement method, seal and submerge in the water bath. Cook for 3 hours.

Once done, remove the bag and drain the beans. Discard the cooking juices. Season with salt. Combine the olive oil and harissa sauce and pour over the beans. Garnish with cilantro.

Buttery Agave Carrots

Prep + Cook Time: 1 hour 25 minutes | Servings: 4

Ingredients

1 pound baby carrots
4 tbsp vegan butter

1 tbsp agave nectar
Salt to taste

¼ tsp ground nutmeg

Directions

Prepare a water bath and place the Sous Vide in it. Set to 186 F.

Place the carrots, honey, whole butter, kosher salt, and nutmeg in a vacuum-sealable bag. Release air by the water displacement method, seal, and submerge the bag in the water bath. Cook for 75 minutes.

Once the timer has stopped, remove the bag and drain the cooking juices. Set aside. Transfer the carrots into a platter and sprinkle with the juices.

Buttery Artichokes with Lemon & Garlic

Prep + Cook Time: 1 hour 45 minutes | Servings: 4

Ingredients

4 tbsp lemon juice
12 baby artichokes
4 tbsp butter

2 minced fresh garlic cloves
1 tsp fresh lemon zest
Salt, to taste

1 tsp dill
Ground black pepper, to taste
Chopped up fresh parsley for serving

Directions

Prepare a water bath and place the Sous Vide in it. Set to 182 F. Combine cold water with 2 tbsp of lemon juice. Peel the artichokes and chop thinly. Transfer to the water and allow resting.

Heat the butter in a skillet over medium heat and cook the dill, garlic 2 tbsp of lemon juice and zest. Season with salt and pepper, allow cooling for 5 minutes. Drain the artichokes and place in a vacuum-sealable bag. Add in butter mixture. Release air by the water displacement method, seal, and submerge the bag in the water bath. Cook for 1 hour and 30 minutes. Once the timer has stopped, remove the artichokes. Top with parsley. Serve.

Tomato & Agave Tofu

Prep + Cook Time: 1 hour 45 minutes | Servings: 6

Ingredients

1 cup vegetable broth
2 tbsp tomato paste
1 tbsp turmeric powder

1 tbsp rice wine vinegar
1 tbsp agave nectar
2 tsp sriracha sauce

3 cloves minced garlic
1 tsp soy sauce
24 oz silken tofu, cubed

Directions

Prepare a water bath and place the Sous Vide in it. Set to 186 F. Combine all the ingredients in a bowl, except the tofu. Place the tofu in a vacuum-sealable bag. Add the mixture. Release air by the water displacement method, seal, and submerge the bag in the water bath. Cook for 1 hour and 30 minutes. Once the timer has stopped, remove the bag. Serve and enjoy!

Sweet Red Beet Dish

Prep + Cook Time: 1 hour 45 minutes | Servings: 4

Ingredients

1 pound red beets, peeled and quartered
2 tbsp butter
2 peeled oranges, chopped
1 tbsp honey

3 tbsp balsamic vinegar
4 tbsp olive oil
Salt and black pepper to taste
6 oz baby romaine leaves

½ cup pistachios, chopped
½ cup Pecorino Romano cheese

Directions

Prepare a water bath and place the Sous Vide in it. Set to 182 F. Place the red beets in a vacuum-sealable bag. Add the butter Release air by the water displacement method, seal, and submerge the bag in the water bath.

Cook for 90 minutes. Once the timer has stopped, remove the bag and discard the cooking juices. Combine the honey, oil and vinegar. Season with salt and pepper. Throw the romaine leaves, orange, beets, and vinaigrette. Garnish with pistachio and Pecorino Romano cheese.

Medley of Root Vegetables

Prep + Cook Time: 3 hours 15 minutes | Servings: 4

Ingredients

1 turnip, chopped
1 rutabaga, chopped
8 carrots, chopped
1 parsnip, chopped

½ sweet onion, chopped
4 garlic cloves, minced
4 sprigs fresh rosemary
2 tbsp olive oil

Salt and black pepper to taste
2 tbsp vegan butter

Directions

Prepare a water bath and place the Sous Vide in it. Set to 186 F.

Place in a vacuum-sealable bag the vegetables and rosemary. Add 1 tbsp of oil and season with salt and pepper. Release air by the water displacement method, seal, and submerge the bag in the water bath. Cook for 3 hours.

Heat a pot over high heat. Once the timer has stopped, remove the bag and transfer the contents to the pot. Cook for 5 minutes until reduced. Add the veggies and stir well. Keep cooking for 5 minutes. Serve.

Provolone Cheese Grits

Prep + Cook Time: 3 hours 20 minutes | Servings: 4

Ingredients

1 cup grits
1 cup cream
3 cups vegetable stock

2 tbsp butter
4 oz grated Provolone cheese
1 tbsp paprika

Extra cheese for garnish
Salt and black pepper to taste

Directions

Prepare a water bath and place the Sous Vide in it. Set to 182 F. Combine the grits, cream and vegetable stock. Chop the butter and add to the mixture. Place the mix in a vacuum-sealable bag. Release air by the water displacement method, seal, and submerge the bag in the water bath. Cook for 3 hours.

Once the timer has stopped, remove the bag and transfer into a bowl. Stir the mixture with the cheese and season with salt and pepper. Garnish with extra cheese and paprika, if preferred.

Effortless Pickled Fennel with Lemon

Prep + Cook Time: 40 minutes | Servings: 8

Ingredients

1 cup apple cider vinegar
2 tbsp sugar

Juice and zest from 1 lemon
Salt to taste

2 bulb fennels, sliced
½ tsp fennel seeds, crushed

Directions

Prepare a water bath and place the Sous Vide in it. Set to 182 F. Combine well the vinegar, sugar, lemon juice, salt, lemon zest and fennel seeds. Place the mixture in a vacuum-sealable bag. Release air by the water displacement method, seal, and submerge the bag in the water bath. Cook for 30 minutes. Once the timer has stopped, remove the bag and transfer to an ice-water bath. Allow cooling. Serve and enjoy!

Simple Broccoli Rabe

Prep + Cook Time: 20 minutes | Servings: 2

Ingredients

½ pound broccoli rabe
1 tsp garlic powder

1 tbsp vegan butter
½ tsp sea salt

¼ tsp black pepper

Directions

Prepare a water bath and place the Sous Vide in it. Set to 192 F. Place the broccoli rabe, garlic powder, sea salt, and black pepper in a vacuum-sealable bag. Release air by the water displacement method, seal, and submerge the bag in the water bath. Cook for 4 minutes. Once the timer has stopped, remove the broccoli to a serving plate.

Garlicky Truffled Potatoes

Prep + Cook Time: 1 hour 50 minutes | Servings: 4

Ingredients

8 oz red potato wedges
3 tbsp white truffle butter

1 tbsp truffle oil
Salt and black pepper to taste

1 garlic clove, minced

Directions

Prepare a water bath and place the Sous Vide in it. Set to 182 F. Place the truffle butter, red potatoes and truffle oil in a vacuum-sealable bag. Season with salt and pepper. Shake well. Release air by the water displacement method, seal, and submerge the bag in the water bath. Cook for 90 minutes. Once the timer has stopped, remove the potatoes and transfer to a hot skillet. Cook for 5 minutes more until the liquid evaporated.

Homemade Giardiniera Picante

Prep + Cook Time: 1 hour 20 minutes | Servings: 8

Ingredients

2 cups white wine vinegar
1 cup water
½ cup sugar
Salt to taste

1 tbsp whole black peppercorns
2 pounds Brussels sprouts, shredded
1 seeded bell pepper, chopped
1 cup carrots, chopped

½ thinly sliced white onion
2 seeded Serrano peppers, chopped

Directions

Prepare a water bath and place the Sous Vide in it. Set to 182 F.

Combine the vinegar, sugar, salt, water, pepper, Brussels sprouts, onion, serrano pepper, bell pepper, and carrots in a vacuum-sealable bag. Release air by the water displacement method, seal and submerge in the bath. Cook for 60 minutes. Once the timer has stopped, remove the bag and transfer to a bowl.

Crispy Garlic Potato Purée

Prep + Cook Time: 1 hour 20 minutes | Servings: 2

Ingredients

1 pound sweet potatoes
5 cloves smashed garlic

2 tbsp olive oil
Salt to taste

1 tsp rosemary, chopped

Directions

Prepare a water bath and place the Sous Vide in it. Set to 192 F. Combine all the ingredients and place in a vacuum-sealable bag. Release air by the water displacement method, seal, and submerge the bag in the bath. Cook for 1 hour. Once the timer has stopped, remove the potatoes and transfer to a baking tray foil-lined. Cut the potatoes in rounds and sprinkle with garlic oil. Bake for 10 minutes in the oven at 380 F. Garnish with rosemary.

Easy Two-Bean Salad

Prep + Cook Time: 7 hours 10 minutes | Servings: 6

Ingredients

4 oz dry black beans
4 oz dry kidney beans
4 cups water

1 minced shallot
Salt to taste
1 tsp sugar

1 tbsp champagne
3 tbsp olive oil

Directions

Prepare a water bath and place the Sous Vide in it. Set to 90 F. Combine the black beans, 3 cups of water and kidney beans in 4-6 mason jars. Seal and submerge the jars in the water bath. Cook for 2 hours.

Once the timer has stopped, remove the jars and top with shallots, kosher salt and sugar. Allow resting. Seal and immerse in the water bath again. Cook for 4 hours. Once the timer has stopped, remove the jars and allow chilling for 1 hour. Add olive oil and champagne and shake well. Transfer to a bowl and serve.

Tasty Spicy Tomatoes

Prep + Cook Time: 60 minutes | Servings: 4

Ingredients

4 pieces cored and diced tomatoes
2 tbsp olive oil

3 minced garlic cloves
1 tsp dried oregano

1 tsp rosemary
1 tsp fine sea salt

Directions

Prepare a water bath and place Sous Vide in it. Set to 146 F. Place all the ingredients in a vacuum-sealable bag. Release air by the water displacement method, seal and submerge in the bath. Cook for 45 minutes. Once the timer has stopped, remove the tomatoes and transfer to a plate. Serve with toast French bread slices.

Easy Vegetable Alfredo Dressing

Prep + Cook Time: 1 hour 45 minutes | Servings: 6

Ingredients

4 cups chopped cauliflower
2 cups water
2/3 cup hazelnuts

2 cloves garlic
½ tsp dried oregano
½ tsp dried basil

½ tsp dried rosemary
4 tbsp nutritional yeast
Salt and black pepper to taste

Directions

Prepare a water bath and place the Sous Vide in it. Set to 172 F.

Place the hazelnuts, cauliflower, oregano, water, garlic, rosemary, and basil in a vacuum-sealable bag. Release air by the water displacement method, seal, and submerge the bag in the water bath. Cook for 90 minutes. Once the timer has stopped, remove the contents and transfer into a blender and blend until pureed. Serve with pasta.

Garlicky Snow Bean Sauce

Prep + Cook Time: 1 hour 50 minutes | Servings: 4

Ingredients

4 cups halved snow beans
3 minced garlic cloves

2 tsp rice wine vinegar
1 ½ tbsp prepared black bean sauce

1 tbsp olive oil

Directions

Prepare a water bath and place the Sous Vide in it. Set to 172 F. Combine well all the ingredients with the snow beans and place them in a vacuum-sealable bag. Release air by the water displacement method, seal, and submerge the bag in the water bath. Cook for 1 hour and 30 minutes. Serve and enjoy!

Lovely Kidney Bean & Carrot Stew

Prep + Cook Time: 3 hours 15 minutes | Servings: 8

Ingredients

1 cup kidney beans, soaked overnight
1 cup water
½ cup olive oil
1 carrot, chopped

1 celery stalk, chopped
1 quartered shallot
4 crushed garlic cloves
2 fresh rosemary sprigs

2 bay leaves
Salt and black pepper, to taste

Directions

Prepare a water bath and place the Sous Vide in it. Set to 192 F.

Strain the beans and wash them. Place in a vacuum-sealable bag with olive oil, celery, water, carrot, shallot, garlic, rosemary, and bay leaves. Season with salt and pepper. Release air by the water displacement method, seal, and submerge the bag in the water bath. Cook for 180 minutes. Once the timer has stopped, remove the beans. Discard bay leaves and the rosemary.

Flavorful Vegan Stew with Cannellini Beans

Prep + Cook Time: 3 hours 15 minutes | Servings: 8

Ingredients

1 cup cannellini beans, soaked overnight
1 cup water
½ cup olive oil

1 peeled carrot, chopped
1 stalk celery, chopped
1 quartered shallot
4 cloves crushed garlic

2 sprigs fresh rosemary
2 bay leaves
Salt and black pepper to taste

Directions

Prepare a water bath and place the Sous Vide in it. Set to 192 F.

Strain and wash the beans and place with the remaining ingredients in a vacuum-sealable bag. Release air by the water displacement method, seal, and submerge the bag in the water bath. Cook for 3 hours. Once the timer has stopped, remove the bag and dash the consistency. If you want more soften cook for another 1 hour. Serve.

Spicy Black Beans

Prep + Cook Time: 6 hours 15 minutes | Servings: 6

Ingredients

1 cup dry black beans
3 cups water
1/3 cup lemon juice

2 tbsp lemon zest
Salt to taste
1 tsp cumin

½ tsp chipotle chili powder

Directions

Prepare a water bath and place Sous Vide in it. Set to 193 F. Place all the ingredients in a vacuum-sealable bag. Release air by the water displacement method, seal, and submerge the bag in the water bath. Cook for 6 hours. Once the timer has stopped, remove the bag and transfer into a hot saucepan over medium heat and cook until reduced. Remove from the heat and serve.

Glazed Pickled Carrots

Prep + Cook Time: 1 hour 45 minutes | Servings: 1

Ingredients

1 cup white wine vinegar
½ cup beet sugar
Salt to taste

1 tsp black peppercorns
1/3 cup ice-cold water
10 carrots, peeled

4 sprigs fresh sage
2 peeled garlic cloves

Directions

Prepare a water bath and place the Sous Vide in it. Set to 192 F. Heat a pot over medium heat and pour the vinegar, salt, sugar and peppercorns. Stir well until boiling and sugar dissolved. Remove from the heat and pour cold water. Allow cooling.

Place the sage, carrots, garlic and the mixture in a vacuum-sealable bag. Release air by the water displacement method, seal, and submerge the bag in the water bath. Cook for 90 minutes. Once the timer has stopped, remove the bag and transfer to an ice-water bath. Plate and serve.

Delightful Tofu with Sriracha Sauce

Prep + Cook Time: 1 hour 10 minutes | Servings: 10

Ingredients

1 cup vegetable broth
2 tbsp tomato paste
1 tbsp grated ginger
1 tbsp ground nutmeg

1 tbsp rice wine
1 tbsp rice wine vinegar
1 tbsp agave nectar
2 tsp Sriracha sauce

3 minced garlic cloves
2 boxes cubed tofu

Directions

Prepare a water bath and place the Sous Vide in it. Set to 186 F.

Combine well all the ingredients, except for the tofu. Place the tofu with the mixture in a vacuum-sealable bag. Release air by the water displacement method, seal, and submerge the bag in the water bath. Cook for 60 minutes. Once the timer has stopped, remove the bag and transfer into a bowl.

Cheesy Arugula & Beet Salad

Prep + Cook Time: 1 hour 10 minutes | Servings: 4

Ingredients

1 pound baby beets, chopped
Salt to taste

½ cup baby arugula
¼ pound cream cheese

2 mandarin oranges, cut up into wedges
¼ cup slivered almonds

Directions

Prepare a water bath and place the Sous Vide in it. Set to 182 F.

Season beets with salt. Place them in a vacuum-sealable bag with orange juice. Release air by the water displacement method, seal, and submerge the bag in the water bath. Cook for 60 minutes.

Once the timer has stopped, remove the beets and discard the juice. Transfer to serving plates and garnish with cream cheese, mandarin oranges wedges, arugula, and almonds. Serve and enjoy!

Herby Balsamic Mushrooms with Garlic

Prep + Cook Time: 1 hour 15 minutes | Servings: 4

Ingredients

1 pound Portobello mushrooms, sliced
1 tbsp olive oil
1 tbsp apple balsamic vinegar

1 minced garlic clove
Salt to taste
1 tsp black pepper

1 tsp minced fresh thyme

Directions

Prepare a water bath and place the Sous Vide in it. Set to 138 F. Combine all the ingredients and place them in a vacuum-sealable bag. Release air by the water displacement method, seal, and submerge the bag in the water bath. Cook for 60 minutes. Once the timer has stopped, remove the bag and transfer to a serving bowl.

Pickled Cucumbers Pots

Prep + Cook Time: 30 minutes | Servings: 6

Ingredients

1 cup white wine vinegar
½ cup sugar
Salt to taste

1 tbsp pickling spice
2 English cucumbers sliced
½ white thinly sliced onion

3 tsp dill seeds
2 tsp black peppercorns
6 cloves garlic, peeled

Directions

Prepare a water bath and place the Sous Vide in it. Set to 182 F.

Combine sugar, vinegar, salt, pickling spice, dill seeds, black peppercorns, cucumber, onion, and garlic and place in a vacuum-sealable bag. Release air by water displacement method, seal and submerge in the water bath. Cook for 15 minutes. Once done, transfer to an ice-water bath. Serve in mason jars.

Coconut Potato Mash

Prep + Cook Time: 45 minutes | Servings: 4

Ingredients

1 ½ pounds Yukon gold potatoes, sliced
4 ounces butter

8 oz coconut milk
Salt and white pepper to taste

Directions

Prepare a water bath and place Sous Vide in it. Set to 193 F. Place the potatoes, coconut milk, butter, and salt in a vacuum-sealable bag. Release air by water displacement method, seal and submerge in the bath. Cook for 30 minutes. Once done, remove the bag and drain. Reserve butter juices. Mash the potatoes until soft and transfer to the butter bowl. Season with pepper and serve.

Tempting Buttery Cabbage

Prep + Cook Time: 4 hours 15 minutes | Servings: 1

Ingredients

1 head green cabbage, cut up into   wedges   2 tbsp butter

Directions

Prepare a water bath and place the Sous Vide in it. Set to 183 F. Place 1 tbsp of butter and cabbage in a vacuum-sealable bag. Release air by water displacement method, seal and submerge in the water bath. Cook for 4 hours. Once done, remove the cabbage and dry it. Melt butter in a skillet over medium heat and sear the cabbage for 5-7 minutes until golden brown.

Sweet Daikon Radishes with Rosemary

Prep + Cook Time: 40 minutes | Servings: 4

Ingredients

½ cup lemon juice
3 tbsp sugar

1 tsp rosemary
1 large size daikon radish, sliced

Directions

Prepare a water bath and place the Sous Vide in it. Set to 182 F. Combine the lemon juice, rosemary, salt, and sugar. Place the mixture and daikon radish in a vacuum-sealable bag. Release air by the water displacement method, seal, and submerge the bag in the water bath. Cook for 30 minutes. Once the timer has stopped, remove the bag and transfer into an ice-water bath. Serve in a plate.

Shallot Cabbage with Raisins

Prep + Cook Time: 2 hours 15 minutes | Servings: 4

Ingredients

1 ½ pounds red cabbage, sliced
¼ cup raisins

2 sliced shallots
3 sliced garlic cloves

1 tbsp apple balsamic vinegar
1 tbsp butter

Directions

Prepare a water bath and place Sous Vide in it. Set to 186 F. Place the cabbage in a vacuum-sealable bag. Add the remaining ingredients. Release air by the water displacement method, seal, and submerge the bag in the water bath. Cook for 2 hours. Once the timer has stopped, remove the bags and transfer into serving bowls. Season with salt and vinegar. Top with the cooking juices.

Mixed Beans in Tomato Sauce

Prep + Cook Time: 3 hours 10 minutes | Servings: 4

Ingredients

1 pound trimmed green beans
1 pound trimmed snow beans

1 (14-oz) can whole crushed tomatoes
1 thinly sliced onion

3 sliced garlic cloves
3 tbsp olive oil

Directions

Prepare a water bath and place Sous Vide in it. Set to 183 F. Place the tomatoes, snow and green beans, garlic, and onion in a vacuum-sealable bag. Release air by water displacement method, seal and submerge in the water bath. Cook for 3 hours. Once done, transfer into a bowl. Sprinkle with olive oil.

Thai Pumpkin Dish

Prep + Cook Time: 2 hours 20 minutes | Servings: 6

Ingredients

1 medium pumpkin
2 tbsp vegan butter

2 tbsp Thai curry paste
Salt to taste

Fresh cilantro for serving
Lime wedges for serving

Directions

Prepare a water bath and place the Sous Vide in it. Set to 186 F.

Cut the pumpkin into wedges slices and take out the seeds. Reserve the seeds. Place the pumpkin wedges, curry paste, butter, and salt in a vacuum-sealable bag. Release air by the water displacement method, seal, and submerge the bag in the water bath. Cook for 90 minutes.

Once the timer has stopped, remove the bag and squash until softened. If required, cook for 40 minutes more. Transfer to a serving plate and top with curry sauce. Garnish with cilantro and lime wedges.

Lemon-Sage Apricots

Prep + Cook Time: 70 minutes | Servings: 4

Ingredients

½ cup honey
8 apricots, pitted and quartered

2 tbsp water
1 tbsp lemon juice

3 fresh sage sprigs
1 fresh parsley sprig

Directions

Prepare a water bath and place the Sous Vide in it. Set to 179 F. Place all the ingredients in a vacuum-sealable bag. Release air by the water displacement method, seal, and submerge the bag in the water bath. Cook for 45 minutes. Once the timer has stopped, remove the bag and discard the herb springs.

DESSERTS & DRINKS

Fresh Fruit Créme Brulée

Prep + Cook Time: 65 minutes + 5 hours Cooling Time | Servings: 6

Ingredients

1 cup fresh blackberries
6 egg yolks
1⅓ cups sugar + more for sprinkling

3 cups heavy cream
Zest of 2 orange
4 tbsp orange juice

1 tsp vanilla extract

Directions

Prepare a water bath and place the Sous Vide in it. Set to 196 F. In a blender, mix the egg yolks and sugar until creamy. Set aside. Heat a saucepan over medium heat and pour the cream. Add the orange zest and juice and vanilla extract. Lower the heat and cook for 4-5 minutes. Put the blackberries in six mason jars, pour the egg-cream mixture over the blackberries. Seal with a lid and submerge the jars in the water bath. Cook for 45 minutes.

Once the timer has stopped, remove the jars and transfer into the fridge and allow to chill for 5 hours. Remove the lid and sprinkle with sugar. Caramelize the sugar with a blowtorch.

Vanilla Berry Pudding

Prep + Cook Time: 2 hours 32 minutes | Servings: 6

Ingredients

1 cup mixed fresh berries
4 slices challah, cubed
6 egg yolks

1⅛ cups superfine sugar
2 cups heavy cream
1 cup milk

2 tsp almond extract
1 vanilla pod, halved, seeds reserved

Directions

Prepare a water bath and place the Sous Vide in it. Set to 172 F. Preheat the oven to 350 F. Place bread cubes in a baking tray and toast for 5 minutes. Set aside. With an electric mixer, mix the egg yolks and sugar until creamy.

Heat a saucepan over medium heat and pour in cream and milk. Cook until boiled. Add in almond extract, vanilla pod seeds and vanilla pod. Lower the heat and cook for 4-5 minutes. Set aside and allow to cool for 2-3 minutes.

Once the vanilla mixture has cooled, pour a small amount of the cream into the egg mixture and combine. Repeat the process with each egg. Combine the bread cubes with the egg-cream mixture and let the bread absorb the liquid. Add the berries and combine well. Divide the mixture into six mason jars. Seal with a lid and submerge the jars in the water bath. Cook for 2 hours.

Mocha Mini Brownies in a Jar

Prep + Cook Time: 3 hours 17 minutes | Servings: 10

Ingredients

⅔ cup white chocolate, chopped
8 tbsp butter
⅔ cup superfine sugar
2 egg yolks

1 egg
2 tbsp instant coffee powder
1 tbsp coconut extract
1 tbsp coffee liqueur

½ cup all-purpose flour
Ice cream, for serving

Directions

Prepare a water bath and place Sous Vide in it. Set to 196 F. Heat the chocolate and butter in a pot or in the microwave. Fold sugar into the chocolate-butter mixture until dissolved. Pour the egg yolks one by one and stir well. Add in whole egg and continue mixing. Pour in coffee powder, coconut extract and coffee liqueur.

Add in flour and stir until combined well. Pour the chocolate mixture into 10 mini mason jars. Seal with a lid and submerge the jars in the water bath. Cook for 3 hours. Once ready, remove the jars and allow to cool for 1 minute.

Orange Pots du Créme with Chocolate

Prep + Cook Time: 6 hours 5 minutes + | Servings: 6

Ingredients

⅔ cup chopped chocolate	3 cups half and half	⅛ tsp orange extract
6 egg yolks	1 tsp vanilla extract	2 tbsp orange juice
1⅓ cups fine white sugar	Zest of 1 large orange	2 tbsp chocolate-flavored liqueur

Directions

Prepare a water bath and place the Sous Vide in it. Set to 196 F. With an electric mixer, combine the egg yolks and sugar. Mix for 1-2 minutes until creamy. Heat the cream in a saucepan over medium heat and add in vanilla, orange zest and extract. Cook on Low heat for 3-4 minutes. Set aside and allow to cool for 2-3 minutes.

Melt the chocolate in the microwave. Once the mixture has cooled, pour the cream mixture into the egg mixture and stir. Add the melted chocolate and stir until combined. Add in orange juice and chocolate liqueur. Pour the chocolate mixture into mason jars. Seal with a lid and submerge the jars in the water bath. Cook for 45 minutes. Once the timer has stopped, remove the jars and allow to cool for 5 minutes.

Vanilla Ice Cream

Prep + Cook Time: 5 hours 10 minutes | Servings: 4

Ingredients

6 egg yolks	1 ½ tsp vanilla extract
½ cup sugar	2 cups half and half

Directions

Prepare a water bath and place the Sous Vide in it. Set to 180 F. Whisk all the ingredients in a vacuum-sealable bag. Release air by the water displacement method, seal, and submerge the bag in the water bath. Set the timer for 1 hour. Once the timer has stopped, make sure there are no lumps. Transfer the mixture to a container with a lid. Place in the freeze for 4 hours.

Chocolate Pudding

Prep + Cook Time: 55 minutes | Servings: 4

Ingredients

½ cup milk	3 egg yolks	4 tbsp cocoa powder
1 cup chocolate chips	½ cup heavy cream	3 tbsp sugar

Directions

Prepare a water bath and place the Sous Vide in it. Set to 185 F. Whisk the yolks along with sugar, milk, and heavy cream. Stir in cocoa powder and chocolate chips. Divide the mixture between 4 jars. Seal and immerse the jars in the water bath. Set the timer for 40 minutes. Once ready, remove the jars. Let cool before serving.

Honey & Citrus Apricots

Prep + Cook Time: 70 minutes | Servings: 4

Ingredients

6 apricots, pitted and quartered	2 tbsp water	1 vanilla bean pod, halved
½ cup honey	1 tbsp lime juice	1 cinnamon stick

Directions

Prepare a water bath and place the Sous Vide in it. Set to 179 F. Place all the ingredients in a vacuum-sealable bag. Release air by the water displacement method, seal, and submerge the bag in the water bath. Cook for 45 minutes. Once the timer has stopped, remove the bag and discard the vanilla bean pod and cinnamon stick. Serve.

Light Cottage Cheese Breakfast Pudding

Prep + Cook Time: 3 hours 15 minutes | Servings: 3

Ingredients

1 cup cottage cheese	3 tbsp sour cream	1 tsp orange zest
5 eggs	4 tbsp sugar	1 tbsp cornstarch
1 cup milk	1 tsp cardamom	¼ tsp salt

Directions

Prepare a water bath and place Sous Vide in it. Set to 175 F. With an electric mixer, beat the eggs and sugar. Add in zest, milk and cornstarch. Add the remaining ingredients and whisk well.

Grease 3 mason jars with cooking spray and divide the mixture between them. Seal and immerse the mason jars in a water bath. Cook for 3 hours. Once the timer has stopped, remove the jars. Let cool before serving.

Sous Vide Chocolate Cupcakes

Prep + Cook Time: 3 hours 15 minutes | Servings: 6

Ingredients

5 tbsp butter, melted	4 tbsp sugar	1 tsp apple cider vinegar
1 egg	½ cup heavy cream	Pinch of sea salt
3 tbsp cocoa powder	1 tsp baking soda	
1 cup flour	1 tsp vanilla extract	

Directions

Prepare a water bath and place the Sous Vide in it. Set to 194 F. Whisk together the wet ingredients in one bowl. Combine the dry ingredients in another bowl. Combine the two mixtures gently and divide the batter between 6 small jars. Seal the jars and submerge the bag in the water bath. Set the timer for 3 hours Once the timer has stopped, remove the bag. Serve chilled.

Easy Banana Cream

Prep + Cook Time: 60 minutes | Servings: 6

Ingredients

3 banans, mashed	1 cup superfine sugar	1 tsp vanilla extract
12 egg yolks	3 cups heavy cream	1 tsp mint extract

Directions

Prepare a water bath and place the Sous Vide in it. Set to 196 F. With an electric mixer, combine the egg yolks and sugar. Mix for 1-2 minutes until creamy. Heat the cream in a saucepan over medium heat and add in vanilla and mint. Cook on Low for 3-4 minutes. Set aside and allow to cool for 2-3 minutes.

Once the mixture has cooled, pour the cream mixture into the egg mixture and stir. Add in mashed bananas and stir to combine. Pour the mixture into 6 mini mason jars. Seal and submerge in the water bath. Cook for 45 minutes. Once the timer has stopped, remove the jars and allow to cool for 5 minutes.

Apple Pie

Prep + Cook Time: 85 minutes | Servings: 8

Ingredients

1 pound apples, peel and cubed	2 tbsp lemon juice	¼ tsp nutmeg
6 ounces puff pastry	1 tbsp cornstarch	¼ tsp cinnamon
1 egg yolk, whisked	1 tsp ground ginger	
4 tbsp sugar	2 tbsp butter, melted	

Directions

Preheat your oven to 365 F. Roll the pastry into a circle. Brush with the butter and place in the oven. Cook for 15 minutes. Prepare a water bath and place Sous Vide in it. Set to 160 F. Combine all the remaining ingredients in a vacuum-sealable bag. Release air by water displacement method, seal and submerge in the water bath.

Cook for 45 minutes. Once the timer has stopped, remove the bag. Top the cooked pie crust with the apple mixture. Return to the oven and cook for 15 more minutes.

Dulce de Leche Cheesecake

Prep + Cook Time: 5 hours 55 minutes + 4 hours | Servings: 6

Ingredients

2 cups mascarpone, softened   1 cup dulce de leche   3 tbsp butter, melted
3 eggs   ⅓ cup heavy cream   ½ tsp salt
1 tsp almond extract   1 cup graham cracker crumbs

Directions

Prepare a water bath and place the Sous Vide in it. Set to 175 F. With an electric mixer, mix the mascarpone, eggs, and almond in a bowl until smooth. Pour 3/4 cup of dulce de leche and mix well. Add in cream and stir until fully combined. Set aside.

Combine the graham cracker crumbs and melted butter. Divide the crumbs mixture into six mini mason jars. Pour cream cheese mixture over the crumbs. Seal with a lid and submerge the jars in the water bath. Cook for 1 hour and 30 minutes. Once the timer has stopped, remove the jars and transfer into the fridge and allow to cool for 4 hours. Top with the remaining dulce de leche. Garnish with the salted caramel mixture.

Sugar-Free Chocolate Chip Cookies

Prep + Cook Time: 3 hours 45 minutes | Servings: 6

Ingredients

1/3 cup chocolate chips   ½ cup flour   ¼ tsp salt
7 tbsp heavy cream   ½ tsp baking soda   1 tbsp lemon juice
2 eggs   4 tbsp butter, melted

Directions

Prepare a water bath and place the Sous Vide in it. Set to 194 F. Beat the eggs along with the cream, lemon juice, salt, and baking soda. Stir in flour and butter. Fold in the chocolate chips.

Divide the dough between 6 ramekins. Wrap them well with plastic foil and place the ramekins in the water bath. Cook for 3 hours and 30 minutes. Once the timer has stopped, remove the ramekins.

Raisin-Stuffed Sweet Apples

Prep + Cook Time: 2 hours 15 minutes | Servings: 4

Ingredients

4 small apples, peeled and cored   4 tbsp butter, softened   ½ tsp cinnamon
1 ½ tbsp raisins   ¼ tsp nutmeg   1 tbsp sugar

Directions

Prepare a water bath and place the Sous Vide in it. Set to 170 F.

Combine the raisins, sugar, butter, cinnamon, and nutmeg. Stuff the apples with the raisin mixture. Divide the apples between 2 vacuum-sealable bag Release air by the water displacement method, seal and submerge the bags in the water bath. Set the timer for 2 hours. Once the timer has stopped, remove the bags. Serve warm.

Bread Pudding

Prep + Cook Time: 2 hours 15 minutes | Servings: 8

Ingredients

1 cup milk
1 cup heavy cream
10 ounces white bread
4 eggs

2 tbsp butter, melted
1 tbsp flour
1 tbsp cornstarch
4 tbsp sugar

1 tsp vanilla extract
¼ tsp salt

Directions

Prepare a water bath and place the Sous Vide in it. Set to 170 F. Chop the bread into small pieces and place in a vacuum-sealable bag. Beat the eggs along with the remaining ingredients. Pour the mixture over the bread. Release air by the water displacement method, seal, and submerge the bag in the water bath. Set the timer for 2 hours. Once the timer has stopped, remove the bag. Serve warm.

Rice Pudding with Rum & Cranberries

Prep + Cook Time: 2 hours 15 minutes | Servings: 6

Ingredients

2 cups rice
3 cups milk

½ cup dried cranberries soaked in ½
cup of rum overnight and drained

1 tsp cinnamon
½ cup brown sugar

Directions

Prepare a water bath and place the Sous Vide in it. Set to 140 F. Combine all the ingredients in a bowl and transfer to 6 small jars. Seal them and submerge in the water bath. Set the timer for 2 hours. Once the timer has stopped, remove the jars. Serve warm or chilled.

Lemon Curd

Prep + Cook Time: 75 minutes | Servings: 8

Ingredients

1 cup butter
1 cup sugar

12 egg yolks
5 lemons

Directions

Prepare a water bath and place the Sous Vide in it. Set to 168 F.

Grate the zest from lemons and place in a bowl. Squeeze the juice and add to the bowl as well. Whisk on the yolks and sugar and transfer to a vacuum-sealable bag. Release air by the water displacement method, seal, and submerge the bag in the water bath. Set the timer for 1 hour. Once the timer has stopped, remove the bag and transfer the cooked lemon curd to a bowl and place in an ice bath. Let chill completely.

Crème Brulee

Prep + Cook Time: 45 minutes | Servings: 4

Ingredients

2 cups heavy cream
4 egg yolks

¼ cup sugar
1 tsp vanilla extract

Directions

Prepare a water bath and place the Sous Vide in it. Set to 180 F. Whisk together all the ingredients and transfer into 4 shallow jars. Seal and immerse in the water bath. Cook for 30 minutes. Once the timer has stopped, remove the shallow jars and sprinkle some sugar on top of the brulee. Place under broiler until they become caramelized.

Lemony Muffins

Prep + Cook Time: 3 hours 45 minutes | Servings: 6

Ingredients

2 eggs	1 tbsp lemon juice	2 eggs
1 cup flour	1 tbsp lemon zest	1 tsp baking soda
4 tbsp sugar	1/3 cup heavy cream	½ cup butter

Directions

Prepare a water bath and place the Sous Vide in it. Set to 190 F. Beat the eggs and sugar until creamy. Gradually beat in the remaining ingredients. Divide the batter between 6 mason jars. Seal the jars and submerge the bag in the water bath. Set the timer for 3 hours and 30 minutes. Once done, remove the jars. Let cool before serving.

Raspberry Mousse

Prep + Cook Time: 75 minutes | Servings: 6

Ingredients

1 cup raspberries	2 tbsp cornstarch	1 tsp ground ginger
1 cup milk	½ cup sugar	1 tbsp cocoa powder
1 cup cream cheese	1 tbsp flour	Pinch of sea salt

Directions

Prepare a water bath and place the Sous Vide in it. Set to 170 F. Place all the ingredients in a blender. Blend until smooth and transfer to 6 small jars., Seal the jars and submerge the bag in the water bath. Set the timer for 1 hour. Once the timer has stopped, remove the jars. Serve chilled.

Apple Cobbler

Prep + Cook Time: 3 hours 50 minutes | Servings: 6

Ingredients

1 cup milk	1 tsp butter	4 tbsp brown sugar
2 green apples, peeled and cubed	7 tbsp flour	1 tsp ground cardamom

Directions

Prepare a water bath and place the Sous Vide in it. Set to 190 F.

Whisk together the butter, sugar, milk, and cardamom. Stir in the flour gradually. Fold in the apples and divide the mixture between 6 small jars., Seal the jars and submerge the bag in the water bath. Set the timer for 3 hours and 30 minutes. Once the timer has stopped, remove the bag. Serve warm.

Mini Strawberry Cheesecake Jars

Prep + Cook Time: 90 minutes | Servings: 4

Ingredients

4 eggs	½ cup sugar	1 tbsp flour
2 tbsp milk	½ cup cream cheese	1 tsp lemon zest
3 tbsp strawberry jam	½ cup cottage cheese	

Directions

Prepare a water bath and place the Sous Vide in it. Set to 180 F.

Whisk together the cheeses and sugar until fluffy. Beat in the eggs one by one. Add the remaining ingredients and stir until well combined. Divide between 4 jars.Seal the jars and submerge the bag in the water bath. Set the timer for 75 minutes. Once the timer has stopped, remove the bag. Chill and serve.

Wine and Cinnamon Poached Pears

Prep + Cook Time: 80 minutes | Servings: 4

Ingredients

4 pears, peeled

2 cinnamon sticks

2 cups red wine

1/3 cup sugar

3 star anise

Directions

Prepare a water bath and place the Sous Vide in it. Set to 175 F.

Combine the wine, anise, sugar, and cinnamon in a large vacuum-sealable bag. Place the pears inside. Release air by the water displacement method, seal, and submerge the bag in the water bath. Set the timer for 1 hour. Once the timer has stopped, remove the bag. Serve the pears drizzle with the wine sauce.

Coconut and Almond Oatmeal

Prep + Cook Time: 12 hours 10 minutes | Servings: 4

Ingredients

2 cups oatmeal

2 cups almond milk

3 tbsp shredded coconut

3 tbsp flaked almonds

3 tbsp stevia extract

1 tbsp butter

¼ tsp ground anise

Pinch of sea salt

Directions

Prepare a water bath and place the Sous Vide in it. Set to 180 F. Combine all the ingredients in a vacuum-sealable bag. Release air by the water displacement method, seal, and submerge the bag in the water bath. Set the timer for 12 hours. Once the timer has stopped, remove the bag and divide into 4 serving bowls.

Banana Buckwheat Porridge

Prep + Cook Time: 12 hours 15 minutes | Servings: 4

Ingredients

2 cups buckwheat

1 banana, mashed

½ cup condensed milk

1 tbsp butter

1 tsp vanilla extract

1 ½ cup water

¼ tsp salt

Directions

Prepare a water bath and place the Sous Vide in it. Set to 180 F.

Place the buckwheat in a vacuum-sealable bag. Whisk the remaining ingredients in a bowl. Pour this mixture over the buckwheat. Release air by the water displacement method, seal, and submerge the bag in the water bath. Set the timer for 12 hours. Once the timer has stopped, remove the bag. Serve warm.

Coffee Buttery Bread

Prep + Cook Time: 3 hours 15 minutes | Servings: 4

Ingredients

6 ounces white bread

¾ cup butter

6 tbsp coffee

½ tsp cinnamon

1 tsp brown sugar

Directions

Prepare a water bath and place the Sous Vide in it. Set to 195 F. Slice the bread into strips and place in a vacuum-sealable bag. Whisk the other ingredients in a bowl and pour the mixture over the bread. Release air by the water displacement method, seal, and submerge the bag in the water bath. Set the timer for 3 hours. Once the timer has stopped, remove the bag. Serve warm.

Almond Nectarine Pie

Prep + Cook Time: 3 hours 20 minutes | Servings: 6

Ingredients

3 cups nectarines, peeled and diced
8 tbsp butter
1 cup sugar

1 tsp vanilla extract
1 tsp almond extract
1 cup milk

1 cup flour

Directions

Prepare a water bath and place the Sous Vide in it. Set to 194 F. Grease small jars with cooking spray. Gather the nectarines amongst the jars. In a bowl, mix sugar and butter. Add the almond extract, whole milk and vanilla extract, mix well. Stir the self-rising flour and blend until solid. Place the batter into the jars. Seal and submerge the jars in the water bath. Cook for 180 minutes. Once the timer has stopped, remove the jars. Serve.

Basic Oatmeal from Scratch

Prep + Cook Time: 8 hours 10 minutes | Servings: 4

Ingredients

1 cup oats
3 cups water

½ tsp vanilla extract
Pinch of sea salt

Directions

Prepare a water bath and place the Sous Vide in it. Set to 155 F. Combine all the ingredients in a vacuum-sealable bag. Release air by the water displacement method, seal, and submerge the bag in the water bath. Set the timer for 8 hours. Once the timer has stopped, remove the bag. Serve warm.

Mini Cheesecakes

Prep + Cook Time: 45 minutes | Servings: 3

Ingredients

3 eggs
5 tbsp cottage cheese

½ cup cream cheese
4 tbsp sugar

½ tsp vanilla extract

Directions

Prepare a water bath and place the Sous Vide in it. Set to 175 F. Place all the ingredients in a mixing bowl. Beat with an electric mixer for a few minutes, until soft and smooth. Divide the mixture between 3 mason jars., Seal the jars and submerge the bag in the water bath. Set the timer for 25 minutes. Once the timer has stopped, remove the jars. Chill until ready to serve.

Bubble Raspberry Lemonade

Prep + Cook Time: 3 hours 10 minutes | Servings: 1

Ingredients

2 cups fresh raspberries
3 cups vodka

3 ounces lemonade
1 tbsp champagne

Directions

Prepare a water bath and place the Sous Vide in it. Set to 130 F. Put 1 cup of raspberries in each of two mason jars. Smash some of the raspberries. Pour the vodka and seal with a lid and submerge the jars in the water bath,

Cook for 3 hours. Once the timer has stopped, remove the jars and transfer to an ice water bath. Drain the raspberries. Place into a cocktail shaker some ice, 1 1/2 ounces of raspberry-infused vodka and lemonade. Shake for 30 seconds. Pour into a martini glass. Top with the champagne. Garnish with raspberries.

Carrot Muffins

Prep + Cook Time: 3 hours 15 minutes | Servings: 10

Ingredients

1 cup flour
3 eggs
½ cup butter

¼ cup heavy cream
2 carrots, grated
1 tsp lemon juice

1 tbsp coconut flour
¼ tsp salt
½ tsp baking soda

Directions

Prepare a water bath and place the Sous Vide in it. Set to 195 F. Whisk the wet ingredients in one bowl and combine the dry ones in another. Gently combine the two mixtures together. Divide the mixture between 5 mason jars (Do not fill more than halfway. Use more jars if needed). Seal the jars and submerge in the water bath. Set the timer for 3 hours. Once the timer has stopped, remove the jars. Cut into halves and serve.

Peach and Almond Yogurt

Prep + Cook Time: 11 hour 20 minutes | Servings: 4

Ingredients

2 cup whole milk
4 ounces ground almonds

2 tbsp yogurt
¼ cup mashed peeled peaches

¼ tsp vanilla sugar
1 tbsp honey

Directions

Prepare a water bath and place the Sous Vide in it. Set to 110 F. Heat the milk in a saucepan until the temperature reaches 142 F. Let cook at 110 F. Stir yogurt, honey, peaches and sugar. Divide the mixture between 4 jars. Seal the jars and immerse in the water bath. Cook for 11 hour. Once timer has stopped, remove the jars. Stir in almonds and serve.

Raspberry Lemon Créme Brulée

Prep + Cook Time: 6 hours 5 minutes | Servings: 6

Ingredients

6 large egg yolks
1 1/3 cups sugar
3 cups heavy whipping cream

Zest of 2 lemons
4 tbsp freshly squeezed lemon juice
1 tsp vanilla extract

1 cup fresh raspberries

Directions

Prepare a water bath and place the Sous Vide in it. Set to 194 F.

In a mixer, combine the egg yolks and sugar until creamy. Set aside. Heat a pot over medium heat and cook the creamy mixture, lemon zest, lemon juice, and vanilla. Stir for 4-5 minutes in lower heat. Remove from the heat and allow cooling. Combine well the egg mix with the creamy blend.

Put the raspberries in six mason jars and pour over the mixture. Fill with more raspberries. Seal and submerge the jars in the water bath. Cook for 45 minutes. Once the timer has stopped, remove the jars. Allow chilling for 5 hours. Caramelized the sugar and serve.

Fresh Cocktail with Ginger Beer

Prep + Cook Time: 2 hours 30 minutes | Servings: 8

Ingredients

2-3 cups sliced seedless white grapes
1 ¼ cups vanilla sugar
½ cup bourbon
½ vanilla bean, split

1 lemon, peeled
1-star anise pod
1 cardamom pod
½ cup ginger beer per serving

Fresh mint leaves to garnish
Lemon twists to garnish
Sliced grapes to garnish

Directions

Prepare a water bath and place the Sous Vide in it. Set to 168 F. Place grapes, sugar, vanilla, bourbon, star anise, lemon peel, and cardamom in a vacuum-sealable bag. Release air by water displacement method, seal and submerge in the water bath. Cook for 2 hours.

Once the timer has stopped, remove the bag and transfer into an ice-water bath. Transfer to the fridge and allow chilling. Drain the grape mix and reserve the fruit. In a rock glass, add ginger beer and fruit liquid. Garnish with mint and lemon twist. Top with grapes.

Oatmeal with Prunes and Apricots

Prep + Cook Time: 8 hours 15 minutes | Servings: 4

Ingredients

2 cups milk
2 cups oatmeal
3 tbsp chopped prunes

¼ cup dried apricots
2 tbsp sugar
1 tbsp heavy cream

1 tbsp butter
1 tsp vanilla extract
¼ tsp salt

Directions

Prepare a water bath and place the Sous Vide in it. Set to 180 F. Place the oatmeal in a vacuum-sealable bag. Whisk together the remaining ingredients in a bowl and pour over the oats. Stir in prunes and apricots. Release air by the water displacement method, seal, and submerge the bag in the water bath. Cook for 8 hours. Once the timer has stopped, remove the bag.

Balsamic Honey Shrub

Prep + Cook Time: 2 hours 10 minutes | Servings: 6

Ingredients

1 cup water
½ cup honey
½ cup balsamic vinegar

1 tbsp freshly grated ginger
Bourbon whiskey
Club soda

Lime wedges

Directions

Prepare a water bath and place the Sous Vide in it. Set to 134 F.

Place the water, vinegar, honey, and ginger in a vacuum-sealable bag. Release air by the water displacement method, seal, and submerge the bag in the water bath. Cook for 2 hours.

Once the timer has stopped, remove the bag and drain the mixture. Allow chilling all night. Serve with one-part whiskey and one-part club soda with ice. Garnish with lime wedges.

Indian Lassi with Papaya

Prep + Cook Time: 32 hours 45 minutes | Servings: 8

Ingredients

3 cups milk
3 tbsp yogurt
2 pitted papaya, diced

¼ cup sugar
1 cup ice
1 tbsp vanilla extract

½ tsp salt
Fresh mint leaves for garnish

Directions

Prepare a water bath and place the Sous Vide in it. Set to 115 F.

Hot a saucepan over medium heat and hot the milk. Pour into canning jars and allow cooling. Pour in yogurt and seal. Submerge the jar in the water bath. Cook for 24 hours. Once the timer has stopped, remove the jar and transfer into an ice-water bath. Transfer to the fridge and allow chilling for 8 hours. Blend the papaya, sugar, ice, vanilla, salt, 2 cups of milk and the yogurt mixture. Mix until smooth. Garnish with mint leaves.

Maple & Cinnamon Steel Oats

Prep + Cook Time: 3 hours 10 minutes | Servings: 2

Ingredients

2 cups almond milk
½ cup steel cut oats

¼ tsp salt
Cinnamon and maple syrup for topping

Directions

Prepare a water bath and place the Sous Vide in it. Set to 182 F. Combine all the ingredients, except the cinnamon and maple syrup and place in a vacuum-sealable bag. Release air by the water displacement method, seal, and submerge the bag in the water bath. Cook for 3 hours. Once the timer has stopped, remove the oats and transfer into a serving bowl. Garnish with cinnamon and maple syrup.

Asian-Style Rice Pudding with Almonds

Prep + Cook Time: 7 hours 30 minutes | Servings: 5

Ingredients

5 tbsp basmati rice
2 (14-oz) cans coconut milk

3 tbsp sugar
5 cardamom pods, crushed

3 tbsp cashews, chopped
Slivered almonds for garnish

Directions

Prepare a water bath and place the Sous Vide in it. Set to 182 F.

In a bowl, combine the coconut milk, sugar, and 1 cup water. Pour the rice and mix well. Divide the mixture between the jars. Add a cardamom pod to each pot. Seal and submerge in the bath. Cook for 3 hours. Once the timer has stopped, remove the jars. Allow cooling for 4 hours. Serve and top with cashews and almonds.

Gingered Peaches with Cardamom

Prep + Cook Time: 1 hour 15 minutes | Servings: 4

Ingredients

1 pound peaches, halved
1 tbsp butter

1 tsp cardamom seeds, freshly ground
½ tsp ground ginger

½ tsp salt
Fresh basil, chopped

Directions

Prepare a water bath and place the Sous Vide in it. Set to 182 F. Combine the butter, peaches, ginger, cardamom, and salt. Place in a vacuum-sealable bag. Release air by the water displacement method, seal, and submerge the bag in the water bath. Cook for 60 minutes. Once the timer has stopped, remove the bag and transfer into a bowl. Garnished with basil and serve.

Maple Potato Flan

Prep + Cook Time: 1 hour 10 minutes | Servings: 6

Ingredients

1 cup milk
1 cup heavy whipping cream
3 whole eggs

3 egg yolks
½ cup sweet potatoes puree
¼ cup maple syrup

½ tsp pumpkin spice
Sugar for garnish

Directions

Prepare a water bath and place Sous Vide in it. Set to 168 F. Combine the milk, heavy cream, whole eggs, egg yolks, sweet potatoes puree, maple syrup, and pumpkin spice. Mix until smooth. Pour into mason jars. Seal and submerge in the water bath. Cook for 1 hour. Once ready, remove the jars and allow chilling. Sprinkle with sugar, place under broiler until the sugar is caramelized, and serve.

Homemade Vanilla Pudding

Prep + Cook Time: 55 minutes | Servings: 6

Ingredients

1 cup whole milk
1 cup whipping cream
½ cup sugar

3 large eggs (2 additional egg yolks)
3 tbsp cornstarch
1 tbsp vanilla extract

½ tsp salt

Directions

Prepare a water bath and place the Sous Vide in it. Set to 182 F.

In a blender, mix all the ingredients and pulse until smooth. Transfer to a vacuum-sealable bag. Release air by the water displacement method, seal, and submerge the bag in the water bath. Cook for 45 minutes. Shake a few times. Once the timer has stopped, remove the bag and transfer the contents to the blender. Mix until smooth. Allow chilling in a bowl. Top with strawberries.

Honey Tangerines

Prep + Cook Time: 1 hour 15 minutes | Servings: 4

Ingredients

1 pound tangerines

¼ cup honey

½ tsp salt

Directions

Prepare a water bath and place the Sous Vide in it. Set to 193 F. Slice the tangerines and remove stems and seeds. Combine the honey, tangerines and kosher salt. Place in a vacuum-sealable bag. Release air by the water displacement method, seal, and submerge the bag in the water bath. Cook for 60 minutes. Once the timer has stopped, remove the bag and cool it. Serve.

Coconut Banana Oatrolls with Walnuts

Prep + Cook Time: 6-10 hours 5 minutes | Servings: 4

Ingredients

2 cups rolled oats
3 cups coconut milk

3 cups skimmed milk
3 mashed bananas

1 tsp vanilla extract
1 cup of walnuts, chopped

Directions

Prepare a water bath and place the Sous Vide in it. Set to 182 F.

Combine all the ingredients and place in a vacuum-sealable bag. Release air by the water displacement method, seal, and submerge the bag in the water bath. Cook for 6-10 hours. Once the timer has stopped, remove the bags and transfer the oats into serving bowls. Top with walnuts.

White Chocolate & Banana Popsicles

Prep + Cook Time: 40 minutes | Servings: 6

Ingredients

3 bananas

3 tbsp peanut butter

3 tbsp white chocolate chips

Directions

Prepare a water bath and place the Sous Vide in it. Set to 138 F.

Cut the banana in slices. Place them in a vacuum-sealable bag with white chocolate chips and peanut butter. Release air by the water displacement method, seal, and submerge the bag in the water bath. Cook for 30 minutes. Once the timer has stopped, remove the bag and transfer into popsicles molds. Allow cooling. Pop-out and serve.

Cinnamon Quince Bourbon

Prep + Cook Time: 2 hours 20 minutes | Servings: 8

Ingredients

2 cups bourbon

2 quinces, peeled and sliced

1 cinnamon stick

Directions

Prepare a water bath and place the Sous Vide in it. Set to 150 F. Place all the ingredients in a vacuum-sealable bag. Release air by the water displacement method, seal, and submerge the bag in the water bath. Set the timer for 2 hours. Once the timer has stopped, remove the bag. Strain the bourbon through a cheesecloth.

Rum Cherries

Prep + Cook Time: 45 minutes | Servings: 6

Ingredients

3 cup cherries, pitted

1 cup rum

1 tsp agar

¼ cup sugar

2 tsp sour cherry compound

1 tsp lime zest

Directions

Place all the ingredients in a vacuum-sealable bag. Shake to combine well. Prepare the water by preheating it to 142 F. Divide between 6 serving glasses.

Pumpkin Mini Pies with Pecans

Prep + Cook Time: 9 hours 10 minutes | Servings: 6

Ingredients

1 (15-oz) can pumpkin puree

½ tsp salt

½ cup brown sugar

1 egg

1 tbsp pumpkin pie spice

Whipped cream

3 egg yolks

1 (14-oz) can evaporate milk

4 tbsp pecans, chopped

2 tbsp flour

½ cup white sugar

Directions

Prepare a water bath and place the Sous Vide in it. Set to 175 F

Combine well the butternut squash puree, flour, salt, pumpkin-pie spice, egg, yolks, and evaporated milk. Pour into mason jars. Seal and submerge the jars in the water bath. Cook for 1 hour. Once the timer has stopped, remove the jars and allow chilling 8 hours. Top with whipped cream and pecans.

Savory Banana & Nuts Cups

Prep + Cook Time: 2 hours 25 minutes | Servings: 12

Ingredients

½ cup butter

1 tsp vanilla

½ tsp baking soda

½ cup brown sugar

½ tsp salt

2 cups all-purpose flour

½ cup honey

3 tbsp milk

½ cup nuts

2 eggs

3 mashed bananas

Directions

Prepare a water bath and place the Sous Vide in it. Set to 172 F.

Heat a pot over medium heat and cook the butter with the brown and white sugar. Remove from the heat and allow cooling. Stir in the egg, vanilla, milk and honey. Cook until the sugar dissolved. Add the banana, flour, baking soda, and salt. Mix well. Pour the mixture into mason jars. Seal and submerge the jars in the water bath. Cook for 2 hours. Once the timer has stopped, remove the jars and serve.

Homemade Compote of Strawberries

Prep + Cook Time: 75 minutes | Servings: 8

Ingredients

½ cup sugar
1 tbsp freshly squeezed lemon juice

1 tbsp lemon zest
1 tbsp cornstarch

1 pound strawberries

Directions

Prepare a water bath and place the Sous Vide in it. Set to 18F. Combine well the sugar, lemon juice, lemon zest and cornstarch. Add strawberries and mix well. Place it in a vacuum-sealable bag. Release air by the water displacement method, seal, and submerge the bag in the water bath. Cook for 60 minutes. Once the timer has stopped, remove the bag and transfer to a serving plate. Serve warm.

Orange Cheesy Mousse

Prep + Cook Time: 1 hour 25 minutes | Servings: 8

Ingredients

2 cups milk
6 tbsp white wine vinegar
4 oz chocolate chips

¼ cup powdered sugar
Grand Marnier liquor
1 tbsp orange zest

2 oz goat cheese

Directions

Prepare a water bath and place the Sous Vide in it. Set to 172 F.

Place the milk and vinegar in a vacuum-sealable bag. Release air by the water displacement method, seal, and submerge the bag in the water bath. Cook for 60 minutes. Once the timer has stopped, remove the bag and reserve the curds. Discard the remaining liquid. Strain the curds for 10 minutes. Allow chilling for 1 hour.

Prepare a water bath to medium heat and add the chocolate chips. Cook until melted. Transfer to a blender and stir the sugar, orange zest, grand Marnier, goat cheese. Mix until smooth. Serve into individual bowls.

Vanilla Apricot Crumble

Prep + Cook Time: 3 hours 15 minutes | Servings: 6

Ingredients

1 cup self-rising flour
1 cup granulated sugar

1 cup milk
1 tsp vanilla extract

8 tbsp melted butter
2 cups chopped apricots

Directions

Prepare a water bath and place the Sous Vide in it. Set to 194 F. Grease 6 canning jars with butter.

Combine flour and sugar. Add in milk and vanilla. Mix in butter and apricots. Pour the mixture into the jars. Seal and submerge in the bath. Cook for 3 hours. Once done, remove the jars and allow cooling.

Vanilla Cava Fudge

Prep + Cook Time: 60 minutes | Servings: 6

Ingredients

1 cup whipping cream
½ cup cava

½ cup sugar
4 egg yolks

1 tsp vanilla extract
½ tsp salt

Directions

Prepare a water bath and place the Sous Vide in it. Set to 194 F. Blend all the ingredients for 30 seconds. Place it in a vacuum-sealable bag. Release air by the water displacement method, seal, and submerge the bag in the water bath. Cook for 45 minutes. Once the timer has stopped, remove the bag and transfer into an ice-water bath.

Vanilla Cheesecake

Prep + Cook Time: 1 hour 45 minutes | Servings: 6

Ingredients

12 oz cream cheese, softened
½ cup sugar

¼ cup mascarpone, softened
2 eggs

Zest of 1 lemon
½ tbsp vanilla extract

Directions

Prepare a water bath and place the Sous Vide in it. Set to 175 F.

Combine cream cheese, mascarpone and sugar. Mix well. Stir in the eggs. Add in lemon zest and vanilla extract. Mix well. Pour the mixture in 6 mason jars. Seal and submerge in the water bath. Cook for 90 minutes. Once the timer has stopped, remove the jars and allow chilling. Top with fruit compote.

Coconut Blackberry Tart

Prep + Cook Time: 1 hour 10 minutes | Servings: 4

Ingredients

1 egg
¼ cup heavy cream
¼ cup almond flour

1 tbsp sugar
2 tsp coconut flour
¼ tsp baking powder

¼ tsp vanilla extract
½ cup fresh blackberries
Granulated sugar to garnish

Directions

Prepare a water bath and place the Sous Vide in it. Set to 186 F. Combine well all the ingredients, except the blackberries. Grease the mason jars with cooking spray and pour in the mixture. Top with 2 tbsp of blackberries each jar. Seal and submerge the jars in the water bath. Cook for 60 minutes. Once the timer has stopped, remove the jars. Garnish with sugar.

Grand Marnier & Rhubarb Mousse

Prep + Cook Time: 1 hour 25 minutes | Servings: 6

Ingredients

1 pound trimmed rhubarb, chopped
½ cup packed light brown sugar
1/3 cup freshly squeezed lemon juice

1 tbsp Grand Marnier
½ tsp salt
¼ tsp ground cinnamon

2 eggs, separated
½ cup heavy cream
1 tsp vanilla extract

Directions

Prepare a water bath and place the Sous Vide in it. Set to 182 F. Place the rhubarb, 1/4 cup of brown sugar, lemon juice, salt, Grand Marnier, and cinnamon in a vacuum-sealable bag. Release air by the water displacement method, seal, and submerge the bag in the water bath. Cook for 60 minutes.

Once the timer has stopped, remove the bag and transfer the contents into a blender and mix until smooth. Heat a pot over medium heat and pour the rhubarb mix, the egg yolks and 1/4 cup of brown sugar. Cook for 3 minutes until thickens. Set aside. Stir the egg whites until soft and put in the rhubarb mixture. Combine well. Stir the cream and vanilla until soft and put in the rhubarb mixture. Combine well. Place in serving pots.

Spiced Pears with Raisins

Prep + Cook Time: 2 hours 15 minutes | Servings: 4

Ingredients

4 peeled pears
1 lemon juice
3 tbsp butter
2 tbsp light brown sugar

2 whole fresh dates pitted
2 tbsp raisins
1 tbsp ground cinnamon
¼ tsp sea salt

¼ tsp grated nutmeg
1/9 tsp vanilla extract

Directions

Prepare a water bath and place Sous Vide in it. Set to 194 F. Brush the pears with lemon juice. Combine the butter, brown sugar, dates, raisins, cinnamon, salt, vanilla, and nutmeg. Mix until creating a paste.

Fill the pears with the mixture and place in a vacuum-sealable bag. Release air by the water displacement method, seal, and submerge the bag in the water bath. Cook for 2 hours. Once the timer has stopped, remove the pears and transfer to serving plates.

Greek Yogurt Cheesecake with Raspberries

Prep + Cook Time: 10 hours 25 minutes | Servings: 12

Ingredients

9 oz goat cheese	2 eggs	¼ tsp vanilla extract
1 cup granulated sugar	1 egg yolk	1 ½ cups graham crackers
7 oz soft cream cheese	Finely grated zest one lemon	1/3 cup butter
½ cup full-fat Greek yogurt	2 tbsp lemon juice	2 cups fresh raspberries
½ cup heavy cream	2 tbsp all-purpose flour	

Directions

Prepare a water bath and place the Sous Vide in it. Set to 172 F.

Preheat the oven to 375 F. Combine the goat cheese, 2/3 cup of sugar, cream cheese, Greek yogurt, heavy cream, egg yolks, lemon zest, lemon juice, 1 tbsp of flour, vanilla and 1/2 tbsp of salt. Place in a vacuum-sealable bag. Release air by the water displacement method, seal, and submerge the bag in the water bath. Cook for 2 hours.

Meanwhile, prepare the crust, mixing the graham cracker crumbs, butter, 1/3 cup of sugar, pinch of salt, and 1 tbsp of flour. Combine well and put into bake pan, pressing well. Bake for 7-10 minutes until browned. Once the timer has stopped, remove the bag and dry it. Cut a little hole from the bag and fill over the crust. Put the raspberries on top and allow chilling for 8 hours.

French Vanilla Custard Dessert

Prep + Cook Time: 5 hours 25 minutes | Servings: 6

Ingredients

8 large egg yolks	1 tsp vanilla bean paste	1 cup whipping cream
½ cup granulated sugar	½ cup milk	

Directions

Prepare water bath and place Sous Vide in it. Set to 182 F. Whisk egg yolks, sugar, and vanilla paste.

Heat whipping cream and milk in a pot over high heat. Mix in the egg mixture and allow cooling for 20 minutes. Put the mixture in 6 glass jars. Seal and submerge in the water bath. Cook for 45 minutes. Once the timer has stopped, remove the jars and allow cooling for 10 minutes. Transfer into an ice-water bath and allow chilling.

Mint Rum Pineapple

Prep + Cook Time: 2 hours 15 minutes | Servings: 12

Ingredients

1 pineapple, chopped	1 cup sugar
1 bottle dark rum	6 Fresh mint leaves

Directions

Prepare a water bath and place the Sous Vide in it. Set to 135 F. Place the pineapple, rum and sugar in a vacuum-sealable bag. Release air by the water displacement method, seal, and submerge the bag in the water bath. Cook for 2 hours. Once the timer has stopped, remove the bag and add mint leaves. Drain the mix and allow chilling.

Cream Chocolate Pudding

Prep + Cook Time: 60 minutes | Servings: 6

Ingredients

1 cup whole milk
1 cup whipping cream
½ cup ultrafine sugar

1/3 cup cocoa powder
1/3 cup semisweet chocolate chips
3 eggs

2 egg yolks
½ tsp salt

Directions

Prepare a water bath and place the Sous Vide in it. Set to 194 F. Blend all the ingredients until smooth. Place it in a vacuum-sealable bag. Release air by the water displacement method, seal, and submerge the bag in the water bath. Cook for 45 minutes. Once the timer has stopped, remove the bag and transfer to a blender and mix until smooth. Serve in a bowl and chill.

Cinnamon Pineapple with Cheese Yogurt

Prep + Cook Time: 12 hours 10 minutes | Servings: 8

Ingredients

1 whole pineapple
1 tsp Chinese five-spice
2 tsp orange zest

1 tsp crushed pink peppercorns
¼ tsp nutmeg
¼ tsp cinnamon

1 tsp allspice
1 cup white wine
3 ½ oz dark brown sugar

For Whipping Cheese Yogurt

1 ½ tbsp vanilla yogurt
Grated star anise

9 oz whipping cheese
3 ½ oz natural yogurt

3 ½ oz crushed ginger nut biscuits

Directions

Prepare a water bath and place the Sous Vide in it. Set to 186 F. Combine all the ingredients and place in a vacuum-sealable bag. Release air by the water displacement method, seal, and submerge the bag in the water bath. Cook for 12 hours. Blend all the ingredients for the cheese yogurt cream and allow chilling in the fridge. Once the timer has stopped, remove the pineapple and transfer to plates. Serve topped with cheese yogurt cream.

Lemon & Berry Mousse

Prep + Cook Time: 65 minutes | Servings: 8

Ingredients

1 pound raspberries, halved
¼ cup light brown sugar
3 tbsp freshly squeezed lemon juice

½ tsp salt
¼ tsp ground cinnamon
1 cup heavy cream

1 tsp vanilla extract
1 cup crème fraiche

Directions

Prepare a water bath and place the Sous Vide in it. Set to 182 F.

Place the raspberries, brown sugar, lemon juice, salt, and cinnamon in a vacuum-sealable bag. Release air by water displacement method, seal, and submerge the bag in the water bath. Cook for 45 minutes. Once the timer has stopped, remove the bag and transfer the contents to a blender. Stir until smooth. Whisk the heavy cream and vanilla. Pour in the raspberries mix with the créme fraiche and combine well. Transfer into 8 serving bowls.

Creamy Blueberry Mousse

Prep + Cook Time: 60 minutes | Servings: 8

Ingredients

1 pound blueberries
¼ cup sugar

3 tbsp lemon juice
¼ tsp ground cinnamon

1 cup heavy cream
1 tsp vanilla extract

Directions

Prepare a water bath and place the Sous Vide in it. Set to 182 F.

Combine blueberries, sugar, lemon juice, and cinnamon and place in a vacuum-sealable bag. Release air by the water displacement method, seal, and submerge the bag in the water bath. Cook for 30 minutes.

Once ready, remove the bag and transfer the contents to a blender. Stir until smooth. Whisk the cream and vanilla. Pour in the blueberries mix and combine well. Transfer into 8 serving bowls. Allow chilling.

Fruity Chocolate Flan

Prep + Cook Time: 4 hours 50 minutes | Servings: 12

Ingredients

1 cup fruit-forward red wine	8 oz white chocolate, chopped	8 egg yolks
½ cup granulated sugar	1 cup milk	
12 oz white chocolate chips	½ cup heavy cream	

Directions

Prepare a water bath and place the Sous Vide in it. Set to 182 F.

Heat a saucepan over medium heat and pour the wine and sugar. Stir for 20 minutes until reduced. Allow cooling for 10 minutes. Transfer to a blender and put the chocolate chips, milk, cream, and egg yolks. Mix until smooth.

Place the mixture in a vacuum-sealable bag. Release air by the water displacement method, seal, and submerge the bag in the water bath. Cook for 45 minutes. Once the timer has stopped, remove the bag and transfer the contents to a blender and mix for 2 minutes. Share into 12 ramekins and cover with plastic. Serve chilled.

Maple Lemon Brioche Pudding

Prep + Cook Time: 2 hours 20 minutes | Servings: 4

Ingredients

1 cup whole milk	¼ cup maple syrup	1 tsp vanilla bean paste
1 cup heavy cream	2 tbsp lemon juice	4 cups brioche, cubed
½ cup granulated sugar	1 tbsp lemon zest	

Directions

Prepare a water bath and place the Sous Vide in it. Set to 172 F.

Combine well the milk, heavy cream, sugar, maple syrup, lemon zest, lemon juice, vanilla bean paste. Put the brioche and mix together. Pour the mixture into 4 mason jars. Seal and submerge the jars in the water bath. Cook for 2 hours. Once the timer has stopped, remove the jars and transfer to the broiler. Bake for 3 minutes and serve.

Cinnamon Almond Rice

Prep + Cook Time: 2 hours 20 minutes | Servings: 6

Ingredients

1 cup rice	4 cups almond milk	1 tbsp pumpkin piece spice
4 cups water	1 cup sugar	

Directions

Prepare a water bath and place the Sous Vide in it. Set to 192 F.

Combine the rice, water, almond milk, sugar, and pumpkin pie spice and place in a vacuum-sealable bag. Release air by the water displacement method, seal, and submerge the bag in the water bath. Cook for 1 hour and 30 minutes. Once the timer has stopped, remove the rice and season with salt.

Aromatic Nectarines with Mascarpone Topping

Prep + Cook Time: 35 minutes | Servings: 4

Ingredients

2 halved and pitted nectarines
1 tbsp dried lavender buds

¼ cup water
¼ cup honey

For Mascarpone topping

1/3 cup mascarpone cheese
½ cup coconut cream

1 tbsp maple syrup
½ tsp lavender extract

Directions

Prepare a water bath and place the Sous Vide in it. Set to 182 F.

Combine nectarines, lavender. water, and honey in a bowl, then place in a vacuum-sealable bag. Release air by the water displacement method, seal, and submerge the bag in the water bath. Cook for 20 minutes.

Once the timer has stopped, remove the bag and transfer into an ice bath water and allow chilling in the fridge for 1 hour.

For the mascarpone cheese, combine all the ingredients until uniform mixture obtained. Serve the nectarines topped with the mascarpone mixture.

Sweet Potatoes with Maple & Cinnamon Sauce

Prep + Cook Time: 2 hours 45 minutes | Servings: 8

Ingredients

2 pounds sweet potatoes, sliced
½ cup butter
¼ cup maple syrup

2 lemons, juice and zest
1 cup chopped walnuts
1 cinnamon stick

¼ cup brown sugar

Directions

Prepare a water bath and place the Sous Vide in it. Set to 155 F. Place the potatoes and 1/4 cup of butter in a vacuum-sealable bag. Release air by water displacement method, seal and submerge in the water bath. Cook for 2 hours. Once done, remove the potatoes and pat them dry. Transfer to a baking tray.

Preheat the oven to 350 F. Heat a saucepan and stir 1/4 cup of butter, brown sugar, maple syrup, lemon zest and juice, walnuts, salt, and cinnamon stick. Pour the sauce over the potatoes and discard the cinnamon stick. Bake for 30 minutes. Serve warm.

Cinnamon Poached Pears with Ice Cream

Prep + Cook Time: 1 hour 15 minutes | Servings: 4

Ingredients

3 peeled pears
3 cups hard apple cider
1 cup sugar

Zest of 1 lemon
1 vanilla bean, split
1 cinnamon stick

Ice cream for serving

Directions

Prepare a water bath and place the Sous Vide in it. Set to 194 F.

Place all the ingredients in a vacuum-sealable bag. Release air by the water displacement method, seal, and submerge the bag in the water bath. Cook for 60 minutes.

Once the timer has stopped, remove the pears and set aside. Drain the juices into a hot pot. Cook for 10 minutes. Cut the pears by the half and remove the seeds. Serve ice cream and top with the pears.

Simple Lemon Jam

Prep + Cook Time: 2 hours 55 minutes | Servings: 6

Ingredients

1 cup sugar
8 tbsp butter, melted

6 egg yolks
¼ cup lemon juice

Directions

Prepare a water bath and place the Sous Vide in it. Set to 182 F. Blend all the ingredients for 20 seconds. Place in a vacuum-sealable bag. Release air by the water displacement method, seal, and submerge the bag in the water bath. Cook for 45 minutes. Shake a few times. Once the timer has stopped, remove the bag and transfer into an ice-water bath. Allow chilling for 2 hours and serve.

Rich Orange Curd

Prep + Cook Time: 60 minutes | Servings: 2

Ingredients

6 tbsp butter, melted and cooled
4 orange juice

6 large egg yolks at room temperature
1 cup sugar

Directions

Prepare a water bath and place the Sous Vide in it. Set to 179 F. Combine the sugar, butter and orange juice. Stir until the sugar dissolved and add the egg yolks. Mix well.

Place the egg mix in a vacuum-sealable bag. Release air by the water displacement method, seal, and submerge the bag in the water bath. Cook for 45 minutes. Once the timer has stopped, remove the bag and transfer into an ice bag. Shake well. Allow chilling all night.

Vanilla Ice Cream with Mango Jam

Prep + Cook Time: 30 minutes | Servings: 2

Ingredients

2 mangos, sliced
2 tbsp granulated sugar

1 tbsp freshly squeezed orange juice
2 tbsp vanilla ice cream

Fresh mint leaves

Directions

Prepare a water bath and place the Sous Vide in it. Set to 194 F. Combine well the mango slices, sugar and orange juice. Place it in a vacuum-sealable bag. Release air by the water displacement method, seal, and submerge the bag in the water bath. Cook for 20 minutes. Once the timer has stopped, remove the bag and transfer to a bowl. Put the ice cream and garnish with fruit and mint leaves.

Cinnamon & Citrus Yogurt

Prep + Cook Time: 3 hours 15 minutes | Servings: 4

Ingredients

½ cup yogurt
½ tbsp orange zest

½ tbsp lemon zest
½ tbsp lime zest

4 cups full cream milk
1 tsp cinnamon

Directions

Prepare a water bath and place the Sous Vide in it. Set to 113 F. Warm the milk in a pot until 182 F. Transfer to an ice bath and allow cooling until reached 110 F. Pour in yogurt and cinnamon. Add the citrus zest. Put the mixture into 4 canning jars and seal. Immerse the jars in the water bath. Cook for 3 hours. Once the timer has stopped, remove the jars and serve.

Banana Cream

Prep + Cook Time: 60 minutes | Servings: 4

Ingredients

5 bananas, chopped
1 cup brown sugar
2 cinnamon sticks

5 drops vanilla extract
6 whole cloves
Whipped cream for serving

Vanilla ice-cream for serving

Directions

Prepare a water bath and place the Sous Vide in it. Set to 182 F.

Place banana, brown sugar, vanilla, cinnamon sticks, and cloves in a vacuum-sealable bag. Release air by the water displacement method, seal, and submerge the bag in the water bath. Cook for 40 minutes. Once the timer has stopped, remove the bag and allow cooling. Discard the cinnamon sticks and cloves. Top with whipped cream.

Lime Thyme Liquor

Prep + Cook Time: 1 hour 50 minutes | Servings: 12

Ingredients

Zest of 8 limes
4 sprigs fresh thyme

1 cup sugar
1 cup water

1 cup vodka

Directions

Prepare a water bath and place the Sous Vide in it. Set to 182 F. Combine all the ingredients and place in a vacuum-sealable bag. Release air by the water displacement method, seal, and submerge the bag in the water bath. Cook for 90 minutes. Once the timer has stopped, remove the bag and drain the mixture. Allow chilling.

Rum Raisin Rice Pudding

Prep + Cook Time: 2 hours 10 minutes | Servings: 4

Ingredients

½ cup dark rum
1 tbsp Turkish raisins
½ tsp vanilla extract

3 cups milk
2 tbsp butter
2 cups rice

½ cup sugar
Cinnamon for serving

Directions

Prepare a water bath and place the Sous Vide in it. Set to 138 F.

Combine all the ingredients, except the cinnamon and place in a vacuum-sealable bag. Release air by the water displacement method, seal, and submerge the bag in the water bath. Cook for 2 hours. Once the timer has stopped, remove the bag, stir and transfer to a serving bowl. Garnish with cinnamon.

Incredible Coffee Dessert

Prep + Cook Time: 3 hours 10 minutes | Servings: 8

Ingredients

1/3 cup espresso
¾ cup milk
1 cup heavy cream

6 oz white chopped chocolate
1/3 cup sugar
½ tsp salt

Whipped cream
4 large egg yolks

Directions

Prepare a water bath and place the Sous Vide in it. Set to 182 F. Heat a saucepan over medium heat and stir the heavy cream, espresso and milk. Remove from the heat and add the chocolate. Cook for 15 minutes.

Combine egg yolks, salt, and sugar in a bowl. Mix in the chocolate mixture. Allow cooling. Place the mixture in a vacuum-sealable bag. Release air by water displacement method, seal and submerge in the bath. Cook for 30 minutes. Once done, transfer contents to small ramekins. Chill for 2 hours.

Warm Vanilla Quince

Prep + Cook Time: 50 minutes | Servings: 2

Ingredients

2 peeled quince
1 vanilla bean

2 tbsp dark brown sugar
½ tsp salt

1 tbsp butter
Vanilla ice cream

Directions

Prepare a water bath and place the Sous Vide in it. Set to 175 F. Slice the quince by the half. Remove the core. Combine the vanilla bean with brown sugar and salt. Soak vanilla seeds with the mixture.

Place the quinces and the mixture in a vacuum-sealable bag. Release air by water displacement method, seal and submerge in the water bath. Cook for 45 minutes. Once the timer has stopped, remove the quinces and transfer to a bowls. Sprinkle the quinces with the butter sauce. Serve with vanilla ice cream.

Honey Baked Cheese

Prep + Cook Time: 50 minutes | Servings: 6

Ingredients

2 cups milk
6 tbsp white wine vinegar
2 tbsp honey to serve

2 large eggs
2 tbsp olive oil

Salt and black pepper to taste

Directions

Prepare a water bath and place the Sous Vide in it. Set to 172 F. Place the vinegar and milk in a vacuum-sealable bag. Release air by the water displacement method, seal, and submerge the bag in the bath. Cook for 60 minutes.

Preheat the oven to 350 F. Once the timer has stopped, remove the bag and strain the cuds. Allow to draining for 10 minutes. Transfer to a blender and mix with the eggs, salt, olive oil and pepper for 20 seconds. Put the ricotta in 6 oven ramekins and bake for 30 minutes. Sprinkle with honey.

Berries Vodka Tonic

Prep + Cook Time: 35 minutes | Servings: 2

Ingredients

3 oz vodka
1 tbsp coriander seeds
8 juniper berries

2 pieces dried lavender
5 whole black peppercorns
2 whole cardamom pods

1 bay leaf
Tonic water
Orange wedges for serving

Directions

Prepare a water bath and place the Sous Vide in it. Set to 175 F.

Place the vodka, juniper, coriander, cardamom, peppercorns, bay leaf, and lavender in a vacuum-sealable bag. Release air by the water displacement method, seal, and submerge the bag in the water bath.

Cook for 10 minutes. Once the timer has stopped, remove the bag and drain the mixture. Allow chilling for 15 minutes. Serve with a mixture of tonic water. Garnish with orange wedges.

Maple & Lemongrass Drink

Prep + Cook Time: 1 hour 15 minutes | Servings: 4

Ingredients

4 stalks lemongrass, chopped

1 cup water

1 cup maple syrup

Directions

Prepare a water bath and place Sous Vide in it. Set to 182 F.

Combine all the ingredients and place in a vacuum-sealable bag. Release air by water displacement method, seal and submerge in the water bath. Cook for 60 minutes. Once done, remove the bag and drain the contents. Allow chilling.

Vanilla Coffee Liquor

Prep + Cook Time: 3 hours 10 minutes | Servings: 20

Ingredients

1 bottle vodka
32 oz' strong black coffee

2 cups granulated sugar
½ cup coffee beans

2 tsp vanilla extract

Directions

Prepare a water bath and place Sous Vide in it. Set to 146 F.

Combine all the ingredients and place in a vacuum-sealable bag. Release air by water displacement method, seal and submerge in the water bath. Cook for 3 hours. Once the timer has stopped, remove the bag and strain the mixture. Allow cooling.

Homemade Vanilla Bourbon

Prep + Cook Time: 2 hours 10 minutes | Servings: 6

Ingredients

1 cup granulated sugar
½ cup water

½ cup bourbon
6 split vanilla beans

Soda for serving
Lemon wedges for serving

Directions

Prepare a water bath and place the Sous Vide in it. Set to 135 F.

Combine the sugar, vanilla beans, water and bourbon and place in a vacuum-sealable bag. Release air by the water displacement method, seal, and submerge the bag in the water bath. Cook for 2 hours.

Once the timer has stopped, remove the bag and strain the mixture. Allow chilling all night. Serve with one-part syrup, two parts soda with ice. Garnish with a lemon wedge.

Rhubarb & Blueberry Shrub Cocktail

Prep + Cook Time: 1 hour 45 minutes | Servings: 12

Ingredients

2 cups sugar
2 cups balsamic vinegar

1 cup diced rhubarb
1 cup diced blueberries

1 cup water

Directions

Prepare a water bath and place Sous Vide in it. Set to 182 F. Combine all the ingredients and place in vacuum-sealable bag. Release air by water displacement method, seal and submerge in the bath. Cook for 90 minutes. Once done, remove the bag and drain the contents. Reserve the fruit. Allow chilling.

Christmas Hot Wine

Prep + Cook Time: 1 hour 15 minutes | Servings: 2

Ingredients

½ bottle red wine
Juice of 2 lemons
1 cinnamon stick

1 bay leaf
1 vanilla pod, sliced in half lengthways
1-star anise

2 oz sugar

Directions

Prepare a water bath and place the Sous Vide in it. Set to 138 F.

Combine all the ingredients and place in a vacuum-sealable bag. Release air by the water displacement method, seal, and submerge the bag in the water bath. Cook for 60 minutes. Once the timer has stopped, remove the bag and allow chilling.

Summer Mint & Rhubarb Mojito

Prep + Cook Time: 1 hour 45 minutes | Servings: 12

Ingredients

2 cups diced rhubarb
1 cup sugar

1 cup water
5 sprigs mint

Directions

Prepare a water bath and place the Sous Vide in it. Set to 182 F.

Combine all the ingredients and place in a vacuum-sealable bag. Release air by the water displacement method, seal, and submerge the bag in the water bath. Cook for 1 hour 30 minutes. Once the timer has stopped, remove the bag and drain the contents. Reserve the fruit. Allow chilling.

Gingery Gin Tonic with Lemons

Prep + Cook Time: 2 hours 15 minutes | Servings: 4

Ingredients

1 cup gin
1 cup ice

1 ¼ cups tonic water
1 inch ginger piece, peeled

1 lemon, cut into wedges

Directions

Prepare a water bath and place the Sous Vide in it. Set to 125 F.

Place the gin, ginger and half of the lemon wedges in a vacuum-sealable bag. Release air by the water displacement method, seal, and submerge the bag in the water bath. Set the timer for 2 hours. Once the timer has stopped, remove the bag. Let cool completely. Serve with ice and remaining lemon wedges.

Minty Vodka Melon

Prep + Cook Time: 2 hours 10 minutes | Servings: 4

Ingredients

1 cup melon chunks
1 cup vodka

12 mint leaves
1 tsp sugar

Directions

Prepare a water bath and place the Sous Vide in it. Set to 140 F.

Place all the ingredients in a jar and mix to combine. Seal and submerge the jar in the water bath. Set the timer for 2 hours. Once the timer has stopped, remove the jar. Strain and serve.

Sous Vide Limoncello

Prep + Cook Time: 3 hours 8 minutes | Servings: 6

Ingredients

14 ounces vodka

Zest of 3 lemons

2 ounces sugar

Directions

Prepare a water bath and place the Sous Vide in it. Set to 130 F. Place all the ingredients in a mason jar. Seal and submerge in the water bath. Set the timer for 3 hours. Once the timer has stopped, remove the bag. Serve with ice.

Spicy Agave Liquor

Prep + Cook Time: 55 minutes | Servings: 8

Ingredients

2 cups vodka

½ cup water

½ cup light agave nectar

3 dried Guajillo chili peppers

1 jalapeno pepper, halved and seeded

1 Fresno pepper, halved and seeded

Zest of 1 lemon

1 cinnamon stick

1 tsp black peppercorns

Directions

Prepare a water bath and place the Sous Vide in it. Set to 182 F. Combine all the ingredients and place in a vacuum-sealable bag. Release air by the water displacement method, seal, and submerge the bag in the water bath. Cook for 45 minutes. Once the timer has stopped, remove the bag and drain the contents. Allow chilling.

Citrus Piña Colada

Prep + Cook Time: 2 hours 10 minutes | Servings: 1

Ingredients

1 pineapple, chopped

3 cups white rum

1 tbsp coconut water

1 tbsp orange juice

1 tbsp lemon juice

1 tbsp soda water

Directions

Prepare a water bath and place the Sous Vide in it. Set to 130 F.

Pour the rum and pineapple in two mason jars and seal with a lid and submerge the jars in the water bath. Cook for 2 hours.

Once the timer has stopped, remove the jars and transfer to an ice water bath. Drain the pineapple. Place into a cocktail shaker some ice, 1 ½ oz of pineapple-infused rum, coconut water, orange juice, and lemon juice. Shake for 30 seconds. Pour into a highball glass with ice. Garnish with pineapple chunks.

Made in the USA
Las Vegas, NV
03 December 2024

13249742R10105